The Phenomenological Heart of Teaching and Learning

This book presents a carefully constructed framework for teaching and learning informed by philosophical and empirical foundations of phenomenology. Based on an extensive, multi-dimensional case study focused around the "lived experience" of college-level teaching preparation, classroom interaction, and students' reflections, this book presents evidence for the claim that the worldviews of both teachers and learners affect the way that they present and receive knowledge. By taking a unique phenomenological approach to pedagogical issues in higher education, this volume demonstrates that a truly transformative learning process relies on an engagement between consciousness and the world it "intends."

Katherine H. Greenberg is Professor Emerita in the Department of Educational Psychology and Counseling at The University of Tennessee, Knoxville.

Brian K. Sohn is Assistant Professor in the Department of Education and Counseling, Carsen-Newman University, Jefferson City, Tennessee.

Neil B. Greenberg is Professor Emeritus in the Department of Ecology and Evolutionary Biology at The University of Tennessee, Knoxville.

Howard R. Pollio is Professor Emeritus in the Department of Psychology at The University of Tennessee, Knoxville.

Sandra P. Thomas is Chair of the PhD Program in the College of Nursing at The University of Tennessee, Knoxville.

John T. Smith is Associate Professor of Mathematics at Pellissippi State Community College, Knoxville, Tennessee.

Routledge Research in Education

Counternarratives from Women of Color Academics
Bravery, Vulnerability, and Resistance
Manya C. Whitaker and Eric Anthony Grollman

Working Toward Racial Equity in First-Year Composition
Six Perspectives
Edited by Renee DeLong, Taiyon J. Coleman, Kathleen Sheerin DeVore, Shannon Gibney, Michael C. Kuhne, and Valerie Déus

Conversations on Embodiment Across Higher Education
Teaching, Practice and Research
Edited by Jennifer Leigh

Virtue and the Quiet Art of Scholarship
Reclaiming the University
Anne Pirrie

Global Perspectives on International Student Experiences in Higher Education
Trends and Issues
Edited by Krishna Bista

Data for Continuous Programmatic Improvement
Steps Colleges of Education Must Take to Become a Data Culture
Edited by Ellen B. Mandinach and Edith S. Gummer

Grounding Education in the Environmental Humanities
Exploring Place-Based Pedagogies in the South
Edited by Lucas F. Johnston and Dave Aftandilian

The Phenomenological Heart of Teaching and Learning
Theory, Research, and Practice in Higher Education
Katherine H. Greenberg, Brian K. Sohn, Neil B. Greenberg, Howard R. Pollio, Sandra P. Thomas, and John T. Smith

For more information about this series, please visit: www.routledge.com/
Routledge-Research-in-Higher-Education/book-series/RRHE

The Phenomenological Heart of Teaching and Learning

Theory, Research, and Practice in Higher Education

Katherine H. Greenberg, Brian K. Sohn,
Neil B. Greenberg, Howard R. Pollio,
Sandra P. Thomas, and John T. Smith

First published 2019
by Routledge
52 Vanderbilt Avenue, New York, NY 10017

and by Routledge
2 Park Square, Milton Park, Abingdon, Oxon, OX14 4RN

Routledge is an imprint of the Taylor & Francis Group, an informa business

© 2019 Taylor & Francis

The right of Katherine H. Greenberg, Brian K. Sohn, Neil B. Greenberg, Howard R. Pollio, Sandra P. Thomas, and John T. Smith to be identified as authors of this work has been asserted by them in accordance with sections 77 and 78 of the Copyright, Designs and Patents Act 1988.

All rights reserved. No part of this book may be reprinted or reproduced or utilized in any form or by any electronic, mechanical, or other means, now known or hereafter invented, including photocopying and recording, or in any information storage or retrieval system, without permission in writing from the publishers.

Trademark notice: Product or corporate names may be trademarks or registered trademarks, and are used only for identification and explanation without intent to infringe.

Library of Congress Cataloguing-in-Publication Data
A catalog record for this book has been requested

ISBN: 978-0-8153-7183-0 (hbk)
ISBN: 978-1-351-24590-6 (ebk)

Typeset in Sabon
by Apex CoVantage, LLC

Access the Center for Applied Phenomenological Research at the University of Tennessee at
http://phenomenology.utk.edu

Dedication

This book is dedicated to Howard R. Pollio, Distinguished Professor Emeritus, Department of Psychology, The University of Tennessee, Knoxville, USA

Carl Jung said that "Each of us can carry the torch of knowledge but a part of the way, until another takes it from him." Jung's words aptly capture our debt to Howard R. Pollio, who lit a torch for us. He kindled our excitement about phenomenological philosophy and about phenomenology as it can be *applied* in human science research—and in teaching, counseling, and living. In this book, we have endeavored to take up the torch and pass along what we have learned through our associations with this incredible teacher.

Trained as an experimental psychologist, Professor Pollio had already been teaching, researching, and writing for many years before he discovered phenomenological philosophy. This discovery was profoundly transformational for him and set him on a new course of intensive study. He traveled abroad to the UK, Holland, and Scandinavia to study and consult with other scholars. Eventually, he developed a course in existential phenomenology, which was housed in the psychology department of the university, but soon attracted students from diverse disciplines. It is this course that is described in the book you are about to read.

The authors of this book came to know Howard R. Pollio as his students, mentees, colleagues, co-researchers, and friends. The association of some of us with Professor Pollio has spanned more than 40 years. Throughout our interactions with him, we have been struck by his genuine love of learning and the breadth and depth of his knowledge—well beyond his discipline of psychology—extending to Greek mythology, the sociology of knowledge, the etymology of words, and a host of other topics such as honor, love, beauty, and truth. Within a typical conversation, he might mention Freud, Buber, Gadamer, Skinner, Van den Berg, Heidegger, Yalom, or William James.

Professor Pollio's wide-ranging interests are illustrated by publications on teaching and learning, grading in college courses, humor and comedy, metaphor and symbol, and newspaper editorials after the 9/11 attacks on the USA—and of course, phenomenology and phenomenological research. His approach to conducting research was influenced by his scholarly discussions over the years with psychologists at Duquesne University, but eventually diverged from their approach in several respects. What came to be called the "University of Tennessee Approach" has been employed in several hundred dissertations in fields such as education, psychology, nursing, counseling, geography, forestry, sports psychology, and child and family studies. And, of course, scholars well beyond Tennessee now use it.

To each of us, Howard R. Pollio has been tremendously supportive and genuinely interested in what we are thinking, doing, and writing. He is unfailingly kind and never disrespectful, even when disagreeing with us. He truly exemplified a phenomenological approach to teaching—and to everyday living—with joy, humor, curiosity, and a sense of wonder about it all, as his family can attest. We hope we have conveyed his approach faithfully and well.

Contents

List of Figures, Tables, and Boxes	ix
Foreword	xi
Acknowledgments	xiv
List of Contributors	xv
Abstract	xvii

1	The Lifeworld of the Classroom	1
2	Getting DEEP: The Integrative Biology of Teaching and Learning	27
3	Preparation for Teaching: "What Can They Experience in Class?"	50
4	Teaching as Improvisational Jazz: "To Go Somewhere to Answer a BIG Question"	65
5	Free to Learn: A Radical Aspect of Our Approach	94
6	Student Experiences of Other Students: "All Together in This Space"	109
7	Transcending the Classroom: Student Reports of Personal and Professional Change	125
8	Messing Up and Messing About: Student Needs and Teachers' Adaptation of Our Phenomenological Approach	141

viii *Contents*

9 Contributions of Our Existential Phenomenological
Approach to Higher Education Pedagogy:
Implications for Theory, Research, and Practice   163

References   181
Index   193

Figures, Tables, and Boxes

Figures

4.1	The Thematic Structure of the Professor's Perspective on His Approach	70
6.1	The Thematic Structure of the Student Experience of Other Students	112

Tables

1.1	Case Study Research Questions and Data Collection	8
1.2	Authors' Perspectives Regarding Phenomenological Concepts That Inform Our Teaching Approach	10
4.1	Descriptors of Classroom Facilitation and Their Relation to Themes	80
4.2	Episode 1 of a Transcript from a Graduate Seminar Dialogue with Process Coding Analysis of Descriptors	82
4.3	Episode 2 of a Transcript from a Graduate Seminar Dialogue with Process Coding Analysis of Descriptors	85
5.1	Themes and Concepts of Phenomenology in Relation to the Student Experience of Learning	102
9.1	Principles at the Phenomenological Heart of Teaching and Learning	166

Boxes

1.1	Reflection, *Kathy Greenberg*	2
1.2	Labels Matter: Teacher vs. Instructor	3
1.3	Reflection, *Howard Pollio*	14
1.4	Reflection, *Neil Greenberg*	15
1.5	Reflection, *Brian Sohn*	16
1.6	Reflection, *Kathy Greenberg*	17

x   *Figures, Tables, and Boxes*

1.7	Reflection, *Howard Pollio*	19
4.1	Class Episode Exploring the Meaning of Time	66
4.2	Class Episode of Teacher and Student Energizing Dialogue with Humor	74
5.1	Reflection, *Brian Sohn*	107

Foreword

This book began during one of the conversations that takes place in the weekly, two-hour meetings of the Transdisciplinary Phenomenology Research Group at The University of Tennessee, Knoxville. At these meetings, faculty and graduate student members from across campus gather to focus on the meaning of the first-person experiences reported by research participants in transcribed interviews. And we make space to acknowledge, share, and then set aside our personal connections to the phenomenon of focus. For example, when analyzing data from a study about teaching and learning, Distinguished Professor Howard Pollio (one of our authors and the focus of the extensive case study presented in this book), confessed his lack of interest in evidence-based pedagogy. His comments startled TPRG members from the field of educational psychology for two reasons.

First, for over 30 years, students from across campus would enroll in his advanced doctoral seminar on *existential phenomenological psychology* and then advise others, "Take this course. It will change your life!" Every year, busy faculty members would make time to join students and Howard—many returning to sit in on the course in later semesters. But, second, there was a deeper and less comfortable reason. For Howard's comment raised questions about the relevance and importance of evidence-based research concerning pedagogy.

Professor of Educational Psychology Kathy Greenberg (one of our authors) and members of her doctoral research team began to ask questions of each other: Should we be questioning the relevance of the scholarship of teaching and learning in higher education? What kind of teaching framework, if any, had Howard developed without any thought to the scholarship of teaching and learning? Had his intuitive style included elements more traditional approaches had missed? Many well-known scholars have written about the art of teaching as intuitive, situational, reflective, and/or mindful, and others have written of the need to create a framework or theory of teaching out of one's practice—to develop a praxis. Hence, Kathy believed we had a near-perfect example of higher education teaching and learning to explore—one in which the teacher

xii *Foreword*

was unencumbered by evidence-based teaching practices yet clearly and consistently provided a transformational learning experience.

But this was not a typical project in which the researcher or research group all share the same sociocultural professional views of their discipline. We deliberately took advantage of the transdisciplinarity of TPRG to develop a collaborative approach to our questions about the relationship of theory to practice and intuition to intentionality in our teaching. Our time together in this research group first gave us a shared vocabulary. And it also enabled us to honor the phenomenological understanding that perception both opens us to phenomena within the world as well as binds us to worldviews. We wanted to challenge each other's assumptions to which we might otherwise be blind.

The members of the TPRG that agreed to work together to write this book vary greatly from each other in life experiences. Two of us spent our younger lives in the Northeast, two in the Midwest, one in the Southeast and one in the Southwest. Four of us hold graduate degrees in education but each with subtle yet important differences in our focus on pedagogy. Three of us have held teaching licenses and bring to this project the influences from our experience teaching children and youth. Another of us, also from an applied field of study, spent 15 years as a practicing nurse. At the same time, two of us come from non-applied fields having spent their entire careers in academia, one in psychology and the other in the interdisciplinary field of ethology that blends psychology and biology. Further, four of our authors began their college studies as first-generation students. Two of us consider our undergraduate experience as rough. Only the parents of only one of our authors held advanced (doctoral) degrees. Two of us have taught for 7 and 10 years in higher education, while the other four have 35 or more years of teaching experience. In regard to the use of a phenomenological approach to research, three of us have done so for 20 or more years, one for 7 years, and 2 others as interested but less involved until this project. All six authors have a high regard for an interdisciplinary focus, some with more involvement than others. Finally, four authors participated throughout the project while two joined much later, bringing fresh worldviews to challenge our assumptions.

We invited others to join our authors as part of our research team. These people contributed time in analysis of our case study data. They included doctoral students and faculty engaged in scholarly study from the fields of child and family studies, cultural studies, teacher education, educational psychology, ethology, nursing, philosophy, psychology, and special education. Several of them participated in conference presentations and were co-authors on published articles related to the project. One served as our primary research assistant during the two semesters in which we collected data and went on to complete her dissertation on Howard's preparation for teaching.

We gathered data for the case study during the last two years that Howard taught—at a time when he had honed his approach to a very high level. He was very involved in the case study and the planning of the text. He provided invaluable input but due to illness, he was unable to participate in the actual writing of this text.

Together, we wrote this book in a collaborative fashion from our trans-disciplinary and sociocultural perspectives. While members took on the job of writing the first draft of one or more chapters, all of us read and edited the entire narrative to ensure we speak as one voice. Through the sharing of the phenomenological attitude, we have reviewed philosophy, analyzed data, interpreted findings, developed principles of our approach, and adapted them to guide our own unique teaching practices. We became, as Dillard (2015) wrote about improvisational jazz musicians, "Improvisation is about seeking connection. . . . It feels safe and exciting at the same time. It's like together, somehow you can open yourselves to the spirit . . . and create work that you could never create on your own in a million years."

This has been a profound experience for us all, bringing us to richer insights about ourselves as well as a deep appreciation for the remarkable privilege of contributing to each other's understanding of teaching and learning, to the trustworthiness of our findings and related implications. It is our intent to communicate all of this to you as well.

Acknowledgments

Herein we acknowledge the continual cross-fertilization among scholars with different perspectives that enriched the authors' thinking throughout the writing of this book. The research reported here is just one product of many years of ongoing and stimulating dialogue and collaboration among the members of the Transdisciplinary Phenomenology Research Group (TPRG) at The University of Tennessee, Knoxville (UTK). The UTK phenomenological approach has been used in hundreds of other student and faculty research projects, reported in the literature of multiple disciplines. This book presents the findings of a unique educational case study, our rigorous examination of a master teacher and the life-altering consequences of his class on the students. Particularly important in the data collection and/or analyses for this project were Karen Franklin, Tiffany Dellard, Kristina Plaas, Brenda Murphy, and Lauren Moret. We are also indebted to Vincent Price, who meticulously edited our book. It is impossible, however, to name all of the other faculty members and students who participated in the TPRG conversations that challenged us, enlightened us, and provided the support (and "gentle push") to complete the book. We are truly grateful to all of you. You know who you are.

Contributors

Katherine H. Greenberg is Professor Emerita, Department of Educational Psychology and Counseling, at The University of Tennessee, Knoxville, where her scholarly interests focus on theoretical approaches to teaching and learning including phenomenology. She received her PhD from Peabody College of Vanderbilt University and was a Fulbright Research Scholar in Israel (1986–1987), where she worked with theorist Reuven Feuerstein. She is the founding director of one of 12 educational models included in the U.S.D.E. National Follow Through Program (1988–1995), partnering with educators in elementary schools serving children from low-income families. Subsequently, she has consulted in more than six countries to share her model, *Cognitive Enrichment Advantage*, for use in K-12 as well as post-secondary settings. Along with her own research and writing, she has directed numerous doctoral dissertations in Educational Psychology as well as developed several graduate degree programs. She joined the Transdisciplinary Phenomenology Research Group in 2000.

Neil B. Greenberg is Professor Emeritus, Department of Ecology and Evolutionary Biology, The University of Tennessee, Knoxville. His PhD is from Rutgers University in psychology and zoology. After five years as a post-doctoral fellow and research ethologist conducting research in behavioral neurology at the National Institute of Mental Health, he joined the faculty at Tennessee, where he continued research, taught, and directed a large curriculum revision in integrative biology; subsequently he became chair of the campus-wide University Studies Interdisciplinary Faculty and Curriculum Development Program. He was elected a Fellow of the American Association for the Advancement of Science for his interdisciplinary efforts on behalf of biology and the humanities. He remains active in teaching and writing.

Howard R. Pollio received his PhD from The University of Michigan and joined the faculty of the Department of Psychology at The University of Tennessee, Knoxville, where he now serves as Professor Emeritus. He is the recipient of numerous awards for research and teaching.

His research emphasizes Human Learning, Symbolic Processes, Figurative Language, Humor and Laughter, Qualitative Methodology, and, especially, Existential Phenomenology. He has published several books, over 100 articles and books, and has directed over 70 dissertations and served on many doctoral committees. For more than 25 years, he mentored faculty members and students as a co-leader of the Transdisciplinary Phenomenology Research Group and facilitator of his own research team.

John T. Smith is an Associate Professor in the Mathematics Department at Pellissippi State Community College in Knoxville, Tennessee. He teaches developmental and introductory undergraduate mathematics and statistics courses. He is also a faculty fellow with the Pellissippi Academic Center for Excellence first-year experience initiative. In 2016, he received his PhD in teacher preparation with a concentration in mathematics education through the Theory and Practice in Teacher Education Department at The University of Tennessee. His research explored the transformative learning experiences of previously unsuccessful low socioeconomic status community college students. His research is informed by an equity focus through the lens of social class, with a particular emphasis on Appalachian first-generation and non-traditional college students.

Brian K. Sohn is an Assistant Professor of Education at Carson-Newman University in Jefferson City, Tennessee. He was a student participant in the case study course of key focus in this book. He then joined the research team, conducting extensive research on the professors' and students' teaching and learning experiences. Brian earned his doctorate from The University of Tennessee, Knoxville, in 2016. His research focuses on phenomenology as a research methodology, on teaching and learning that contributes to transformative learning, and experiences of students leading to, and the application of, a phenomenological approach to teacher education.

Sandra P. Thomas is the Sara and Ross Croley Endowed Professor in the College of Nursing at The University of Tennessee, Knoxville, where she serves as director of the PhD program. She has over 100 publications and an acclaimed book, *Listening to Patients*, which she co-authored with Howard R. Pollio. She is a founding member of the Transdisciplinary Phenomenology Research Group. Together with Howard R. Pollio, Sandra has mentored many faculty members and students as they learned to use phenomenological methodology. She also teaches qualitative methodology courses. Along with colleagues, she developed an online doctoral program in nursing and continues to teach in the program. She also directs many dissertations as well as serves on doctoral committees across the campus.

Abstract

In this volume the authors present a phenomenological approach to teaching and learning in higher education. Guided by the philosophy of Merleau-Ponty, the aim of the approach is to bring more explicit awareness to the lifeworlds of teachers and students in order to balance the utilitarian needs of workforce preparation with the wonder and natural motivation provided by a phenomenological attitude. The theoretical constructs of existential phenomenology are complemented by research from integrative biology, a two-year case study of a successful professor and his students, and other studies. Using a phenomenological methodology, the authors describe the professor's planning and teaching style and analyze transcribed episodes of classroom conversation. Authors discuss how the professor enacted a phenomenological attitude that honored the lifeworld of the classroom while facilitating dialogue that enabled students to weave personally relevant experiences with course content. Also included are studies of the experiences of the students that provide key insights into the relational nature of transformative learning. Additionally, the broad applicability of the phenomenological approach is exemplified with examples of course descriptions that include traditional and online course delivery and work with marginalized and traditionally underserved student populations. The volume concludes with principles of a phenomenological approach that can enrich and enable the unique connoisseurship of teachers' pedagogical practices in higher education.

1 The Lifeworld of the Classroom

Rarely do we teachers in higher education consider the dynamic processes involved in the lifeworld (*Lebenswelt*) of the classroom: "[T]he world of lived experience inhabited by us as conscious beings and incorporating the way in which phenomena (events, objects, emotions) appear to us in our conscious experience or everyday life" (Brooks, 2015, p. 642).

For the primary job of higher education teachers is to impart to students the objective, analytical, and abstract knowledge of our fields of study. Hence, this objectivism turns our attention away from our subjective perceptions. And we contend (along with many phenomenologists) these subjective perceptions are the only way we initially connect with the world and what we know of it. Indeed, we authors (who are also higher education teachers) believe attention to the lifeworld in relation to course content opens teachers and their learners to a deeper realization of abstract knowledge and its meaning in their personal and professional lives.

Picture these brief descriptions of experiences shared by a professor and his students:

Students: I feel I am in it. I am helping to create it and it is helping to create me. . . . It is seeping into a lot of other areas of my life. (Sonia) I really didn't feel like a student. I felt like a learner. (Lois)

Professor: My intent is to go somewhere—where students want to go—[to focus on] what stands out to them. To find an answer to some BIG question related to the topic of that session. . . . I know certain places that I want to go. We go, and we get there. My job is to show them how they can get themselves there. It's the revelation of self.

Students: I think there's a challenge to be more engaged with everything . . . like little things throughout your day even, and just kind of like seeing those things in your life. (James) It's given me a different way to look at the world. (Lois)

Professor: It flows and most everybody's looking at you or toward the person who is talking. And they're not talking to anybody

2   *The Lifeworld of the Classroom*

> else. And I think that basically, there is no resistance in the class. It's going better than you would ever hope. You've got someplace where you never expected.

What could be more gratifying to any teacher than for students to experience a course as these student quotes indicate? And how can we as teachers understand the teaching that fostered such experiences? We, the authors, have explored the answers to these questions through detailed descriptions of the lifeworld of the classroom. By hearing the voices of students and teachers, by foregrounding their first-person perspectives, we believe that research can uncover the heart of teaching and learning.

Lived experiences of students and teachers are frequently ignored by researchers focused on pedagogy. Some of these researchers consider such accounts too subjective or anecdotal. Hence, the implications for evidenced-based methods for teaching are presented objectively, as if those methods represented universal truths. Yet in this book we present an *existential phenomenological approach* to teaching and learning in higher education. It is an approach in which the science of teaching does not supersede its art, an approach based primarily in the philosophy of Maurice Merleau-Ponty (1945/1962) that fosters deep connections between the personal subjective experiences of teachers and students and the abstract theoretical knowledge of course content.

Our approach and the way we present it is intended to provide principles that encourage every teacher to determine their own intuitive style to address the fluid context that is the lifeworld of their particular classroom (see Chapter 9). Unlike much literature offering approaches for higher education pedagogy, where rationality receives attention while intuition is ignored, in our approach we honor both. For teachers who aspire to use best practices frequently find that recommended techniques do not work as planned because they ignore the lifeworld of a specific classroom and the intermingled, subjective perspectives of a unique group of students. The science of teaching without the art can never be truly successful. On the other hand, combining the lifeworld with best practices can lead to startling improvements in teaching (see Box 1.1).

Box 1.1   Reflection, *Kathy Greenberg*

I experienced a powerful transformation in my teaching after participating on a research team focused on the lived experience of black university students on a predominately white campus (Davis et al., 2004; see also Chapter 8). Prior to that research project, I had spent 20 years teaching, researching, and consulting on the effectiveness of an educational approach to help marginalized students, primarily African Americans, develop personalized strategies for school learning. Nevertheless, with the Davis et al. research, I felt I was able for the very first time to walk in the shoes of marginalized students, if only for a few brief moments. Through this research project I developed a much deeper level of understanding as I reflected on the students' lifeworld *from their perspectives*. It dramatically changed my teaching.

To be sure, traditional research in teaching and learning has led to an extensive and valuable literature related to higher education pedagogy. Some of these texts offer principles or techniques derived from implications of research findings about effective learning (e.g., Ambrose, Bridges, DiPietro, Lovett, & Norman, 2010). Some texts share pedagogical approaches based on implications from fields of study such as brain research (e.g., Taylor & Marienau, 2016). Still others combine implications from personal experience and related research (e.g., James & Brookfield, 2014; Weimer, 2013). These authors discuss their pedagogical ideas from their unique perspectives and often provide examples from classroom settings.

We the authors of this book do not reject such research. But when we examine phenomenological research based on teachers' and students' first-person descriptions of their experiences in teaching and learning contexts, we discover a broader focus on aspects of learning beyond the utilitarian focus of acquisition of knowledge and skills. In this book, we look beneath the surface—to the phenomenological heart of teaching and learning—to provide a balanced approach to researching the living, dynamic, and sensitive system of the lifeworld of the classroom. (Note: Some readers may be wondering why we use the term *teacher* to describe higher education "instructors" and/or "professors." See Box 1.2 for our explanation.)

Box 1.2 Labels Matter: Teacher vs. Instructor

We chose to focus on the more concrete role of *teaching* and move away from the underlying meaning of *instructing*. For instructing implies lack of interest in the lifeworld of the classroom. It also implies lack of balance between first-person experience and the utilitarian focus on mastery of abstract knowledge and skills. The only exception in labels we chose to use when referring to those who teach in higher education is our use of *professor* when referring to our case study teacher. We want to make clear when we are referring to our teacher who served as our research participant and whose practice is at the heart of this text.

4 *The Lifeworld of the Classroom*

The case study research we conducted permits a more intimate glimpse of what is actually happening from the teacher's preparation for class to the moments of mutual excitement and discovery during class interactions, as well as the first-person descriptions shared by the professor and his students. We believe our work allows teachers to make both personal and professional connections that will enhance teaching and learning.

Using the phenomenological research methodology developed at The University of Tennessee, Knoxville (UTK) (Sohn, Thomas, Greenberg, & Pollio, 2017), this book provides an opportunity for readers to walk in the shoes of our case study professor and his graduate students. But we also include teachers and students' first-person descriptions in a variety of higher education settings that demonstrate the feasibility of our approach in other contexts.

We do not recommend a set of techniques or activities. Instead, we share a phenomenological *approach* that can inform the unique connoisseurship of good teachers—the sensitivity to subtle variations of the lifeworld of the classroom—informed by a *phenomenological attitude* (Churchill, 2012; Dirkx, 1998; Finlay, 2008). We include in-depth examples of the approach from the case study (Chapters 3, 4, 5, 6, and 7) but also descriptions of our approach and its use in community college and university settings across numerous fields of study (Chapter 8). We also compare and contrast our findings and framework to that of more mainstream research and other pedagogical approaches (Chapter 9).

Our Case Study

We began our case study because of consistent anecdotal reports that students of a certain graduate seminar were telling other people, "take this course, it will change your life." Throughout the 30 years it was taught, a sizeable number of students and also faculty members participated in the course more than once. Although the professor taught graduate courses focused on learning theory, he claimed little interest in any of the related pedagogical research that might inform his teaching. Clearly, something special was happening in this course—unaffected as it was by mainstream pedagogy—that led to students' reports of transformative learning.

Our curiosity developed into a study of the lived experience of this professor and his students in the graduate seminar—as it occurred—week by week. Our case study was *empirical*—in the sense of using data based on first-hand experience. It was *descriptive*—in that for most of our data, participants were asked to describe their experience in careful detail, while with our analysis of transcribed classroom episodes, we provide evidence of the way in which teaching and learning occurred during class sessions. It was *personal*—in that our findings are presented in the first-person language of participants before we discuss our interpretation of them in more abstract language. Finally, it was *comprehensive*—in that we studied

The Lifeworld of the Classroom   5

the course in its entirety (over two sections of the course in subsequent years) and focused on the experiences of the professor, his students, and third-person observations.

The case study had five goals:

1. Describe the lived experience of a professor and his students in a semester-long, graduate level seminar derived from transcribed interviews and excerpts of class sessions.
2. Derive implications from findings that illuminate a framework of teaching principles.
3. Explore the potential contributions of existential phenomenology to the science and art of teaching and learning.
4. Compare and contrast this approach to teaching and learning with evidence-based practices and theory regarding other approaches to higher education pedagogy.
5. Determine the applicability of this approach in other higher education teaching/learning settings by exploring the experiences of other teachers and learners in community college and university settings at undergraduate and graduate levels and in diverse programs of study.

With these goals in mind, we undertook a phenomenological study combined with case study methods. Our hermeneutic phenomenological approach is built on years of development at The University of Tennessee, Knoxville (Thompson, Locander, & Pollio, 1989; Pollio, Graves, & Arfken, 2006; Pollio, Henley, & Thompson, 1997; Sohn et al., 2017; Thomas & Pollio, 2002). There are many approaches to phenomenological research discussed in the literature (see Finlay, 2012 for an overview). Nevertheless, Natanson (1973) described features of phenomenological research that apply to all or most of these approaches:

> one learned what phenomenology is step by step, through reading, discussion, and reflection. . . . What is needed is rather simple: to learn what is meant by the natural attitude, to practice *epoché*, to attempt descriptions of presentations without prejudicing the results by taking for granted the history, causality, intersubjectivity, and value we ordinarily associate with our experience, and to examine with absolute care the fabric of the world of daily life so that we may grasp its source and its direction. . . .
>
> (p. 8)

The UTK approach stands out from others most clearly in three ways. First, research participants are given freedom to describe what stood out to them as meaningful in their experience. At UTK we ask one open-ended question and only include additional questions for clarification as the

6 The Lifeworld of the Classroom

interview proceeds. Second, a significant amount of analysis is conducted through dialogue in our Transdisciplinary Phenomenology Research Group (TPRG) that provides multiple perspectives on the transcribed texts. Third, thematic findings are typically reported in the first-person words of participants—that represent a common essence of the experience shared by all participants in each study—choosing words and phrases where possible that are poetic in nature and/or share meaningful metaphors (cf. Lakoff & Johnson, 1980).

Over two semesters, our research team collected data. Reports on various aspects of the emerging research are available in greater detail elsewhere (the professor's experience of preparing for class [Franklin, 2013], student experiences of other students [Sohn, 2016], and students' experiences of the course overall [Sohn et al., 2016]). The most relevant findings from these studies are included in the chapters of this text along with related studies conducted by various members of the TPRG over the past 25 years.

The Course and Its Professor

The seminar was titled *Existential Phenomenological Psychology*. The professor designed the course for upper level doctoral students who came from psychology and philosophy as well as applied fields such as business, counseling, education, nursing, and sports psychology; the course was also taken by master's degree students and an occasional undergraduate. The content focused on the philosophy of existential phenomenology from a psychological perspective, primarily the ideas of French philosopher Maurice Merleau-Ponty. Essentially, the professor guided seminar discussions by focusing student attention on descriptions of their own or others' lived experience as it related to course readings and also by engaging students in practicing phenomenological research during class.

The professor assigned readings to be completed prior to each class session. Whole books or excerpts included numerous authors, such as Merleau-Ponty (*Phenomenology of Perception*, 1945/1962), Ihde (*Experimental Phenomenology*, 1986), Berger and Luckmann (*The Social Construction of Reality*, 1967), and Tuan (*Space and Place*, 1977). The professor told students that their only obligation for the course was to read: there would be no graded assignments. Few students had background in philosophy; most found the readings, particularly those of Merleau-Ponty, initially difficult to understand.

We describe the professor's teaching in much greater detail in Chapter 4 and provide only a brief overview here. Rather than beginning with lectures that explained ideas from readings, he typically invited students into a dialogue by asking what stood out to them from the texts. He encouraged students to "say more" about the meaning of passages and only afterwards shared his own deeper or alternative understanding. The professor not only led but also followed students into deep reflection on descriptions of personal experience as it related to the subject matter. In addition, he led them toward the key concepts he wanted them to learn by preparing stories, activities, and questions that he then used to launch them into the world of those ideas.

The professor strived in every class to engage students in awareness of being-in-the-world, being in a living experience in the classroom. He did this often through playfulness, by frequently making fun of himself, "This is getting worser and worser!" (as he discussed a complicated concept) or by adding levity and/or drama to student stories.

Attendance and class participation were high. Field notes from class sessions often included documentation of engagement such as laughter, note taking, or silent pauses after dialogue or *mini-lectures* (typically 2- to 15-minute explanations of abstract knowledge). Audio recordings captured the energy and deep reflection participants displayed in their tones of voice. Student reflections immediately after each class revealed what stood out to them in each session. From personal insights to professional applications, profound thoughtfulness to practical implementation, these data were part of the overall data collection scheme, as detailed below.

Research Questions and Data Collection

For the case study, the research team members worked together to develop the research questions, participant prompts, and other data collection procedures suited to the case study (see the Foreword for a discussion of author positionality). Our goal throughout was to create prompts that would allow participants to comment on whatever it was within their experience of the course that stood out. Table 1.1 lists specific research questions and our procedures for collection of data.

Data Analysis

The UTK data analysis methods are enriched by the dialogical, hermeneutic process used by the TPRG wherein transcripts of data are read aloud. Researchers stop periodically to share interpretations: they make connections to empirical studies, philosophical scholarship, literature, or even a recent radio or television program and also to personal experiences. They seek to continually keep in mind the context of their interpretations through bracketing—they consider the various contexts of the study, the participants, the specific words and phrases they use, and why or why not certain elements of a transcript may stand out to members of the TPRG. The themes, like specific interpretations, attempt to keep a sense of the whole. Drawing from Merleau-Ponty's philosophy and Gadamer's (1960/2013) focus on the *hermeneutic circle*, we interpreted data to find not only what participants considered *figural* but the often-implicit *ground* from which the figure stands out (see Sohn et al., 2017, for greater detail).

8 The Lifeworld of the Classroom

Table 1.1 Case Study Research Questions and Data Collection

Research Questions	Data Collection
What was the experience of the professor as he prepared for and reflected on his teaching?	Audio recordings of planning sessions before each class session and immediately after each session
What processes did the professor use during class sessions?	Audio recordings of class sessions. Selection of 3–5 episodes in each session that stood out as particularly meaningful. A 2-hour audio recorded phenomenological interview of his experience
What were the students' experiences of each class session?	Written reflections prepared by students at the conclusion of each class session to include what stood out to them as particularly meaningful
What were the experiences of students of the course as a whole?	Audio recordings of individual student interviews and two focus group interviews at the conclusion of the course
What were students' experiences of other students?	Gathering of all student data in which students focused on their experience of other students

For the case study, the research team reached consensus on themes that represented a given experience across participants. We confirmed that each theme related to other themes and the context in which they were experienced. We used the words of the participants where possible to represent each theme. For example, in one of our studies of black students on a predominately white university campus (Davis et al., 2004), we could have labeled one theme using a jargon construct, "marginalized." But we wanted to help readers get inside the meaning of marginalization to these students. Hence, we selected a metaphor stated by one participant that best represented the meaning for all student participants: "A fly in the buttermilk."

To increase the trustworthiness of our research, again we submitted our findings to the scrutiny of the TPRG. This process enabled us to revise our findings until they provided the best possible representation of the data from the case study. In this manner the rigor and coherence of our findings were enhanced. In this book we summarize the studies that inform our implications and contribute to a phenomenological approach for teaching and learning.

The research we describe, along with application of philosophical concepts from existential phenomenology, are the bases of our approach for teaching and learning. From the findings and the specific philosophical ideas we detail below, we support our phenomenological framework. In

The Lifeworld of the Classroom   9

the next section, we provide an overview of what stands out to us from the field of existential phenomenology and its relevance in teaching and learning.

Our Perspective on Existential Phenomenology

> [T]he world is what [I] perceive. To seek the essence of perception is to declare that perception is, not presumed true, but defined as access to truth. . . . The world is not what I think, but what I live through.
>
> (Merleau-Ponty, 1945/1962, pp. xvi–xvii)

In this book, we focus on the teacher and student experience in the lifeworld of the classroom as informed by the field of existential phenomenology (for a detailed history, see Bakewell, 2016; Moran, 2000; Sokolowski, 2000). Note that unless otherwise indicated, when we say "phenomenology," we mean existential phenomenology in regard to our understanding of Merleau-Ponty's (1945/1962) perspective.

Most especially, we draw our inspiration from the writings of Maurice Merleau-Ponty (e.g., 1945/1962). But we include the explanations of others (often writing about Merleau-Ponty's views as well as additional phenomenologist philosophers) when we find their statements helpful in relation to teaching and learning in higher education (see Table 1.2 for a brief overview of each of our key concepts).

What draws us to existential phenomenology is its emphasis on human experience:

> [An existential phenomenologist] does not view experience (or consciousness in more technical terms) as a consequence of some internal set of events such as mind or brain but as a relationship between people and their world, whether the world at that moment consists of other people, nature, time, one's own body, personal or philosophical ideas or whatever. What is sought by both existentialism and phenomenology is a rigorous description of human life as it is lived and reflected upon in all its first-person concreteness, urgency, and ambiguity. For existential phenomenology, the world is to be lived and described, not explained.
>
> (Pollio et al., 1997, pp. 4–5)

Many scholars have written extensively about implications of existential phenomenology for education (e.g., Friesen, Henriksson, & Saevi, 2012; van Manen, 2017), but their focus has primarily been on phenomenology's relevance for teachers of children and youth. There are many phenomenological researchers that apply phenomenology to their scholarship on teaching in higher education (e.g., Adams & van Manen, 2017; Barritt, Beekman, Bleeker, & Mulderij, 1984; Halling, 2012; Hultgren, 1987, 1995;

Table 1.2 Authors' Perspectives Regarding Phenomenological Concepts That Inform Our Teaching Approach

Concept	Authors' Perspective
Perception	The subjective means by which we become aware of the world, forever bound by what stands out to us within a given context. By its nature, perception necessarily narrows our perspectives in ways we are often unaware. "What we see is always a function of 'how' we are looking" (Churchill, 2006, p. 89).
Intentionality	A quality of the mind that drives us in a certain manner, in ways we are often unaware. Bakewell (2016) discusses intentionality as the constant relationship of our minds with the world, in which "our thoughts are invariably *of* or *about* something" (p. 44); embracing "the whirl of our minds as they seize their intended phenomena one after the other and whisk them around the floor. . . ." (p. 46). According to Searle (1999), intentionality involves subjective states including, "beliefs and desires, intentions and perceptions, as well as loves and hates, fears and hopes" (p. 85).
Lifeworld	The lived experience of a human-being-in-the world, co-constituting the world as subjective meaning emerges from situated context. "It is a social, historical, and cultural world [that] includes individual, social, perceptual, and practical experiences" (from Alan Parson's course notes on *Lebenswelt*, 2016).

Intertwined influences on our perception, intentionality, and lifeworld of which we are often unaware:

	Embodiment	The body as a lived, experiential structure and as the context of cognitive mechanisms. Our lived experience always includes embodied aspects of development, cognition, physical sensations, and emotions of which we may or may not be aware.
	Sociocultural embeddedness	Existence within a particular sociocultural milieu. Our personal, professional, familial, linguistic, and societal experiences create a worldview, a lens that necessarily limits what and how we see the world.
	Intersubjectivity	The connection of humans to each other in some form of mutuality that can provide a sense of community or alienation, but that by our nature remains subjective. With an *egalitarian stance*, a teacher joins students as another learner exploring course content and personal experiences, where the teacher's and students' paths "intersect and engage each other like gears" (Merleau-Ponty, 1945/1962, p. xx).

Ambiguity	The fundamental indeterminacy of experience that can provide a sense of awe and mystery about course content as well as engender creativity. When ignored, it can lead to an *utilitarian attitude* that prioritizes specific practical applications of knowledge and skills related to content with little thought to their phenomenological meaning that transcends the classroom.

Selvi, 2008), but this body of work focuses almost exclusively on the teaching of the methodology and/or philosophy of phenomenology rather than the application of the phenomenological method to a broader framework for teaching and learning, which is our intent (see Chapters 8 and 9).

Our knowledge of the world comes primarily through our first-person experience of it, through our perceptions and the *intentionality* through which our subjective states connect us with the world. For Merleau-Ponty (1945/1962) intentionality is part of "an ever-flowing energy, a *network of relations*" (p. xx) between a person and the world—driven by "a psychological and historical structure . . . a way of existing, or a style" (p. 455).

As humans, we experience and learn about the world through perception and intentionality. "The world is not what I think, but what I live through" (Merleau-Ponty, 1945/1962, pp. xvi–xvii). But perception and intentionality are subjective; thanks to academia's rationalist, objectivist focus, we are typically unaware of their influence. As Hass (2008) states, perception "opens up in perspective [figures within some ground] . . . overflowing with half-hidden things that overlap, hide, and allude to other things" (p. 58).

If as teachers we understand the meaning and importance of the lifeworld, we can nurture a feeling or approach in ourselves and our students that opens the lifeworld of the classroom for examination. For it is with this approach, including the phenomenological attitude, that we can go to the heart of teaching and learning and *realize* the objective world of course content in all its subjectivity.

The Phenomenological Attitude

Our understanding of the phenomenological attitude falls in with views of the existential phenomenology of Merleau-Ponty. Finlay (2008) describes the phenomenological attitude as a dance "engaging a certain sense of wonder and openness to the world while, at the same time, reflexively restraining pre-understandings" (p. 2). In this manner, people can "[open] themselves to being moved by the Other, where evolving understandings are managed in a relational context" (p. 3). For humans connect with the

12   *The Lifeworld of the Classroom*

world through our senses, filtered through the subjective lenses of our attitudes, values, and beliefs that have evolved through individual experience. To live with this attitude, it is necessary that we acknowledge and constantly work to be aware of our subjectivity. Through the intersubjectivity inherent in a relational context, shared feelings or meanings lead to an increased sense of empathy, a *listening to be influenced*.

A relational stance and cultivation of empathy are common elements in descriptions of the phenomenological attitude. Churchill (2012), for example, described his provision of learning experiences for "cultivating an empathic presence to the world" (p. 3). He talked about his students "becoming enthralled to discover that they can tap into their own experience to open themselves to new worlds" (p. 3). Likewise, Dirkx (1998) discusses how a phenomenological attitude creates space for transformational learning experiences as meaning-making processes instrumental in fostering "a democratic vision of society and self-actualization of individuals" (p. 9).

A phenomenological attitude extends beyond relations with other people, however. Henriksson (2012) recalled being asked by a student if she felt like she was a better person, now that she has found phenomenology. Henriksson (2012) responded, "if better means more thoughtful, more willing to question the taken-for-granted, more open to others' experiences, then yes, phenomenology makes us better persons and probably also better teachers" (p. 122). She stated that phenomenology has the "the potential to create a sense of wonder, openness, change, and readiness to reflect on pedagogical matters" (p. 123). The findings we share in this book related to student experiences support those reported by other researchers and illustrate how students open to a phenomenological attitude when in learning environments that honor the lifeworld of the classroom.

Our particular existential phenomenological approach to teaching and learning in higher education rests on several intertwined aspects that stood out to us from Merleau-Ponty's philosophy. We believe they can help teachers deepen their understanding of what influences perception and intentionality: *embodiment, sociocultural embeddedness, ambiguity, intersubjectivity*. For these four influences, always in play in the lifeworld of the classroom and of each individual student and teacher, can lead to exploration of assumptions and intuitive thoughts that might otherwise go unnoticed and interfere with learning, and with teaching. We discuss these concepts next.

Intertwined Influences of Perception

At first glance, an emphasis on perception seems rather obvious and of limited value to teaching and learning—as perception is a naturally occurring act. But Merleau-Ponty (1948/2004) describes our apparent

The Lifeworld of the Classroom 13

familiarity with the world as "a delusion" and commented, "the world of perception is, to a great extent, unknown territory as long as we remain in the . . . utilitarian attitude" (p. 39).

In the current culture of higher education, the teacher's role is often utilitarian in the negative sense Merleau-Ponty describes (see Chapter 7 for a discussion). Many higher education "instructors" focus almost exclusively on training students, on transmitting the knowledge and skills of course content. Indeed, the job of the college instructor is to impart a given world of abstract knowledge, of explanation and analysis of subject matter—which may engage students in deep reflection, or merely provide an opportunity to demonstrate their ability to repeat back in some manner the information instructors transmit. Perception of each student's human experience seems a distraction. But Merleau-Ponty (1945/1962) says direct personal perception is of *primary* importance in developing knowledge:

> All my knowledge of the world, even my scientific knowledge, is gained from my own particular point of view, or from some experience of the world without which the symbols of science would be meaningless. The whole universe of science is built upon the world as directly experienced, and if we want to subject science itself to rigorous scrutiny and arrive at a precise assessment of its meaning and scope, we must begin by reawakening the basic experience of the world of which science is the second order expression.
>
> (p. viii)

Students may not believe, think, or *realize* (make real for themselves) the ideas their teachers want them most to learn—at least not in the manner that can expand and possibly transform their lives. But because abstract knowledge is built upon students' "basic experience of the world," our framework hinges upon perception.

Student perceptions, whether or not teachers are aware of them, can enhance or inhibit their ability to understand course content. For perception involves a given perspective, and some perspectives hide alternative views. But if teachers exclusively hold a utilitarian perspective, even when students are eager to learn, their goal may be to "cover" the content. They may believe they should not "waste" time helping students consider alternative perspectives related to course content, or helping students experience the inevitable ambiguity of new perceptions in a constructive way. Unfortunately, rather than address these issues, most of the literature on "best practices" takes a top-down stance on "correcting misconceptions," implying student perceptions and experiences are wrong. Further, recommendations for higher education increasingly call for a utilitarian attitude rather than the broader goal of higher education (Biggs & Tang, 2011; Cangemi, 2001; see also Chapter 7).

14   *The Lifeworld of the Classroom*

As we detail in other chapters, with our approach we seek to harness perception in such a way that students are *launched into the world* of the course subject matter. Our case study helped us understand how describing experiences relevant to course content prior to explaining abstract concepts allowed the case study professor and his students to explore their perceptions and meaning at a deeper level (see Box 1.3). Assumptions were questioned, alternative ideas discussed, and realizations frequently took place. We address the value of description in various chapters through our case study and related research findings.

Box 1.3   Reflection, *Howard Pollio*

Instead of beginning with an explanation of the meaning of space and place in the lived experience of humans, I brought five landscape paintings to class and asked several students to describe what stood out for them and then encouraged all students to pay attention to the similarities and differences among these descriptions. Only then did I connect these descriptions to the assigned reading of Tuan's *Space and Place* (1977) and the connections of Tuan's ideas to those of Merleau-Ponty.

Merleau-Ponty's ideas about four aspects of perception contributed greatly to our development of an existential phenomenological approach. As mentioned above, they include *sociocultural embeddedness, embodiment, intersubjectivity*, and *ambiguity*. Each presents a facet, like those of a diamond, that brings out heretofore hidden depths and enhances illumination of the human experience of being-in-the-world. In this section we define these concepts and provide a brief overview of their relation to the lifeworld of the classroom. We develop them further in later chapters.

Sociocultural Embeddedness

Merleau-Ponty (1945/1962) discusses the role of sociocultural development as a key context through which we learn to interpret the world. Sociocultural embeddedness refers to this context, which includes language, culture, and history. Although the particular term "sociocultural embeddedness" is not one Merleau-Ponty (1945/1962) uses, he writes extensively about the ways sociocultural development in childhood determines how we interpret the world. Bakewell (2016) discusses his remarkable insight:

> Of course, we have to learn this skill of interpreting and anticipating the world, and this happens in early childhood. . . . We fall for optical

illusions because we once learned to see the world in terms of shapes, objects, and things relevant to our own interests. . . . We rarely stop to think that [the thing or thought] is partly constituted by our way of paying attention or reaching out to things.

(pp. 231–232)

In particular, Bakewell (2016) discusses the social/cultural/historical influences from past experience. But these influences do not end with early childhood. If we become experts in some field of study, we co-create our perception of it with tacit and intuitive knowledge beyond its decontextualized subject matter. No teacher can fully step outside their own pre-academic development, their intuition (see Box 1.4), nor the assumptions and structures of their field of inquiry; neither can students that are confronted with novel information. Being aware of our own and students' sociocultural embeddedness can assist us in achieving our goals.

Box 1.4   Reflection, *Neil Greenberg*

As an ethologist by training with a research career in academia, I teach graduate and undergraduate biology courses that include content far removed from ethology. Nevertheless, my lectures and responses to student inquiry are always connected in a subtle if not overt manner to my understanding of this discipline of biology by first describing behaviors (actions) of organisms, followed by looking for patterns of relationships and connections and only then inferring causation. The assumptions, questions, and ways of inquiry of ethology infuse all my work.

Sociocultural embeddedness contributes to the lifeworld of the classroom in deeper ways as well (see Box 1.5). The term "unconscious/implicit bias" recently became a popular term, appearing frequently in the media (e.g., Spinney, 2014) and popular books (e.g., Kahneman, 2011) reviewing extensive research in this area. Merleau-Ponty's philosophical ideas about sociocultural embeddedness are manifest and confirmed in social psychology research (e.g., Haidt, 2001; Kahneman, 2011). Humans have prejudices and misconceptions. We cannot avoid it. As teachers, we view our students through unconscious bias, through stereotypes of race, class, gender, and what we think they are like as more or less responsible learners. As Mackh (2018) states, "We must first recognize our own biases, presumptions, and the impact of culture in our own lives so that we can genuinely, respectfully, humbly do the

16 *The Lifeworld of the Classroom*

most good for the people whose lives we hope to improve" (p. 199). Our students, too, are embedded in a sociocultural milieu, and they enter our classrooms with their own perspectives they developed through experiences in their families, earlier schooling, and the communities in which they live. These influences affect how they approach the teacher and the course content.

Box 1.5   Reflection, *Brian Sohn*

As I teach courses regarding the professional obligation of teacher candidates to do their part to dismantle systemic racism and work for social justice, I encounter resistance. There have been times when this resistance comes across as bigoted. When I hear phrases such as "I'm not racist, I have friends that are black," "Some of the gay kids just want attention," and other such banalities, it is difficult to maintain an open relational stance. At times I do so and find my negative assumptions to be correct, but at other times I learn from my students in unexpected ways. In one instance, a student responded negatively to a video in which black youth are described by a school principal as "victims." After dialogue with the student, I found, rather than latent racism, this student had suffered abuse from her domestic partner: in facing him in court, she was referred to repeatedly as a victim and had come to hate the term. She preferred survivor. Without an openness to student perspectives, I would have made the grave error of thinking I knew when I was influenced by my own bias. As my ignorance was alleviated, my understanding of the student grew and as a result I was better able to serve her learning needs.

As we describe in later chapters, our approach focuses on sociocultural embeddedness in order to broaden our own and our students' awareness of their social, historical, and cultural situations. We work to reveal underlying assumptions and use lived experience to more deeply reach our students.

Embodiment

Perhaps Merleau-Ponty's (1945/1962) most notable contribution to philosophy was his elucidation of embodiment and its clear refutation of the Cartesian dualism of mind and body. He stresses that "thinking is never devoid of context; it is always shaped by my history, language, interpersonal influences, and my *bodily attunement* [emphasis added] toward a meaningful and structured world or environment" (p. x). His ideas are especially important to consider in the classroom due to their implications for expression, language, and meaning (Adams, 2014; Hass, 2008):

> My body is the seat or rather the very actuality of the phenomenon of expression. . . . My body is the fabric into which all objects are woven. [So] my body is . . . that strange object which uses its own parts as a general system of symbols for the world, and through which we can consequently "be at home" in that world, "understand" it and find significance in it.
>
> (Merleau-Ponty, 1945/1962, p. 235)

All lived experience, even thinking, is embodied. Everything we as humans do—and are—involves our physical body and our senses, including our interoceptive and proprioceptive interaction with cognitive processes. Our engagement with the internal as well as the external world is fundamental to who we are as human-beings-in-the-world. Our feelings, imaginings, intuition, and many psychological and environmental influences are a part of us and, of course, influence teaching and learning (see Box 1.6).

Box 1.6 Reflection, *Kathy Greenberg*

I recall a time as a student when embodiment dramatically affected my learning. My professor was well known in his field and was teaching an introductory graduate course on a particular theory of learning. I was excited to be studying under an esteemed researcher. But I felt my body tense as the teacher began to speak rapidly about basic tenets of the theory. I sensed defensiveness in his demeanor which I took to mean the class was not a safe environment in which students could openly question any of the tenets. Later I learned the professor was coping with recent criticism of this once highly esteemed theory. Although I was able to do well on tests, I found I could not creatively engage with the content—I could not *mess about* (Hawkins, 1974) with the implications for teaching that the theory was supposed to make obvious.

In the lifeworld of the classroom, bodies and embodiment are often ignored, but always influential. When teachers and students are aware of emotions and other sensations, they become more mindful of the present moment. When the classroom is open to humor, to acceptance of feelings ranging from excitement to frustration or confusion,

18   *The Lifeworld of the Classroom*

the classroom becomes more "real." With our approach we appreciate, rather than ignore, the key role the body plays in teaching and learning. For embodiment is not simply some kind of affect or motivation. It is more. For it is the seat and site of our lived experience. In later chapters we discuss the role of embodiment in the lifeworld of the classroom and ways teachers can create a safe atmosphere in which it is acceptable for all participants to share what they experience in its wholeness (see also Chapter 2 for a discussion of embodiment from a scientific perspective).

Intersubjectivity

While there are many definitions of intersubjectivity within various disciplines, the term generally refers to agreement—mutual understanding—between individuals that leads to shared feelings or meanings. Intersubjectivity is related to empathy, understanding another individual's feelings from their point of view. But discussions of empathy are often limited to the realm of the cognitive. Intersubjectivity includes as integral the embodied individuals who share a world together with some degree of safety and/or conflict and sometimes with the synergy of something created between us. Merleau-Ponty (1945/1962) describes the ways in which reflection ultimately reveals not only a self, but a self that is in a world in which other selves exist: "The world is an indivisible unity of value shared" by all those with consciousness (p. xi). And in the lifeworld of the classroom, this shared indivisible world, this basis for intersubjectivity, can be seen most clearly in language. Hass (2008) states,

> In language, in dialogue, self and other communicate, that is, they "come together in one": conversation sweeps us into a common experience in which "subject" and "object" have no place, in which we are reciprocally drawn out of ourselves and our former thoughts toward the other.
>
> (p. 110)

Regarding others, Merleau-Ponty took a decidedly egalitarian stance. He viewed other people as "fellow travelers in life's journey" (Thomas, 2005, p. 71) and wrote, "my own and other people's [paths] intersect and engage each other like gears" (Merleau-Ponty, 1945/1962, p. xx). As humans, we are very good at categorizing and comparing ourselves to others but rather wary when facing the others' uniqueness, which can complicate teacher-student and student-student relationships. With our approach, we discuss ways to personalize relationships with students, so we can build trust and find the bridges to connect with each other (see Box 1.7).

Box 1.7 Reflection, *Howard Pollio*

I often share stories about how I acquired my knowledge, illustrating how I came to realize the abstract concepts of the subject matter. I present those stories in a self-deprecating manner as another learner working to expand his understanding of the world. My stories and my stance as an advanced student of the course content help create a sense that my students and I are all learners, we all have weaknesses, and we can all work together to pursue the challenges of learning.

Through our framework, we honor intersubjectivity by joining our students as learners in order to lead them to deeper understandings of course content (see especially Chapters 4 and 8).

Ambiguity

According to Hass (2008), Merleau-Ponty uses ambiguity "literally to denote that our experience of the world is pregnant with multiple meaning-directions . . . with multiple things calling for our attention" (p. 62). Ambiguity is part of the mystery of lived experience. Merleau-Ponty saw the ultimate role of the philosopher to always question assumptions and approach even "well-known" phenomena with wonder and openness. Perpetual questioning leaves the fixed accounts of objectivity open to flexibility and uncertainty and allows for a sense of excitement and discovery within everyday life.

To be sure, the particular sociocultural backgrounds and bodies of teachers and students leave open the potential for chaotic and infinitely differentiated interpretations of course content. But far from suggesting students will not learn what we teach, we believe implications of Merleau-Ponty's ideas tell us that students will have their own perspectives, and while these may cohere through our guidance, we can create opportunities to navigate multiple meanings within the classroom, assured that no phenomenon is ever known in a complete way.

Ambiguity may seem counter to the typical enterprise of teaching and learning. Most students, perhaps due to their past learning experiences in the school setting, want to attain a fixed set of knowledge from their teachers. "Just give me the answer," a student may say. But from science to the humanities, ambiguity can be linked to important cautions in scholarship, such as tentativeness, interpretation, and appropriation when considering research results. Failure to realize the ubiquity of ambiguity is a barrier to deep learning (see chapter 5). From the author of a textbook, to a teacher lecturing, to a student learning, course content may be seen as objective and rigid. Students become distracted from sensing the mystery

20   *The Lifeworld of the Classroom*

in our experience of learning something; they may remain unaware of their co-constitution of it.

Within our approach, the ambiguity that exists in all fields of study is not only acknowledged but used to develop powerful learning. We value the mystery and curiosity that accompanies ambiguity and share more about its power in later chapters. These four influences on perception, crucial to our approach to teaching and learning, are not isolated from each other. Ambiguity is intertwined with embodiment, sociocultural embeddedness, and intersubjectivity. For perception underlies the mind's intentionality.

Intentionality

At the heart of teaching and learning—as with all human experience— lies an ever-flowing energy, a *network of relations* (Merleau-Ponty, 1945/1962, p. xx) between a person and the world. Most philosophers call this situated perspective *intentionality*, adopted by Husserl to address the mind's disposition to be *about* something. Although much controversy exists among philosophers over the particularities of intentionality, Searle (1999) describes intentionality in a manner that is helpful in relation to our focus on teaching and learning:

> The primary evolutionary role of the mind is to relate us in certain ways to the environment, and especially to other people. My subjective states relate me to the rest of the world, and the general name of that relationship is "intentionality." These subjective states include beliefs and desires, intentions and perceptions, as well as loves and hates, fears and hopes. "Intentionality," to repeat, is the general term for all the various forms by which the mind can be directed at, or be about, or of, objects and states of affairs in the world.
>
> (p. 85)

By its very nature, intentionality is always a first-person perspective; "What we see is always a function of 'how' we are looking" (Churchill, 2006, p. 89). For

> [w]e learn and relearn who we are on the basis of our encounters with objects, ideas, and people—in short, with every different kind of "otherness". . . . What we are aware of in a situation reveals something important about who we are.
>
> (Pollio et al., 1997, p. 8)

Indeed, according to Merleau-Ponty (1945/1962), the human experience involves a structure of intentionality, and "All of my actions and thoughts are related to this structure" (p. 455). And first-person descriptions are the

The Lifeworld of the Classroom 21

way to understand the structure, to reveal it. For we do not deliberately control our intentionality. Based on the intertwined aspects of perception, we may be completely unaware of its structure.

Merleau-Ponty makes the following connections between intentionality and Gestalt psychology: figure-ground relationships (critical in Gestalt psychology) provide a window into intentionality by revealing what stands out in a lived experience and what recedes to the background. Merleau-Ponty (1945/1962) describes the all-encompassing role of intentionality and its subjective states:

> The fact remains that I am free, not in spite of, or on the hither side of, these motivations, but by means of them. For this significant life, this certain significance of nature and history which I am, does not limit my access to the world, but on the contrary, is my means of entering into communication with it. It is by being unrestrictedly and unreservedly what I am at present that I have a chance of moving forward; it is by living my time that I am able to understand other times, by plunging into the present and the world, by taking on deliberately what I am fortuitously, by willing what I will and doing what I do, that I can go further.
>
> (pp. 455–456)

Hence, in the lifeworld of the classroom, all participants—teacher and students—have their own, personal network of relations with other participants, the physical environment, and course content. Each participant's intentionality in turn becomes a part of the lived experience of the other participants. What participants are aware of and how they are aware of it reveal what is important to them. Intentionality connects a multitude of processes with each other and the world. It influences their demeanor, how participants connect or disconnect with others, and their perceptions of teaching and learning as they live the moments of the class. Intentionality is—and figure and ground are—fundamental to human experience and led us to Merleau-Ponty's work on the nature of perception. It is our intent that other chapters in this book will make these concepts come alive.

In summary, our approach seeks to go to the phenomenological heart of teaching and learning in higher education. We believe an understanding of the intertwined influences on perception of sociocultural embeddedness, embodiment, intersubjectivity, and ambiguity can help teachers better understand the phenomenological attitude, including related intentionality. Teachers who are open to the meaning of the lifeworld of the classroom will display a much more egalitarian than authoritarian stance as they embrace intersubjectivity in their relationship with students and toward course content. Although usually a more knowledgeable other, this kind of teacher invites students to share-or points out in class-alternative views and the ambiguity natural to our exploration of any objective

22 *The Lifeworld of the Classroom*

knowledge. This kind of teacher joins students in exploring the wonder of course content, rather than maintaining a strict focus on the "facts." Further, teachers with a phenomenological attitude can better balance the utilitarian demands of helping students master knowledge and skills needed in some future career with the importance of exploring personal experience in relation to course content. In this manner, such teachers help students find deep meaning at the heart of learning.

Our intent is to connect philosophy, research, and implications for practice. The purpose of each chapter is to help readers follow us through these lines of thinking so that our existential phenomenological approach becomes clear and useful to higher education teachers.

Organization of This Text

The goal of our organization is to help the reader live through the case study course from planning, to teaching and learning, to the outcomes of learning and implications for all teaching in higher education. Chapter 1 presented an overview of this text, information about our research procedures and extensive case study, a description of related research we include in the text, and our perspective on existential phenomenology and its important implications for higher education teaching and learning. But two chapters focus to a greater (Chapter 2) or a lesser (Chapter 9) degree on alternative views related to teaching and learning. Coming from a phenomenological attitude, towards other perspectives, we want to remain open to alternative ideas so they may provide insight and help us contrast the perspective of existential phenomenology.

Chapter 2. Getting DEEP: The Integrative Biology of Teaching and Learning

In this chapter we explain how transformative learning emerges out of the convergence of phenomenological experience and biological factors in a teachable moment. We describe such moments as deeply rooted in the integrated, biological domains of development, ecology, evolution, and physiology that include cognition, emotions, intuitions, and other aspects of the whole person. And we discuss implications of this knowledge for transformative learning in particular and higher education pedagogy in general.

Chapter 3. Preparation for Teaching: "What Can They Experience in Class?"

This chapter focuses on the findings from a study of the instructional planning practices of our case study professor. The data analysis examined transcripts of the professor's audiotaped pre-class and post-class conversations with a graduate assistant (Franklin, 2013). Verbatim transcripts of the actual class sessions were also examined. Six figural themes were identified, grounded in the professor's philosophical orientation in existential phenomenology. Although meticulous and detailed plans were outlined for each seminar session, these plans always included several options, so that the professor could choose the best approach according to the lifeworld of the classroom as it was occurring. We compare the professor's approach to instructional planning with current recommendations in higher education pedagogy.

Chapter 4. Teaching as Improvisational Jazz: "To Go Somewhere to Answer a BIG Question"

This chapter presents a comprehensive picture of how one master teacher used a phenomenological approach to focus on the lifeworld of the classroom and engage students in a free-flowing journey to answer a BIG question related course content. We present findings from two research studies related to our case study. We discuss the improvisational jazz teaching style of our case study professor. We present findings from a phenomenological analysis of a 2-hour interview of the professor. Then we present transcripts of two episodes that took place during class sessions and share our process coding analysis of the ways in which the professor enacted his unique approach. The chapter includes a discussion of aspects of our phenomenological approach as they relate to the professor's teaching.

Chapter 5. Free to Learn: A Radical Aspect of Our Approach

In this chapter we share a phenomenological analysis of the student experience of being a learner in the case study course. Student participants in our case study described the course as "different" from other courses they had taken: the atmosphere of the course was "free" and "open," they felt "safe" and "comfortable," and "collaborative" and "connected." What they learned was personally and professionally relevant. Our findings revealed how differently they felt when the institutional role of "student" was removed. Despite the lack of course requirements, these students reported that the course changed their lives. We discuss these findings in relation to the case study professor's approach and the four intertwined concepts of phenomenology we highlight: ambiguity, embodiment, intersubjectivity, and sociocultural embeddedness.

24 *The Lifeworld of the Classroom*

Chapter 6. Student Experiences of Other Students: "All Together in This Space"

In this chapter we share a phenomenological analysis of the student experience of other students, an often-overlooked aspect of higher education pedagogy. Students in the case study course experienced each other as "Genuinely Invested" in the course and "Completely Caught Up" in each other and its content. They also experienced "Coming to Appreciate Diversity," a progression of learning through each other's contributions. These themes emerged from the ground of "All Together in this Space." We discuss the ways in which the professor's approach contributed to a strong sense of intersubjectivity and a classroom climate that encouraged students to share in a common existential project.

Chapter 7. Transcending the Classroom: Student Reports of Personal and Professional Change

In this chapter, we share a phenomenological analysis of student experience focusing on the ways in which they realized course content beyond the classroom. Case study participants described "life-changing" learning experiences that went beyond a narrow definition of success dominated by surface learning. We provide case study participants' descriptions of applications of course content, such as changes in a participant's approach to clinical psychological counseling, another's redesign of his approach to his own teaching, and several participants' descriptions of changes in their ways of seeing the world and others in their personal lives. Students described increased openness, awareness, appreciation, and empathy. We then examine perceptions of students from a different higher education context who were also exposed to a phenomenological approach to teaching and learning. The similarities were striking. We discuss implications of these changes as they relate to the purpose and mission of higher education.

Chapter 8. Messing Up and Messing About: Student Needs and Teachers' Adaptation of Our Phenomenological Approach

This chapter focuses on two aspects of teaching and learning outside of our case study. First, we discuss student perceptions of their experience of teachers messing up, in the context of African American undergraduate students on a predominately white university campus, low socioeconomic status and first generation undergraduate students in community colleges and universities, and international graduate students for whom English was not their native language. Second, we provide six teacher descriptions of courses in which they messed about with their own unique phenomenological style. The descriptions include face-to-face as well as online courses with undergraduates, master's and doctoral level students. We provide implications for teachers in multiple fields working with students at various levels.

Chapter 9. Contributions of Our Existential Phenomenological Approach to Higher Education Pedagogy: Implications for Theory, Research, and Practice

In this chapter, we share overall conclusions regarding how our research and thinking has been inspired and informed by existential phenomenology. We present seven principles of our approach that we derived from implications of both philosophy and our extensive research. Next, we compare and contrast our approach with other higher education phenomenological approaches described in the literature. Then we discuss other pedagogy often recommended for use in higher education, including learner-centered, brain research-based, contemplative, and cognitive theory-based practices. Further, we discuss four implications in pedagogical research that can be addressed by an existential phenomenological framework.

Conclusion

We are comfortable speaking of the *heart* of teaching and learning. Outside of the objective anatomical definition, our favorite dictionary (Merriam-Webster Dictionary, 2018) tells us that heart refers also to the central or innermost, essential or vital part of something. A Hebrew word for heart, *lebab*, is defined in Strong's Concordance (1890) as inner man, mind, will, and heart. The Chinese have one word, *xīn* (心) (Han Trainer Dictionary, 2018), translating to both heart and mind, as well as center or core. If we co-constitute our experience of the world, and this is our only access to abstract knowledge, then teaching in higher education needs to address the lifeworld of the classroom. Our research illustrates how an existential phenomenological framework can help higher education teachers meet students at the heart of teaching and learning.

As with all phenomenological approaches of which we are aware, ours is open to teaching artistry, acting on momentary intuition, and the connoisseurship of the teacher. But it does not distract from the use of pedagogical techniques and activities unless they are in conflict with a phenomenological attitude. Our approach can help higher education teachers better understand the lifeworld of the classroom as it is lived—in its idiosyncratic, fluid context. As Merleau-Ponty argued, perception provides our only access to abstract knowledge. And the phenomenological emphasis on description can help teachers understand influences on their students' perceptions of course content. For real teaching begins with understanding who our students are, what they think, and what they feel. The goal of our existential phenomenological approach to teaching is to further an understanding of pedagogical techniques at a deeper level—so they become flexible, situation-based, personal approaches to fostering transformative learning. And with our approach, we can better develop our connoisseurship as teachers. Even in their "messiness," the lifeworlds of all classrooms can be navigated with basic principles predicated on what is meant to exist in a phenomenal world.

2 Getting DEEP
The Integrative Biology of Teaching and Learning

> The whole of science is built upon the world as directly experienced, and if we want to subject science to rigorous scrutiny and arrive at an assessment of its actual meaning and scope, we must begin by reawakening the basic experience of the world of which science is the second-order expression.
>
> (Merleau-Ponty, 1945/1962, p. viii)

We believe that all teaching can profit from a better understanding of the processes that enable learning, and this involves adopting a phenomenological attitude while remaining open to the biological factors that underlie teaching and learning. The biologist amongst our authors is confident the shared values of phenomenology and science is the opening through which fruitful collaboration will flow. This is, in part, because the *meaning* of his subject matter and what he learns about it is deeply enriched by first order insights, as is true of many scientists. Description, pursued as deeply as possible without bias, and particularly connections with more or less related topics, contributes significantly to this meaning. And as a teacher he is highly motivated to make comparable experiences available to students.

An examination of these processes is, however, a vast task, so in this chapter, we shall focus only on a few key examples of how biological considerations can speak to the phenomenologically inclined teacher. In particular, we focus on the ideas of the transformative learning experience and the teachable moment. Taken together, they also represent an eloquent expression of the reciprocity of internal and external phenomena, an idea valued in both phenomenology and ethology. We turn next to those ideas.

Transformative Learning

We begin with *transformative learning*, which is an internal phenomenon that can be understood in a variety of ways (Taylor, Cranton, &

28   *Getting DEEP*

Associates, 2012). The meaning to which we subscribe was included in an article concerning some of our case study findings (Sohn et al., 2016, and see Chapter 7):

> While thoughtful teachers in higher education strive to help their students master course content, for many, a further goal is to help them transcend it—to help them go beyond transfer of content skills and knowledge—to a transformative understanding of the world and their place within it. . . . This transformation is manifest in students realizing the relevance of course content in their personal and professional lives—in the aesthetic sense of gratification that imparts confidence in one's understanding or insight—an intuitive sense of its truth and worth.
>
> (p. 179)

Learning goes on at every level of organization all the time. Cells learn, tissues and organs learn, connections within and between tissues and organs change as result of experience—we learn. It is an expression of the everyday ongoing processes of change and growth, but in its extreme expression, learning which imparts a distinctive sense that "everything is different" is transformative. Of course, connections are always being created, reconfigured, weakened, and strengthened, as we experience the world and ideas, but in its extremity, the transformative learning experience enables more clarity in our thinking about the circumstances that encourage and enable it. It shares attributes with epiphany ("an experience of sudden and striking realization") and resembles Piagetian "accommodation," the changing of a mental schema under the influence of new information (Piaget, 1947/2003).

In our view and in phenomenological terms, this is exemplified by students experiencing a paradigm shift from merely knowing course content to realizing its relevance in their personal and professional lives. This shift from *knowing* to *realizing* (Greenberg et al., 2015) can be compared to an act of creation (or discovery) that gives course content privileged personal meaning. This "bridge" from disciplinary generalities to an individual's particulars may have been gradually constructed, but often appears suddenly in a student's mind when there is a conscious awareness of energizing connections to other information or to intuitive and affective depths that are not usually available for connecting. The transformation is often (but not only) experienced as a cascade of ideas that has been "triggered" by an ecphoric thought or idea—a stimulus that acts as a trigger for a cascade of memories that can be organized into a coherent whole. The metaphoric implications are interesting: very small adjustments in this cascade can have massive consequences. The phenomenologically informed classroom can make the reservoir of a student's personal resources available for such connections. Students themselves may be unaware of the depth and richness of this reservoir. If we are going to put it in the service of learning, the best the teacher can do is create an enabling environment—potentially teachable moments—in which students feel ownership of canonical content that can create meaning and make the content available to other domains of life, often in highly creative ways.

The Teachable Moment

The environment in which transformative learning occurs emerges from the convergence of internal and external circumstances—biological, phenomenological, and environmental. It has been called the perfect storm of circumstances in which external factors in the moment converge with memory, awareness, and expectations, making a creative, transformative experience much more likely—this is the *teachable moment* (Greenberg et al., 2016).

Like the transformative learning experience, the teachable moment is at the end of a continuum of experiences and evokes unmistakable signs of phenomenological meaning. Teachable moments often appear unpredictable because the circumstances that converge to create them are not—probably *cannot*—be fully understood. It is, however, possible for teachers to reflect upon these circumstances as they plan learning activities. This is not a new insight; according to Plato (n.d.), Socrates appreciated that one could learn the skill of delivering an appropriate comment at precisely the right moment.

Of course, such moments can occur spontaneously, but some (implicit or explicit) understanding of them—the *phenomenological attitude*—can enable the teacher to maximize the possibilities for them. Our case study professor has done just that: with insight about each student's personal history, an expectation that in a specific place at a specific time they all have a measure of shared beliefs and values; in an environment he made "safe" for spontaneous discussion, he could guide students toward the moment. In his intuitive deployment of DEEP thinking (see DEEP ethology, below) in a phenomenologically inclined classroom, his understanding of development and environment could guide students toward a teachable moment, much like "the pedagogical moment" of van Manen (1991), in which a teacher must act (or withhold acting) at a time that manifests both great sensitivity to the context and the life story and circumstances of the student (see Chapter 4).

Existential Phenomenology

Phenomenology emphasizes the perceptions of the individual and the description rather than the explanation of experience. This view, complemented by existentialism, informs the thinking of the authors of this volume, some of whom have implemented it in their qualitative research,

30 *Getting DEEP*

some of which is summarized or reported here (see Chapter 1). It is helpful to distinguish this school of thought, with its emphasis on uniquely individual sources of authority and meaning, from its predecessors such as transcendental phenomenology, concerned principally with *essences*. This is an important distinction because the implicit points of view that inform transcendental philosophy still haunt teacher education and the classroom.

This is the problem Jean-Paul Sartre (1943/1956) sought to solve: the *"existence"* of his *existentialism* was ventured to contrast with the *essence* of his philosophical predecessors (the motto became, *l'existence précède l'essence*)—in other words, the real takes priority over the ideal, restoring authority (and responsibility) to the individual by emphasizing how things *are* rather than how they *should be*. This is most acutely manifest at times when, for example, a student experiences a transformative learning experience—for it is *the learner's* experience, not anyone else's.

Naturalizing Phenomenology

The distances between philosophy and science are significant and often contentious. For example, the claim in phenomenology that every experience is irreducible is difficult to reconcile with the scientific paradigm. Fortunately, there are significant efforts to *naturalize* phenomenology (Petitot, Varela, Pachoud, & Roy, 1999). Merleau-Ponty was stretching towards such an optimistic state in his emphasis on the "embodied mind" (Levin, 2016), a key topic we shall return to when discussing cognition. Naturalizing mental traits reflects efforts to increase confidence in an intuitive belief that there is a continuity between philosophy and science, and as such, it is an important step in avoiding the sterility of the ancient biases regarding dualism, epitomized for our era by Cartesian dualism. In Merleau-Ponty's (1945/1962) view, philosophy

> is not the reflection of a pre-existing truth, but, like art, the act of bringing truth into being. . . . We witness every minute the miracle of related experience, and yet nobody knows better than we do how this miracle is worked, for we *are ourselves* [emphasis added] this network of relationships.
>
> (p. xx)

Naturalizing the phenomenological perspectives makes them accessible to science at the same time as it infuses science with an appreciation for and implementation of the phenomenological attitude. Our view accepts that in teaching and learning, biological corollaries of consciousness (and in many cases its prerequisites) occur at all levels, from simply the evoking of attention to an internal or external stimulus to what it feels like to be one's self. This is a view encouraged by Merleau-Ponty's *Phenomenology of Perception* and the waves of subsequent works in philosophy and science (see Marconi, 2012), confirming and extending its insights (Carel & Meacham, 2013; cited in Petitot et al., 1999). The ways of thinking encouraged by these views involves an understanding of the forms of consciousness and cognition by means of which, and in which, all dimensions of the *lifeworld* are integrated (see Chapter 1).

Lifeworld

The idea of the *Lifeworld* (*Lebenswelt*) has been influential since introduced in the 1930s by Edmund Husserl, who conceptualized it as pre-reflective—that is, our focus is on *what* we are perceiving rather than *how* we are perceiving it (Brooks, 2015). As discussed in Chapter 1, the lifeworld is "the world of lived experience inhabited by us as conscious beings and incorporating the way in which phenomena (events, objects, emotions) appear to us in our conscious experience or everyday life" (Brooks, 2015, p. 642). As such, "It is a social, historical, and cultural world [that] includes individual, social, perceptual, and practical experiences" (from Alan Parsons's course notes on *Lebenswelt*, 2016). We can compare it to the *umwelt* proposed earlier by Jakob von Uexküll (1982) to describe the fact that each kind of organism lives in its own perceptual world and will interpret the same information in different ways (Eagleman, 2011). For example, the sensory world is a combination of information from all senses, internal and external, and each has a unique trajectory through the nervous system, extracting different kinds of information from the aspect of the environment to which it is responsive. And it is the intertwining, integrative aspects that compose the lifeworld that leads us to consider existential phenomenology in relation to integrative biology.

Existential Phenomenology and Integrative Biology

Deploying all the study and scholarship resources of the several key biological disciplines that converge on behavior, we find an often neglected dynamic comes to the foreground: every aspect of an individual's cognitive processing is manifest as an outcome of the interactions that are part of the very definition of life. Arguably, these processes are not things that happen to people, they *are* people.

It is the unity of action which emerges from this multiplicity that encourages the holistic impulse. And a familiar theme in holistic thought is emergence, the idea that no whole can be defined by only its components (Humphreys, 2018). In this, phenomenology has an aesthetic quality, another aspect that is often neglected (Levin, 2016), but deeply appreciated by Merleau-Ponty (Crowther, 1982). Something unspecified (or unspecifiable) about the elements of which any distinctive entity is

32 *Getting DEEP*

constituted enables the existence of that particular whole. We can take some philosophical heart, however, from Yoshimi's (2011) juxtaposition of two relevant comments:

> Every entity that is valid for me [is] . . . an index of its systematic multiplicities. Each one indicates an ideal general set of actual and possible experiential manners of givenness . . . every actual concrete experience brings out, from this total multiplicity, a harmonious flow.
>
> (Husserl, 1970, p. 166)

And

> human cognition involves . . . many hundreds, perhaps even thousands, of internal cognitive "spaces," each of which provides a proprietary canvas on which some aspect of human cognition is continually unfolding.
>
> (Churchland, 2002)

Yoshimi juxtaposes Husserl (the "transcendental idealist") and Churchland (the "reductive physicalist") to comfort us. Their thoughts enjoy a resonance that is also a tenet of aesthetics: "unity in multiplicity" (see Greenberg, 2018b).

As mentioned earlier, the first task of the phenomenologist (and, as we will see, the ethologist) is to *describe*. Ethologists often begin by describing as much of their subject's repertoire as possible (creating an "ethogram") and then tend to emphasize a behavioral pattern of interest that might range from a muscle twitch to an entire constellation of closely related patterns (Greenberg, 1978). The ultimate goal is further insight about the likely causes and consequences of what they are able to observe about the way individuals and groups (not least, teachers and students) acquire, organize, and act upon information. These phenomena are inevitable in the architecture of life—that is, the aggregate of traits that enable individuals to meet their biological needs in changing environments—both the environment within (physiological) and that outside the organism (environmental). This, in the spirit of true science, is a hypothesis, not an indubitable truth. Time has mitigated the rigidity attributed to science by researchers, who were persuaded by positivism and the seeking of a "true truth." Science has become progressively and more frequently viewed as a human endeavor (Greenberg, 1986). Science, echoing the function of everyday thinking, must remain open to revision as new information is received and old information is reinterpreted or disqualified.

There is an empowering ambiguity in the egalitarian attitude Merleau-Ponty (1945/1962) espouses, not the least of which is creativity (see Chapter 1). Hence, phenomenologists describe, but in a different fashion. For they are looking for what stands out to the individual, in an unreflected manner, related to a particular phenomenon—in an effort to find the meaning held by the individual. Ethologists, on the other hand, assume (and this may be bias) that non-humans are necessarily unreflective and that meaning resides in the pursuit of evolutionary fitness. It is further assumed that in humans as well as non-humans, the deepest biases, those that are constitutional parts of the brain's organization, have been selected by evolution because of their adaptive contribution to fitness. Certainly, meeting that essential need also motivates humans, when meaning, reflected upon, may contribute to the integration of an individual's self.

In other words, importantly and in great service to efforts to mitigate Cartesian dualism, all the discriminable components and processes of an organism have evolved over generations and developed over a lifetime as elements in each individual's environment:

> Parts and wholes evolve in consequence of their relationship, and the relationship itself evolves. These are the properties of things that we call dialectical: that one thing cannot exist without the other, that one acquires its properties from its relation to the other, that the properties of both evolve as a consequence of their interpenetration.
>
> (Levins & Lewontin, 1985, p. 3)

Gadamer's observation about the process of interpretation is significant for our view of interpretation within ethology and phenomenology:

> The anticipation of meaning in which the whole is envisaged becomes actual understanding when the parts that are determined by the whole themselves also determine this whole. . . . The movement of understanding is constantly from the whole to the part and back to the whole.
>
> (cited by Robinson & Robinson, 2013, p. 291)

In this sense, and in agreement with Merleau-Ponty's view, the "phenomenological method is a process of reconciliation rather than an instrument for restricted descriptive-analytic purposes. What needs reconciling are, at first approximation, the objective world and its subjective interpretation" (Natanson, 1973, p. 28).

Both these ideas evoke concern about the tension between holism and reductionism, both enshrined in implicit bias as well as scholarly tradition. Gadamer (1960/2013) may have a satisfying solution, however: *the hermeneutic circle*, in which one treats a whole with reference to its parts, while simultaneously mindful that each part exists in the context of the whole. Gadamer envisioned the circle as a dynamic and progressive "conversation" with data that builds consensus and is more accessible to practical application. This process is at the heart of the research methodology utilized by most of our authors. But we

34   *Getting DEEP*

briefly introduce now the field of ethology and its contributions to our understanding of individual behavior as it relates to the lifeworld of the classroom.

We believe that efforts to create such an empowering lifeworld in the classroom are facilitated by an understanding of ethology, an approach to the biology of behavior that integrates several key sibling disciplines within biology. These are developmental biology, ecology, evolutionary biology, and physiology, represented by the acronym DEEP. We will return to these after commenting on our understanding of embodiment and cognition/consciousness, key ideas in phenomenology that are also our best bridge from the philosophical views to biology.

Embodiment

Maurice Merleau-Ponty (1945/1962) states that "There is no inner man, man is in the world, and only in the world does he know himself" (p. xi). But knowledge, from the perspective of behavioral biology, involves cognition, and being in the world involves it in the context of that cognition. *Embodiment* refers to giving concrete form to an abstraction, to making an idea or feeling tangible. In phenomenology, as Merleau-Ponty (1945/1962) frames it, "a nexus of living meanings" (p. 151). Our engagement with the internal as well as the external world is fundamental to who we are as human-beings-in-the-world. Our feelings, imaginings, intuition, and many psychological and environmental influences are a part of us and, of course, influence teaching and learning.

Embodied cognition is the term adopted by scholars and researchers seeking to emphasize the extent to which cognitive processes in particular are intimately interwoven with the fabric of the body—a body that influences and is influenced by the environment into which it is born and hopefully prospers. This idea, derived from existential phenomenology, informs and energizes our reports of the experiences discussed in this volume (see Chapter 1). It refers to the always present involvement of every cognitive function, and every level of consciousness, from intuition to epiphany, with the state and functions of the body. These are communicated by a large array of internal sensory receptors (interceptors and proprioceptors), as well as countless specific chemicals that have more or less access to the brain where they participate in organizing and initiating (or suppressing) specific actions, including learning (e.g., Laureys & Tononi, 2008; Merleau-Ponty, 1945/1962) and the expression of what is learned, even by means of intuition, which involves access to cognitive resources of which an individual is unaware and typically precedes conscious reasoning (Haidt, 2012).

Whatever we know depends on our body that enables life and also builds on its constituent elements. Merleau-Ponty (1945/1962), from whom we have taken much direction, states that "The body is our general medium for having a world" (p. 146). The functions of body he includes in his conception of embodiment are those "necessary for the conservation of life," those that "elaborate upon primary actions" and those that "build itself an instrument, and it projects thereby around itself a cultural world" (p. 146).

We use the term embodied in the sense that cognition depends upon the "kinds of experience that come from having a body with various sensorimotor capacities, and second, that these individual sensorimotor capacities are themselves embedded in a more encompassing biological, psychological and cultural context" (Varela, Thompson, & Rosch, 1991/2016, p. 173). Further, as Brown (2017, p. 871, citing Greeno, 1998) observes, "if we are embodied selves then we are also always somewhere embedded in some situational context. Thus, the theory of embodied cognition can also entail what is known as situated cognition." This is a position that regards the social and cultural context both as formative and as a resource (Cobb, 2001). As in ethology, situated context is concerned with authenticity—real-life contexts, a point emphasized in teachers who find inspiration in this idea for their instructional design. Cognition is one of the most striking elements of embodiment, and we turn next to that.

Cognition and Consciousness

Cognition is sometimes thought of as everything that happens in the brain between input of sensory information and output of actions. But this neglects the extent to which these processes are affected by perception and action. A more useful view is that cognition refers to "the mechanisms by which animals acquire, process, store, and act on information from the environment. These include perception, learning, memory, and decision making" (Shettlesworth, 1998, p. 5). These are the processes that enable us to cope with vagaries and exigencies of the world from the most subtle to the most challenging. It is how we meet our needs as an organism. Perception is included as a participant in cognition because the processing of stimuli—its suppression or enhancement and the extraction of various kinds of information—begins at the instant of detection by a sensory receptor and also at every successive processing module along the path to awareness. Processing and the constructing, deconstructing, and reconstructing of connections is especially affected by past experience and contributes to future perceptions and their perceived meanings. The structures and processes of cognition, while almost impenetrably complex, manifest layers of organization of relative complexity, mostly by virtue of the more or less interconnected nature of its constituent elements. For example, cells, aggregates of functionally related cells, and interconnected systems of varying complexity, are each distinguishable components whose actions alone or in concert affect the state of mind.

36   *Getting DEEP*

Cognition is also wholly dependent on the processes of *perception*, in the foreground of phenomenological thinking. When a sense organ is stimulated, and information enters the nervous system, a percept is created. Before there is any conscious awareness, the information is analyzed, information extracted, and reconstructed within the brain. It is the active deconstruction and restructuring of percepts that allows us to regard perceptual experience as a cognitive process. In William James's (1911) view the supervenient phenomenon is a concept; as he put it,

> The intellectual life of man consists almost wholly in his substitution of a conceptual order for the perceptual order in which his experience originally comes. . . . Percepts and concepts interpenetrate and melt together, impregnate and fertilize each other. Neither, taken alone, knows reality in its completeness. . . . The world we practically live in is one in which it is impossible (except by theoretic retrospection) to disentangle the contributions of intellect from those of sense.
>
> (pp. 51–52)

Maintaining that "the *perceived* world is the always presupposed foundation of all rationality, all value and all existence" (p. 13), *Merleau-Ponty (1964) sought* to develop a descriptive philosophy of *perception*, our kinesthetic, prescientific, lived-bodily experience and cognition of the world—the unification. And as James (1911) reminds us,

> The deeper features of reality are found only in perceptual experience. Here alone do we acquaint ourselves with continuity, or the immersion of one thing in another, here alone with the self, with substance, with qualities, with activities in its various modes, with time, with cause, with change, with novelty, with tendency, and with freedom.
>
> (p. 97)

Perception, the critical bridge between the cognizing individual and their environment, includes other individuals in one's environment, indispensable to our ability to navigate and meet our needs in the world.

Amongst the many crucial processes that cognition entails, two of particular interest are memory and foresight. In one sense this is exactly what learning is about, but in our species, it goes much further. It is interesting that much of the neural basis of both memory and foresight—past and future—is shared in the brain (Schacter & Addis, 2007). Awareness of such a connection, played out in practice, could guide a teacher seeking student engagement with content. For example, both memory and creativity would be engaged when asking students where knowledge of some aspect of course content could lead in the future.

Consciousness is sometimes viewed as the inevitable consequences of our complexity or an unexpected irreducible *emergent* quality that could never have been predicted on the basis of a perfect knowledge of its subordinate processes. There is an abundance of reasonable paths within cognition which can compete as well as cooperate with each other to evoke an optimal response. Although at its best all processes function well together, there are nevertheless multiple functions, which, like all other traits described earlier, have each their own developmental and evolutionary histories. This is a principal contribution to our uniqueness.

The expressions of consciousness at different levels—from coma to the fullest measure of attention and thought—are tuned by intimate relations with the environment. Consciousness is often regarded as the most complex of human attributes, possibly emergent from cognition at its most complex. It is the embodiment of these processes that occupies many phenomenologists, and past and anticipated work of several highly productive research groups in cognitive neuroscience is gradually leading to a rapprochement between the fields. Traditional scientific methods integrating brain and behavior studies (neuroscience, cognitive science) have made remarkable progress but are at present stymied by a problem that would resonate with phenomenologists.

This is the "hard problem" of consciousness: how is subjective state derived from objective entities? How are feelings related to survival needs? Although a question that has deep roots in history, just the naming and framing of this problem by the distinguished philosopher of mind, David Chalmers (1995), has been the catalyst for an abundance of diverse studies. The richness of the methods developed and the analyses of consciousness in the last few generations of phenomenology would seem an invaluable resource for those approaching consciousness from a scientific viewpoint. Indeed, collaboration would, in Zahavi' s (2003) view, be highly beneficial to both. The study of these processes is plagued by an array of congenital and acquired biases, ranging from our competence to perceive and process selected aspects of our environment through those attributable to cultural traditions such as education and language. But, however they are viewed, their dependence on the environment throughout development and subsequent sensitivity to bodily functions energizes our confidence in embodiment. And it is helpful to consider embodiment and the teachable moment in relation to levels of organization.

Levels of Organization

Cultivating an appreciation for embodiment is highly desirable for the phenomenologically inclined teacher (Stolz, 2015). Placing a mental phenomenon within the brain, body, and environment also underscores the utility of thinking in terms of *levels of organization*, where the elements at given levels (for example, systems that serve receptivity, attention, integration of information, and action) communicate with levels both above and below them in complexity. A few examples: access to information from

38 Getting DEEP

the sensory world of the classroom or from memory, and acting on that information, may be at different levels of organization within an individual. Similarly, a raw stimulus and its meaning are at different levels of organization, achieved as its information is extracted and then integrated with other cognitive processes at more complex areas of the brain. And in a classroom, a student having an idea to express and actually articulating it, involves different levels of organization: First, she must retrieve and hold the thought in memory, but then when expressing that idea, she must move to a more complex level of controlling muscles involved in speaking while thinking. Also, an individual student's attention in the classroom could be affected by a subordinate level (say, the student is too cold or hungry) or a superordinate level (say, the classroom climate feels safe, or the teacher is particularly compelling).

The connections within and between these levels can easily be bewilderingly complex, but two general principles that appear to govern this complexity are deceptively simple. We accept easily that traits are the result of the actions of genes, activated or suppressed by their immediate environment. But most of these traits are affected by multiple genes—they are *polygenic*. In concert with a complementary phenomenon: most genes have multiple functions—they are *pleiotropic*. Taken together these attributes of traits and genes create an inseparable fabric of structures and functions that is deeply appealing: unimaginable complexity reduced to simple rules. As an analogy in the classroom, an idea or concept in mind may take its specific form from a multitude of variables, many unique to the student; the idea may then influence a multitude of other thoughts and ideas by a process recalling ecphory, the retrieval of a constellation of memories evoked by a new fragment of information. In some cases, this is highly creative if the memories recovered were not previously related but now present themselves to consciousness as a coherent whole.

We appreciate that there are layers above and beneath every specific phenomenological observation. Not least, how the environment and body collaborate with cognition and the cognitive processes that then interact with the body and through it, the environment. Of course, there are always more layers, and so the endpoint of our inquiries—where we choose to stop—involves a judgment about the usefulness of the layers of organization we emphasize versus the cost of looking further, either down to more fundamental, possibly enabling levels, or up to supervenient layers. The levels of organization we are mostly concerned with in the classroom emphasize perception and cognition at the center, and the immediate aspects of body just beneath (embodied cognition) and the immediate aspects of the environment just above—including intersubjectivity and sociocultural embeddedness (socially situated cognition)—all are incorporated in the lifeworld.

At the highest level of organization are the connections we can discover between knowledge and its place in our lifeworld—ability to meet our needs—that provides *meaning*: and, in Mark Johnson's (2007) incisive terms, "Meaning is more than words and deeper than concepts" (p. 1). The central thesis of Johnson's book is consistent with our operating assumptions about cognition. And they bring another dimension to this idea: not only is "what we call 'mind' and what we call 'body' not two things, but rather aspects of one organic process." Johnson (2007) goes on to emphasize that

> all our meaning, thought, and language emerge from the *aesthetic* [emphasis added] dimensions of this embodied activity. Chief among those aesthetic dimensions are qualities, images, patterns of senso-rimotor processes, and emotions. . . . Coming to grips with your embodiment is one of the most profound philosophical tasks you will ever face.
>
> (p. 1)

And in pursuit of meaning we are presented with another optimality—cost versus benefit—problem, familiar to ecologists and economists (see below). But given the pleasures of participating in this book, the price is not so high. Eager for insights and pleased by surprise, we have observed (with Wilson & Foglia, 2017) that "Sometimes the nature of the dependence of cognition on the body is quite unexpected and suggests new ways of conceptualizing and exploring the mechanics of cognitive processing" (paragraph 2, online).

All connectedness at every level of biological organization exists by virtue of its communications within and between levels. Ultimately communication between organisms (as in the cultivation of intersubjectivity) occurs where the quality of communications is arguably more precise when organisms share aspects of their lifeworlds. And while never complete, we might expect that the quality of communications is precise to that extent. A phenomenological investigation that builds on first-person reports is only possible to the extent that we can describe another person's subjective state while rigorously avoiding our acquired biases, a process emphasized in phenomenology as "*epoché*" or "bracketing" (Hut, 2001). Is this, as Churchill (2012) inquires, asking for empathy? Feeling what the subject feels about what they say? Or as one of our authors puts it, "walking in their shoes" (see Chapter 1). Learning is generally understood to represent adaptive change. That this change can occur at all levels of organization, each in their own way, is suggested by the observation that it is a property of all organisms, and even those without organized nervous systems (Tennenhouse, 2017).

To "walk in another's shoes" is the beginning of understanding of shared worlds (see Chapter 1 for a description of the experience of one of our authors who walked in the shoes of students and changed her teaching). In 1974, Nagel asked the question that still energizes consciousness

40   *Getting DEEP*

studies: "What is it like to be a bat?" He spoke of a host of related issues about how much we can share with the self-centered world of another organism. This is comparable to the lifeworld of Husserl, which we discuss below in relation to ecology.

Another dimension that helps coordinate levels of organization and ramifies through the disciplines integrated in ethology, as we shall see, is the meeting of biological needs, to which we now turn.

Biological Needs

A hierarchy reflecting relative priorities in meeting needs was designed originally by humanist psychologist Abraham Maslow (1943) as a theory of motivation. It effectively connects disciplines at different levels of organization. Needs must be met for organisms to survive and thrive in any given environment, and the body is finely attuned to (a) detect which biological needs at a given moment are not being met, and (b) their priorities for survival and self-actualization. At every point, mindfulness of a particular component of DEEP ethology must include at least an intuition of the biological need(s) of the individual. Needs are often understood as a linear hierarchy of biological urgency, but generally proceed also in parallel, sometimes competing: it is a familiar idea to sacrifice health or safety to more firmly secure self-actualization.

Meeting these needs—whether real or perceived—is the primary conscious or nonconscious aim of all individuals. It is important to note that real or perceived threats to being able to meet a need evoke more or less of a physiological stress response that is able to reconfigure one's conscious or nonconscious activities to better meet that need. The phenomenologically understood first-person experiences of students with unmet needs is a first step in enhancing the effectiveness of teaching (see Chapters 1 and 4 and studies we report in Chapter 8 that support this contention).

The most basic level is that of life itself. In Maslow's (1943) original hierarchy, this is best represented by the maintenance of a dynamic balance (homeostasis) of functions that enables health and welfare. The healthy individual next aims for safety, as in protection from elements or predators or competitors. But this is also manifest in a classroom where students feel personally safe to express themselves. We are a social species and require sociality for mutual safety and for reproduction. It is frequently argued that our remarkable progress as a species is attributable to our sociality (Henrich, 2017, citing Laland, 2017). For security within a social group and to identify and recruit a reproductive partner, esteem is sought, usually by excelling in a particular trait that might provide a recognizable reproductive advantage.

Finally, self-actualization is an expression of what the US Army called "being all you can be." Manifesting your most adaptive traits and transmitting as much as possible in genes or memes to future generations roughly approximates maximizing your biological fitness (see Greenberg, 2016).

With a sense of biological needs and their role in structuring behavior at every level, we can turn to integrative biology of behavior as expressed in ethology. In the spirit of "unity in diversity"—a kind of behavioral *e pluribus unum*—we undertake a focused survey of several principles in ethology that stand out to us by virtue of their heuristic potential in the phenomenologically informed classroom. Where ethological values are brought to bear in phenomenology, and phenomenological values contribute to ethology, the interdisciplinary synergy is manifest in ways that stand out by being applied to meeting fundamental human needs, and in this we could say they have meaning. So we turn now to DEEP ethology.

DEEP Ethology

The first explicit appeal for integrating biology in the service of more fully understanding behavior was that of one of the founders of ethology, Nico Tinbergen (1963), who identified four aims, each corresponding to a traditional discipline. Taken together, our contemporary restatement of Tinbergen's aims—development, ecology, evolutionary biology, and physiology—can characterize any behavioral pattern at any level of organization and in all contexts. As mentioned above, the coordinated consideration of these four disciplines applied to a question of behavior is called DEEP Ethology (Greenberg, 2018a). By history and ethos, ethology is the discipline that best organizes the abundance of variables embraced by the sibling disciplines and which also most fully appreciates the fact that the exclusion of inconvenient variables from a research model often leads to significant error (Greenberg, 1994). Movement toward embracing a phenomenological attitude has been suggested by Burghardt (1997).

Integrating the biological perspectives makes us mindful that *every definable behavioral event or pattern occurs at the intersection of development, ecology, evolution, and physiology*. A crossroads of time and space in which, for the purposes of study, phenomena, dynamic as they are, are necessarily seen as though static, frozen like a photograph. Like time and space, while intuitively obvious, these phenomena are at best inferred from patterns of perception of phenomena (Buzsáki & Llinás, 2017). In resonance with our intersection metaphor is Friesen, Henriksson, and Saevi's (2012) suggestion for conceptualizing the critical shared experience aspect of phenomenological research. It is to "understand the life-world experience as extending or unfolding along four axes, dimensions or 'existentials'": lived space, lived time, lived body, lived relation (p. 43).

If we can visualize our biological traditions as four objective lenses on our microscope, each reveals something about the individual at a different level of organization and with differing degrees of resolution. At each

42 *Getting DEEP*

magnification, fine focus can be sought by means of the process akin to the phenomenologist's collaborative hermeneutic circle.

After briefly characterizing the DEEP disciplines and identifying phenomenological constructs that resonate with them, we will also identify several themes at traverse levels of organization. These themes include the importance of pure description, the integration of "inner" and "outer" influences on behavior, and constraints on behavior.

Development

Development refers to both programs of change encoded in the genes inherited from the previous generation(s) as well as those attributable to individual experiences within one's lifespan. In recent years the field of genetics has given rise to **epigenetics**, providing dramatic new insights into how the environment can activate or suppress genetic activity, often in ways that can be transmitted across generations (Allis & Jenuwein, 2016). Thus, genes that unfold their program in a relatively fixed manner are complemented by changes that occur in a relatively environmentally sensitive manner.

In other words, a core of evolutionarily ancient genetic programs guide the earliest stages of development. In response to their immediate intracellular environment, genes are activated (or suppressed) in the processes of tissue growth and organ formation. But also, the growing individual affects its environment establishing an intimate reciprocity that endures a lifetime. Throughout development both the organism and its environment are in constant change. They are partly fixed but also exquisitely sensitive to change attributable to the vagaries of the environment. Development is, of course, continuous from conception to demise with dramatic surges of responsiveness to the environment, particularly the social environment. We are thus socioculturally embedded—situated in the context of other people, from family to social media and involving countless linguistic and societal experiences to create a personal worldview (Bakewell, 2016; see Chapter 1).

With respect to learning, a once common view led many to believe that development is little influenced after early childhood, but Vygotsky and his followers demonstrated that mediated learning actually leads to further development. A large body of literature supports the idea that opportunities to learn how to learn in concert with high quality mediation are potent at any age (Feuerstein, 1985; Sternberg, 1997). While it may be difficult if not impossible for teachers to become knowledgeable about each student's development, higher education students reported transformational learning occurred when they were engaged in personal reflection (Franklin et al., 2014; Taylor et al., 2012). In other words, students, once they appreciate the role of private experiences in the learning process, can supply that variable on their own (see Owen-Smith, 2018; see Chapter 7).

Further, research demonstrates the feasibility of providing students with a repertoire of metastrategic knowledge from which they can develop and adapt personal learning strategies to overcome challenges in learning (Greenberg, 2014).

Habit is built into all organisms and certainly into perception. After the experiences of discriminating and categorizing our perceptions we can conserve or reallocate our energy and operate intuitively. All conditions of growth and change, such as the classroom, require us, however, to attend to new stimuli. An environment in which growth is sought—in line with basic ideas of optimality—trusts that the current cost is worth the future benefit.

Another important dimension of growth is creativity, enabled by ways of thinking that can be lost over time, but in an appropriately safe classroom, students are emboldened to shake off the previously mentioned "lethargy of custom." Considering even familiar ideas in new contexts, the opportunity for a teachable moment is more likely. Here, the uniqueness of the individual can manifest itself in creative insights and expression. As mentioned earlier, very small variations can have very large consequences in the complex cognitive working of problem solving. As Thoreau (1855) put it, under such circumstances, "It is only necessary to behold the least fact or phenomenon, however familiar, from a point a hair's breadth aside from our habitual path or routine, to be overcome, enchanted by its beauty and significance. . . . To perceive freshly, with fresh senses, is to be inspired" (p. 44).

Ecology

At every level of organization, every distinguishable element of life—from the multiplicity of organelles within a cell through the outermost boundaries of an organism—is embraced—embedded—in protean concentric spheres of the matrix of the world. The emphasis on any particular level of organization or the phenomena within it becomes interesting only when direct effects on us—such as health—are discovered. For example, in recent decades, ecology at its most vast has been found relevant to our thinking about ourselves (exobiology; NASA, 2018) as much as at its most minute (microbes). The familiar dimensions of our ecology with which we occupy ourselves is that which is most obviously relevant to our meeting of biological needs.

The environment includes the temporal and spatial physical and biotic contexts in which organisms must survive and thrive. It is also the source of all perceptions that organisms use to create their reality. In that regard, research indicates that the social environment is a particularly powerful variable, influencing our perception of interpersonal safety. This can be seen in the classroom as trust amongst students and with the teacher (Holley & Steiner, 2005). While it appears that most teachers in higher education pay attention to these factors, this is not always the case. We were amazed at the lack of safety and trust reported by African American students at a predominantly white university (Davis et al., 2004). In this study, for example, the student participants often felt hyper-visible or invisible—both of which stood out to them and reduced the availability of teachable moments (see Chapter 8).

The lifeworld is the phenomenologically relevant dimension of ecology. The collaboration of multiple senses is highly adaptive, but also, it "can create unique experiences that emerge when signals from different sensory channels are bound together" (Stein, Stanford, & Rowland, 2014). Thus, the vast possibilities of the elements of our environment that we are able to perceive contributes in unpredictable ways to our lifeworld. The implication is that even at a basic level of processing this sensory synergy can fuel individual uniqueness. A shared lifeworld fosters *intersubjectivity*, and it is this uniqueness, once appreciated, that can enable particularly effective learning communities (see especially Chapter 6).

For the ecologically informed, phenomenologically inclined teacher, with respect to conspecifics, the intersubjectivity aspect stands out. The crucial nature of sociality to being "fully human" has been recognized since Aristotle, and other individuals in one's environment have long been recognized by phenomenologists as a critical element in fostering insight and cognition (Pollio, Henley, & Thompson, 1997; see Chapter 6).

One of the essential tensions of human development involves the continuing processes of individuation and socialization—whereby individuals learn the appropriate norms, values, behaviors, and interpersonal communicative skills. To the extent this tension is resolved, individuals can retain a sense of their own uniqueness while intersubjectivity is achieved. But in fact, it can never be fully resolved; there remains what is arguably a productive residue of ambiguity. Mutual understanding enables, more or less, unity of actions and can help the mutually involved individuals meet their individual biological needs. The pressure for sociality, presumably to pool our cognitive resources, is manifest in the extraordinary growth of areas of the brain and their connections that form the "social brain," which is uniquely enlarged compared to other social species (summarized by Adolphs, 2009).

But as in every other domain of intersubjective interaction, the *meaning* of shared understanding depends on the interaction of both internal, implicit variables and those that are external and relatively explicit, in *all* parties to the interaction—teacher as well as taught. In other words, to echo a familiar mantra of behavioral science, what we study and the meaning of what we learn is the outcome of the interaction of internal and external processes. Together, these processes engender "the best story we can tell given our beliefs." But beliefs can change, and that is a key theme in our book.

Language is important but does not stand alone in interpersonal communications. While it involves the most advanced cognitive processing, other less clear modes of communication that are typically prereflective can be crucial: body language, touch, eyes meeting (his mouth says "yes" but his eyes say "no"). So lifeworlds are shared to a point, but there are important gaps creating another aspect of phenomenological thought: *ambiguity* (see Chapter 1).

What is shared and what is not or cannot be shared, "intersubjectivity and ambiguity," resonates with individuation and socialization. These processes are related to idiography and nomothetics in an older tradition. Because we appear to share more with each other than with other species, the importance of these differences between us is often lost. On the continuum from idiographic (individual, specific) to nomothetic (shared, general) traits, often seen in tension with each other, the particulars and uniqueness of individuals grades into the generalities and universally shared qualities of our species (Silverstein, 1988). Because these are often related to the antagonism of scientific worldview and that of the humanities, they are worth referencing because study of this tension can flush out implicit bias (Robinson, 2012).

Evolution

Evolutionary biology is concerned with the change in traits and organisms and societies across generations, from ancestors to the present moment, and forward to our direct and indirect descendants. Traits are understood to have their present form because of their preservation through the processes of natural selection of variations that are found adaptive—that is, able to compensate for environmental forces (often called "selection pressure") that impair their ability to meet needs. *Adaptations* are at the center of concern. There are several definitions of the term and all are unified by the idea of compensation for change, either short-term (such as a stimulus or life experience) or long-term adaptations (such as climate change).

Only recently has the expression of emotion, possibly the most ancient of these variables, been implicated in the circumstances of a teachable moment (van de Goor, Sools, Westerhof, & Bohlmeijer, 2017). There is a possible connection in that amongst the adaptive traits that have evolved in humans is a sometimes insatiable pursuit of information. Interestingly, when threads of information converge in specific areas of the brain they act to evoke a distinctively pleasurable response (Biederman & Vessel, 2006). It is likely that this response contributes to their coherence in narratives that enable them to be explored mindfully. This points to adaptive behavioral traits that engage and integrate the perceptual skills of experience and the conceptual skills of argument to establish the most coherent narrative possible with the facts at hand. The world we experience is one in which it is impossible (except by theoretic retrospection) to disentangle the contributions of intellect from those of sense, as described

46   *Getting DEEP*

by William James (1911). Thus, in order to enable profound learning experiences, the teacher needs to allow space for shared descriptions of relevant information prior to any explanation of course content (Greenberg, Greenberg, Patterson, & Pollio, 2015). These can be guided by a sense of constraints—that is, the constitutional limits of competence for any definable trait, to be discussed below.

Physiology

Physiology, the fourth domain of DEEP, also provides insight into the teachable moment. Certainly, physiology provides the means by which acquisition of content and insight at a particular moment in time is framed and formed in conjunction with everything else the organism experiences (or may have experienced in the past). The processes within and between organ systems, including the many functionally specialized components of the brain, are dynamic and in continual pursuit of balance (*homeostasis*) which, because of constant change, can never really be attained. These processes are especially tightly integrated with memory as well as anticipated outcomes of actions. Most of our actions are directly or indirectly necessary to enable these processes necessary to life to have the resources essential to meet their needs—from nutrients to energy. Many actions are, however, by constitution or custom, collateral and incidental to the main function. These actions, and the structures they utilize, contribute to confusion when we try to impute causal relationships. But they are also available for natural selection to utilize them in serving other, often unexpected functions if they contribute to fitness. This is complicated as well by the fact that these structures and functions evolved in environments very unlike anything we might feel familiar with today. As a result, there is often a mismatch between past utility and contemporary function.

Stress, as commented earlier, is evoked by a real or perceived challenge to our ability to meet our real or perceived needs. The physiology of stress and its capacity to balance or reconfigure the cognitive processes associated with motivation can be discussed in conjunction with a biological interpretation of Maslovian needs.

The awareness of a mismatch between circumstances and the prospect of meeting needs creates a dissonance that echoes what occurs at deeper levels of organization: in systems of neurons, detection of mismatches—errors—is absolutely essential to behavior. Most adjustments of posture, micromovements of muscle, and homeostasis are compensated with little or no conscious awareness. But there are important nonconscious signals detected by neurophysiologists, for example "error detection" is a compelling and growing field within behavioral neuroscience (Bach & Dolan, 2012). At another level of organization, error detection is important for teachers as they make intuitive decisions about what to say and do in a given moment in the classroom (see Chapter 9).

Although originally a generalized response to protect the body, stress, as mentioned above, can selectively energize motivational systems to meet needs. This is connected to Festinger's (1957) idea of *cognitive dissonance*—a tension evoked by a mismatch, however slight, between an internal working model of the world and the world as it is perceived, resulting in competing cognitive processes (Boring, 1964). The resulting motivation to restore consonance can range from unreflected through intense and preoccupying and is driven at least in part by the effects of stress on cognitive processes.

While stress energizes motivational systems associated with specific needs, for the most part, the vast detail of life is met by automatic, intuitive, unreflected responses of the body to changes in its environment. For example, when cold, our muscle tension might increase, the circulation of blood might be adjusted, or we might change our postures—all very effective and *not very expensive*. When these responses are insufficient, the failure to cope comfortably may emerge in consciousness, and the highest cognitive resources may be put into the service of solving the problem. Employing these resources may involve significant expense in time and energy and interfere with ongoing activities. A student in a classroom growing chill might even, after some thought, ask the instructor to adjust the thermostat. We are largely on "automatic pilot" until something out of the ordinary gets our attention. Something must, in Coleridge's (1817) now familiar poetic phrase, "awaken the mind's attention from the lethargy of custom."

For our purposes, the effect of stress on cognition is the most salient. Cognition is a complex protean concept as it has developed in scholarship over the generations, but its irreducible core has traditionally consisted of the processes of the nervous system involved in acquiring information from the environment (by means of senses and perception), storing it (several forms of memory), and acting as influenced by this information. Coping with change includes an extraordinary ability for error detection, mentioned earlier. This trait enables a crucial self-correcting mechanism for action that occurs in slightly different form at every level of organization.

The processes of cognition act in exquisite balance to address our real or perceived biological needs. That balance is highly sensitive to stress and can be reconfigured to help one cope. The expression of this response is evoked in modest or dramatic degree—by experiences ranging from an unexpected threat to life through a raised eyebrow, flushed cheek, or awareness that someone is staring at you. Any of these can reconfigure cognitive processes almost instantly (McEwen & Sapolsky, 1995; Greenberg, Carr, & Summers, 2002). Extreme or sustained stress can diminish the quality of life and be life-threatening. But in relation to our focus in this book, all aspects of DEEP ethology emphasize its relations to the existential phenomenological perspective on teaching and learning.

48 *Getting DEEP*

All Moments Are Teachable and All Experiences Are Transformative

We are perpetually challenged to look both above and below whatever level of organization occupies us—the ancient impulse to understand all causes and consequences, the congenital need to find connections, the search for simplicity we intuit lies beneath the complexity we experience. And we look for boundaries, the extremes of the everyday continua we experience. The transformative learning experience is such an extreme, but not really out of reach. And we look for uniqueness that we find in the teachable moment. But to study these we must be mindful of the integrative impulse.

Internal and External Integration

An implicit understanding of the unity of the organism and its environment is manifest in the ethologist's aversion to the study of organisms separated from the environments in which they naturally occur (Greenberg, 1994). Phenomenologists and other qualitative researchers often speak of the lack of focus in pedagogical studies on the lived experience of teacher and learner (see Chapter 1). When we explore how teachers can best create teachable moments and facilitate transformative learning, it makes no sense to look solely at teacher or student behaviors without also exploring their lived experience—the meaning they find in context.

Further, paths and processes are adaptive traits as much as morphology or behavioral patterns and, importantly, each path has its own evolutionary and developmental history. In ethology, an alternative path to an apparently identical behavior pattern may very well have followed a different evolutionary or developmental trajectory and have different relationships with all the systems with which it needs to be balanced in order to function. And this is no less true for teachers and students in the classroom than it is for mice or monkeys. In this spirit, perhaps, (Merleau-Ponty, 1945/1962) famously stated that although always tethered to perception "there are several ways for consciousness to be conscious" (p. 124).

In pursuit of transformative learning, we should appreciate that these two processes of individuation and socialization, mentioned earlier, are often competitive with each other. At such times we may be acutely aware of our limits, the boundaries of our abilities, and the constraints on our behavior.

The biological boundaries of an organism—anatomical, physiological, cognitive—are commonly detected only when they are confronted or compromised, as they may be in the classroom. And in this, expectations are important. Our perceptions of the boundaries of specific traits are typically set by extraordinary individuals under extraordinary circumstances and are constantly being extended such that the most extreme capacity manifested by any one individual, no matter how extraordinary, represents the possibilities of all individuals, no matter how ordinary. An inventory of many specific constraints on behavior, such as those on stimuli and responses or the reinforcing effects of stimuli, have been tentatively identified by Hinde (1973).

Arguably, our lives are devoted to transcending our constraints. They are also a fact of life that haunts us. Even the most hardened logical positivist or existential phenomenologist might pause to ask with Dorothy as she entered the land of Oz, or with Israel "IZ" Kamakawiwo'ole (2010) as he sang, "Birds fly over the rainbow/Why then, oh why can't I?" This, of course, is sentimental, romantic, and an arrow to the heart of what it means to be human. Such questions, when aesthetically framed, highlight the profound influence, if not priority, of prereflective thought on more conscious cognition.

In summary, we hope you will consider the case we make in this chapter: that biology, particularly the integrative biology of ethology, is a valuable complement to phenomenology that can be brought to bear in understanding teaching and learning in the classroom. We characterized our general philosophy as existential phenomenology because in the shared emphasis on the world as we live it, and in the importance of rigorous description of our experience and reflections on its meaning, we find a deep resonance with our personal experiences in the classroom.

The teachable moment and its goal of transformative learning represent the crucial insight that behavior is the result of internal as well as external structures and processes. In traditional teaching we are too often and too easily satisfied by metrics of successful pedagogy. At such times, we may neglect the higher calling of our profession: to engender *meaning*. In this way, course content that is realized beyond mere knowing is owned by the student in ways that enable its creative applicability in other contexts. The difficulty is in the fact that meaning for us and for each individual student are never exactly the same. But as teachers we can launch students into the world where they can grab hold of the abstract knowledge we want them to realize by finding, in their own depths, the ties that bind content to life and foster a life of creative connections. Enabling students to do this is our self-actualization; this is our greatest legacy.

3 Preparation for Teaching
"What Can They Experience in Class?"

> I'm astounded as to how much time I'm spending on organizing the flow of a thing and worrying about things that it never, never occurs to us that we worry about . . . like . . . how does the third week fit with the first week, and how does the whole thing have a sense of—a sensible trajectory?
>
> (from an interview with our case study professor about his class planning; Franklin, 2013)

Since the 1990s, college teachers have been urged to move from instructor-centered to learner-centered approaches (see Blumberg, 2017; Weimer, 2013). Educators were urged to relinquish being "the sage on the stage" and instead to become the "guide on the side" (King, 1993). Literature proliferated about teaching as coaching, guiding, and facilitating. Memorably, Parker Palmer (2007) urged teachers to put the subject "in the center" and then sit together with the students in an egalitarian circle around the subject. Yet, Maryellen Weimer, writing in 2013, concluded that *teacher-centered* instruction continued to be dominant across widely disparate disciplines. Moreover, Bruce Mackh, writing even more recently, in 2018, after years of research and consulting in higher education, asserts that "higher education as a whole has changed little since the mid-20th century" (p. xi). It is still common for faculty to repeat in their lectures the material from the assigned readings in course textbooks and articles, an outmoded practice which surely diminishes the students' motivation to read the material before class. Strongly advocating change, especially in curricular planning and instruction, Mackh (2018) went on to say: "Pedagogical practices dependent on unstudied, deficiently designed, static standards of the past are increasingly irrelevant to today's students" (p. 257).

College teachers do express bewilderment about "today's students," who are smart and capable but sometimes seem apathetic and disengaged. In classrooms that permit laptops and/or smartphones, the students may be more engaged with their devices than with the instructor or their fellow students. Phil Race (2010), who has conducted workshops for faculty in the UK, Australia, Europe, Canada, and elsewhere, reports that faculty frequently ask him, "What can I do if students are sitting like puddings and not responding?" (p. 207). It is likely that these faculty are still relying on the lecture method of teaching despite its dismal efficacy in inspiring students to engage and learn.

Not only do these authors suggest that higher education pedagogy is often uninspiring, but the current assessment-driven milieu is also problematic. Students engage in surface learning that merely enables them to pass the next exam. Asserted Gibbs and Sampson, "The most reliable, rigorous and cheat-proof assessment systems are often accompanied by dull and lifeless learning that has short-lasting outcomes" (as cited in Race, 2010, p. 64). Race (2010), based on receipt of extensive student complaints about assessment and grading practices, recommends to higher education teachers that we "reduce the burden of assessment for learners and for ourselves. . . . We have got our education system into a state where assessment all too often militates against deep learning and takes much of the enjoyment out of learning" (p. 102).

Teachers who desire to recapture the joy that can be found at the heart of teaching and learning—a desire that might have motivated purchase of this book—may wish to consider a *phenomenological approach*. Willis (2012), van Manen (2017), and others have written movingly about philosophically grounded pedagogy with goals *beyond* student acquisition of information and measurement of its retention by traditional classroom tests. The existential experience of learners now assumes prominence—in the words of Willis (2012), our concern is "processes of human being and becoming" (p. 212). We have written this book to share an illustrative case in which a phenomenological approach for higher education produced profound changes in student lives. Furthermore, in Chapter 8 we share descriptions of other teachers in a variety of higher education settings, including online, that demonstrate the feasibility of this approach for use in almost any setting. While this chapter describes the findings from a study of the experience of preparing for class preparation by our case study professor, we do not want to imply that this is the only type of preparation a teacher must do if they want to teach with a phenomenological attitude or use our approach.

Narrowing Our Focus to Instructional Planning

In this chapter, we narrow our focus to one aspect of a phenomenological approach, as exemplified by our case study professor. We carefully examine his specific practice of *instructional planning for class sessions during an academic semester*. First, we make a brief foray into the instructional planning literature that is most relevant to our case. Weimer (2013), in a popular book for faculty new to learner-centered teaching practices,

52 Preparation for Teaching

emphasizes that teachers in higher education must make a commitment to do their instructional design work *more carefully* than they did before. She delineates four characteristics of well-designed learning experiences: (1) the assignments or activities motivate student involvement and participation; (2) students must carry out explorations relevant to their discipline, whether that is biology, philosophy, or engineering; (3) well-designed learning activities take students from their present knowledge/skill level to greater competence; and (4) these experiences simultaneously develop content knowledge and learning skills (e.g., critical thinking, self-reflection). Weimer (2013) recommends that these characteristics become the benchmarks for the class activities that are planned.

Unfortunately, she does not provide readers with many concrete examples of well-designed learning experiences. Most beneficial was her description of an activity she used in her own class, designed to help students develop argumentation skills. She structured the class as a debate in which students took sides about a case in which a fictitious student protested unfair grading on the basis of race. She functioned as a recorder of the debate, listing arguments on the blackboard. After each side had exhausted their arguments, they were assigned to discuss among themselves the *strongest* arguments they could use to refute those of the other side. Finally, a role-play by student volunteers enacted a discussion between the "unfair" teacher and the student challenging the grade. Perhaps the most valuable aspect of this exemplar was Weimer's (2013) honest admission that the exercise required multiple modifications—at least six iterations—before it achieved its goals. Only in a later iteration of the exercise did she realize that the best role for her was as the recorder of the debate. This anecdote bolsters her initial point about the careful attention to design (and redesign) that is required by the learner-centered approach. Student response to an exercise is unpredictable, and teachers must gauge the degree of intervention they are willing to undertake if the planned activity is not proceeding as planned.

Concrete guidance for designing and implementing learner-centered teaching strategies is provided in a self-help workbook by Blumberg, (2017), which includes a set of rubrics depicting incremental steps for teachers to take in course revision. The book features many learner-centered teaching techniques, such as competitive games; service learning projects; small group work to solve problems or analyze case vignettes; and "intra-teach sessions," in which student dyads or triads discuss study questions together before taking quizzes drawn from those study questions. An interesting aspect of Blumberg's (2017) approach is her emphasis on helping students to take increasing responsibility for their own learning as an academic term unfolds. An example is providing *directed* study questions at the beginning of the course, then *helping* the class to develop their own study questions; this process culminates in *autonomous* student development of the study questions.

Contextual Factors Involved in Instructional Planning

Instructional planning does not take place in a vacuum. A college teacher who becomes excited about new pedagogical practices cannot undertake instructional planning before thoughtfully considering a host of contextual factors, such as level and cultural background of students, placement of the course in the program of study, length of the semester, size of the class, frequency and length of class sessions, institutional policies/requirements about grading and course evaluations, and departmental norms (e.g., Does the department favor provision of outlines or PowerPoint slides to the students? Does the department foster competition rather than collaboration among students?). To state the obvious, these contextual factors present both freedom and constraints. It must be acknowledged that the planning for our case study course took place in an environment of fewer constraints than most higher education teachers experience, because the course was a popular, freely chosen, elective at the graduate level. The psychology department in which the course was housed did not mandate grading criteria, and teachers were free to specify course policies regarding attendance, lateness, and class participation. Our case study professor did not require attendance, nor did he assign penalties for lateness or grade the quantity or quality of class participation (see Chapters 1, 4 and 5 for more details).

Personal Factors Involved in Instructional Planning

Personal factors that relate to instructional planning practices include a teacher's theoretical perspective, need for power and control in the classroom, enthusiasm (or lack of enthusiasm) for learner-centered approaches, and willingness to take risks regarding nontraditional teaching strategies. Sometimes an innovative planned activity will fall flat, an anecdote may not be compelling, a visual aid will not resonate with the class. Willingness to take risks was evident in our case study professor, who planned a wide variety of classroom activities (as will be described shortly). Other personal characteristics that undoubtedly contributed to his facility in planning the seminar course included his lengthy teaching experience and comfort in leading an egalitarian seminar-type class. Rather than preferring to be a "sage on the stage"—although he had been the sage at times earlier in his career—he was genuinely interested in exploring the diverse experiences of the students who chose to take this elective course, and in creating the favorable conditions in which they could learn from, and with, one another. He was adept at using self-deprecating humor in the classroom, which he employed to diminish the traditional distance between the "brilliant professor" and the less learned students. Lastly, he had a cherished personal vision of his class as a stimulating "salon" like one that he himself had experienced as a college student. In his view,

54 *Preparation for Teaching*

the ideal class would replicate—to the extent possible—this salon that had such a profound influence on his later teaching:

> I had experienced a salon in New York before I left. The guy who was a friend of mine, a rabbi, used to invite someone he knew, and he would invite students he thought would enjoy it, and I had such a good time that he invited me almost every week. We would sit around in a circle in his living room . . . and this was the time when they were just really unpackaging the Dead Sea Scrolls. So the professor who had done that would come over and talk about the Scrolls, and then a philosopher would come over and talk about some philosophy, and that's where I learned about Buber for the first time. And there was a guy who ultimately wrote a very good biography of Justice Black. It was just an incredible collection. And I couldn't believe that there were such smart people in the world and that they really cared about talking about intellectual stuff. It was one of the great experiences of my life.

Instructional Planning Practices of a Master Teacher

We turn now to the instructional planning practices of the professor in our case study course, a course he had been teaching for 30 years at the time of data collection. Many years had passed since his experience as a young student in the New York "salon." Rightfully, he merited the designation of "master teacher" by this stage in his long career. In this section of the chapter, we share the findings from a dissertation by Karen Franklin (2013), whose involvement in our case study research project began as a graduate research assistant for the team. Prior to the second year of data collection, she had formalized her intention to conduct a dissertation investigating our case study professor's instructional planning. This rigorous and comprehensive examination of planning proved to be unique in its scope and breadth. Her research involved (1) conducting audiotaped interviews with the professor before each weekly class meeting during a 15-week fall semester, (2) attending and making verbatim transcripts of all the actual class sessions, and finally (3) conducting post-class interviews with the professor in which he was asked to reflect on each session and what stood out to him about the session (as noted earlier in Chapter 1, students also completed post-class reflections). Using phenomenological analysis procedures, as developed by Pollio, Henley, and Thompson (1997) and further refined by Thomas and Pollio (2002), a total of 1150 transcript pages were analyzed to ascertain the *contextual ground* and *figural themes* of instructional planning for this graduate course in existential phenomenological psychology (Franklin, 2013). As discussed in Chapter 1, figure and ground are inseparable, and the report of a phenomenological analysis must explicate both.

Next, we review and discuss the results of this analysis. We begin with the contextual ground.

Ground of Phenomenological Attitude

Our case study professor's teaching vividly exemplified his deep personal grounding in the philosophical stance or attitude of phenomenology. Inspired by decades of study of the writings of Merleau-Ponty (e.g., 1945/1962), the professor embodied and brought to life in the classroom Merleau-Ponty's enduring sense of wonder and awe about human existence, along with the philosopher's perpetual humility about knowledge. We recall that Merleau-Ponty, uncharacteristically among the pantheon of eminent philosophers, referred to himself as "the philosopher who does not know" (as cited in Thomas, 2005, p. 73) because he remained a restless seeker of greater knowledge and understanding throughout his life. His continual revisions of his thinking still provoke lively scholarly debate to this day.

The professor hoped that students' experience in the seminar would go beyond mere intellectual engagement into the existential dimension of transformative learning (Sohn et al., 2016). As a phenomenologist, he was committed to the transformational potential of dialogue among people, ever open to the possibility of the Other to "teach me something . . . surprise [me] . . . and allow a transformation in both of us" (Merleau-Ponty, as cited in Switzer, 2001, p. 263). The dialogical seminar that fosters such transformative learning was described by the professor as follows:

> And I ask you a question and you take me, with your answer, someplace I hadn't planned to go, but then I go with you, and we finally get to what we need to get to, and we get to it, and we both learn something from it.

Figural Themes of Instructional Planning

Six themes dominated the data collected by Franklin (2013) about the professor's extensive planning for each week's graduate seminar. All themes are interrelated and emanate from his ontological orientation in phenomenological philosophy. Themes are illustrated with segments of the planning interview data. (Note that inclusion of quotation marks indicates the actual words of the professor within our data.)

"What Can They Experience in Class?"

The cardinal priority in planning a class session was devising a strategy to elicit students' first-person experience of the philosophical concept of interest that week—whether that be the students' experience of their bodies, time, the natural world, or relationships. For example, he might decide to ask the class what it was like to become lost, or to be late, or to

56 *Preparation for Teaching*

work in a restaurant. In this interview excerpt, he considers soliciting student stories about an event that disrupts the ordinary experience of time:

> So I want to ask them about have they ever been in an accident. We can talk about that. What aspect of time is that? It's amazing how out of connection, out of synchrony, my experience is with respect to the clock. . . . It's amazing how different, how out of whack the clock is with my experience.

Eventually, he planned to move the discussion from personal stories to the pertinent phenomenological literature: "So two things are going on. People are talking about their lives. And I want people to keep talking. But I want to move it, insofar as I can, to Merleau-Ponty."

In his weekly planning, he considered a vast array of materials, gathered during years of teaching, which could stimulate student discussion and reflection about their lived experience, such as poems, paintings, recorded music, and intriguing objects (e.g., a rotating trapezoid, AKA the Ames Window). He also considered whether student experience would be enriched by small group work in dyads or triads. For example, he anticipated that invaluable learning about phenomenological interviewing would be gained by having students interview one another. In addition, having the students discuss difficult philosophical concepts in small groups would allow them to be honest about areas of confusion, and to help one another achieve understanding and insight. Unlike more typical college teachers debating how to construct their own lively lectures, he focused his planning on what the *students would be doing* in the class. He did utilize mini-lectures from time to time, but they were not designed to summarize material from the readings. Knowing the class would be dialogical, the students knew that they must do the readings before class.

"Playing With Possibilities"

The content for the course, including dense, complex readings by Ihde, Merleau-Ponty, William James, and other authors, might be considered quite heavy going for college students. The writings of Merleau-Ponty, in particular, are widely regarded as difficult, because he struggled to express the fullness of his thought (Thomas, 2010). Therefore, it may strike the reader as incongruous that a key aspect of the professor's planning for a class was "playing with possibilities." Yet he wanted the students to interact in a somewhat playful way with the serious writings of the eminent scholars. He was convinced that a class session could be intellectually challenging but also *enjoyable*. It was the professor's custom to re-read every one of the course materials along with the students, speculating about passages that could be opaque or confusing and then envisioning various ways in which the class could struggle together—and have fun together—in arriving at greater understanding. Together, professor and student could play with the ideas, achieve new insights, and resolve philosophical and practical puzzles.

Perception exercises were often playful, designed to elicit alternative interpretations of ambiguous visual phenomena. In the pre-class planning sessions, the professor would ask Franklin (the research assistant) to examine a stimulus image he was considering. In one case, she variously interpreted an image as an animal, wheelbarrow, basket, child's toy, and a frog; this image actually turned out to be the logo for Peruvian Airlines (illustrating the diversity of stimulus images he might select). An interesting homework assignment for students challenged them to set aside their customary way of viewing trees, attempting to "pull the sky through trees":

> If you look at a tree and you've got all the green stuff . . . there is a lot of green stuff then there are like little holes in it that show the sky. The sky is clearly behind the tree. I don't know exactly what Don Juan told Castaneda, but I have taken it, and I bring the stuff that's behind, forward. In other words, you've got this tree, and you've got all the spaces between it, and I want to say "squeeze" so hard, and I have the white come through the tree. It seems easy, but it is not. . . . Do you want to try this? This week I want you to go out and pull the sky through trees.

Perception exercises such as these helped students in the class to accomplish what Merleau-Ponty was advocating in the course readings, a radical re-seeing: "in learning how to *see*, we learn how to *be*, how to be something other than what we were when we remained blind to a new way of seeing" (Macann, 1993, p. 170). Data about the student reaction to these perception exercises (see Chapters 5, 6, and 7) provides evidence that radical re-seeing did take place in the class sessions.

"Blow Them Away!"

Never would a seminar led by our case study professor be characterized as boring, with students "sitting like puddings" (Race, 2010, p. 207). Compelling demonstrations, candid sharing of life experiences, and surprising revelations were the order of the day. It is unlikely the students ever realized, however, what detailed pre-planning undergirded the exciting class sessions. As documented in the audio recorded planning meetings, the professor was determined to "blow them away" with the activities that would take place.

For example, he would speculate about students' potential reactions, "I think they'll want to do that," but then ask the research assistant for her opinion. He would ask her if she found a reading interesting, a joke funny,

58 Preparation for Teaching

or a psychological test useful. On one occasion he pondered whether "the way we're going at it is boring . . . the stuff that we're asking them to do may not *capture* them, which is what we want to do." Note that the focus of the theme "Blow them away" is *not* on the professor himself, and whether he will be perceived as the creator of classroom "magic," but on the *students*—and whether the class exercises are meaningful to the students.

"A Good Question"

During instructional planning, the professor placed great emphasis on careful crafting of the questions he would pose to students in the upcoming seminar. Unlike the detested practice of "cold-calling," when college teachers plan difficult questions to spring on vulnerable students who may not have done the readings, his questions were not designed to play "Gotcha" or to elicit predetermined "right" answers. Understandably, many college students have learned to dread faculty questions, feeling insecure about disclosing their opinions or about the inadequacy of their knowledge base. Some students may have experienced highly critical—even abusive—faculty, causing them to be reticent about responding to teacher questions. As discussed in Chapter 4, our case study professor worked from the first day of class to establish a safe atmosphere in his classroom, in which questions would not be viewed as threatening. Nor would students receive points for speaking a certain number of times in class, a practice of some very behaviorally oriented teachers.

Commenting in a recent interview about his teaching (see Chapter 4), the professor said, "I kind of study more intensively and think about questions that I could ask and everyone could answer . . . that I could reasonably expect students to answer." This expectation was based in his respect for students' ability to grapple with difficult readings—and in his trust that they would do the readings. Other types of questions might invite students to reflect on significant lived experiences outside the classroom, such as 9/11, viewing the Grand Canyon, or childbirth. As depicted in Chapter 5, sharing personal stories of such universal human situations permitted students to make meaningful connections to the critically important phenomenological tenets and concepts. Often, the professor's questions were designed to evoke reactions to dramatic readings or demonstrations taking place in the classroom. In his view, a good question should ask for specifics: "What aspects of the structure did you notice?" and "What stands out to you in the painting?" It was important to the professor that questions be non-trivial and genuine. On one occasion documented in a recorded planning meeting, the professor decided to ask the students a question *that he himself had no answer for*. The phenomenon of concern was the self appearing in two places at one time, such as when a reader

Preparation for Teaching 59

is deeply engrossed in another world in a book while solidly sitting in a reading chair:

> How can you be in two places at the same time? How can there be two of you? The next [situation] is when I am centered in my work, and everything else disappears, most notably time. How could that be?

The professor's planning for his college "salon" was grounded in his conviction that dialogue among class members could permit *discovery of new knowledge*, not merely transmission of existing knowledge in a boring monologue by the learned professor.

"All the Stuff"

This theme describes the variety and volume of teaching materials used by our case study professor, which he referred to as "all the stuff." Paintings, poetry, or recorded music might be employed to evoke emotions or memories. As expected in a course on existential phenomenological psychology, many of the materials were short text excerpts from published articles and books, or photocopied tables, diagrams, graphs, and charts depicting the thematic structures of diverse phenomena that had been explored by his doctoral students and research collaborators over the years. Use of technology was minimal (for example, the professor never showed Power-Point slides). Diagrams might simply be drawn on the blackboard or Scotch-taped to the blackboard. A weekly planning session with Franklin often ended with the professor's review of the "stuff" to be used in the upcoming seminar: "So let's see what we've got. . . . We've got all these stories, clocks, calendars, van den Berg, Andy's story, and then the T.S. Eliot poem and that picture."

Invariably, there was far more "stuff" than could possibly be used in the available time, but it was the professor's custom to accrue this abundance of materials, permitting him to choose among them during the class according to the flow of the discussion.

"Going With the Flow"

Perhaps the most remarkable aspect of our case study professor's teaching is his comfort with abandoning carefully crafted lesson plans and props when the mood or interests of the class merited doing just that. As one student commented:

> I could see all the props on the table beside [the professor]—a giant beer bottle, stacks of handouts . . . yet we hadn't gotten to any of them, and we were past our usual break time. My own sense of time urgency was kicking in. The side trip we had taken from the topic of

60 *Preparation for Teaching*

the day was fascinating, but I wanted to know what that giant beer bottle was about. I wanted to receive all those handouts before class time ran out. Glancing at [the professor], it was obvious that he did not share my sense of time urgency. He was totally in the moment, hanging on every word of the student who was speaking. I set aside my antsy feelings and emulated his absorption in the discussion.

In stark contrast to this student depiction of the professor's apparent ease in "going with the flow" was the systematic and detailed written plan he had actually prepared in his weekly pre-class planning meeting with the research assistant. A typical plan for a class session involved compilation of a numbered list of class activities, with estimation of the time required for each. Items on the outline were logically sequenced so that he would focus more on concrete material before abstract, experiential before didactic. More time was allowed for students to react to emotionally provocative pieces of art or poems. "Getting the order right" was a frequent motif in the audio recorded planning sessions with the research assistant. Yet he often reminded himself "We don't want this to be too organized, you know, lockstep"—because he enjoyed being surprised by an unanticipated tangent in the class discussion. An ever-present concern was allocating too much time to his mini-lectures. He was acutely aware of his own love of talking and explaining, but also realized that if he simply "got out of their way" the students would offer valuable contributions to the discussion, even enlightening one another at times if he remained silent.

A Post-Class Reflection by the Professor

The reader may wonder if every class fulfilled the professor's planned aims. Franklin's (2013) post-class interviews often revealed his propensity to be self-critical: "I knew it wasn't as good as it could be. It could have been better." An excerpt from one of the post-class interviews is illustrative of his ability to self-analyze, reflect, and learn from an experience when the class did *not* go well:

The first part of the class only got going in fits and starts. We never got a consistent excitement level. . . . It wasn't bad, but it was just sort of slow, and it was not quite as funny, and not quite as lively . . . and I don't think the material was organized well. And I didn't spontaneously move from one thing to the other. I kind of went through my plan. And going through the plan is never as satisfying (laughs) as having something pick up and fly on its own. I think I wanted to cover material today. It had the format in my head of a lecture, but that's not good for this class. This class needs an easy slip and slide to different topics. Second part did better, I thought . . . I wanted them to be talking, and so the second half I changed what I was going to do. I am a much better teacher when I am not a "real teacher." Using a lecture mentality in a seminar class is non-effective; that's not what it should be. And that was the change that I made between the first and second half. I made the change from having a lecture notion in my head, and I'm going to give them facts, to saying, "This is preposterous. I'm going to do what I do best and what the class does best."

(Franklin, 2013)

When reading this honest reflection, we can walk in the shoes of our case study professor, who—despite his ambitious and careful pre-planning for class—almost slipped back to the posture of the lecturer dispensing facts. It is likely that all of us who teach are tempted at times to be "the sage on the stage." But the results of our case study research make a convincing case that the sage should be permanently retired from service.

Comparison of Findings to Extant Literature

In this chapter, we have observed a creative master teacher as he planned for a graduate seminar class, a singular opportunity. No comparable elucidation of a higher education teacher's planning was found in the literature. Comparing the practices of our case study professor to the recommended practices for planning effective instruction in a 2018 book by Mackh for higher education faculty, the following similarities can be found:

- Excellent lessons begin with a "hook" (story, artifact, image, anecdote)
- Instructional activities should include a combination of approaches, including demonstrations and active student participation
- Post-class student reflections (termed "exit slips" by Mackh) are valuable for assessing student understanding (and, we would add, also for discovering what stood out as meaningful in students' perceptions—see Chapter 8 descriptions of teaching that included the importance of student reflections)
- Post-class assignments should foster real-world application of the concepts

Interestingly, although Mackh (2018) provides step-by-step, concrete guidance for creating a lesson plan, including a template, he does not expect most college teachers to actually *do* it—because it requires a "substantial investment of time and energy" (p. 105). In fact, he commends the (apparently rare) teacher who does so: "You're also moving beyond common practice, taking your teaching to an advanced level, which is definitely an admirable and worthy goal" (Mackh, 2018, p. 105). In contrast, our professor commented recently, "It is often recommended that

62 Preparation for Teaching

students study 2–3 hours for every hour spent in class. We would recommend the same for teachers and planning."

Discrepant from our case study professor's lesson planning is Mackh's (2018) extensive focus on the quizzes, projects, or presentations that will be employed to assess student learning. In fact, Mackh (2018) advises that "planning *begins* [emphasis added] with the development of assessments, working backwards to the level of individual lessons" (p. 109). This procedure is ubiquitous in the assessment-dominated K-12 environment (e.g., Wiggins & McTighe, 2005). As noted previously, our case study professor eschewed formal assessments and grading, which does represent a unique feature of our exploration of university pedagogy (see Chapter 5 for further discussion of his decision not to assign student grades). In situations where grading cannot be abandoned, readers may wish to thoughtfully consider having students submit learning portfolios, written or other types of project results, or other materials that show the depth and richness of what they have learned.

Many commonalities can be found between our case study professor's planned experiential learning activities and the "rich learning experiences" recommended in Fink's (2003) textbook about designing college courses. Specifically, Fink (2003) recommends giving students more hands-on "doing" and "observing" experiences during class, as well as indirect, vicarious experiences such as simulations, role plays, and films. Outside-of-class learning activities can be designed as well. Like our professor's assignment to go outside the classroom and try to "pull the sky through the trees," Fink (2003) suggests that students in a sociology class be assigned to observe and make notes on human behavior in a crowd.

Similar to the post-class student reflections collected during our case study, Fink (2003) recommends "one-minute papers" as a brief form of reflective writing after a class session. The students can be asked to respond to a question, such as "What was the muddiest point in today's lecture?" or "What important questions remain unanswered for you?" The "one-minute paper," analogous to Mackh's (2018) above-mentioned "exit slip," prompts students to actually reflect on what they were thinking (and feeling!) during the lesson, before they rush to the next class, hastily checking text messages on their cell phones. More extensive reflective writing, in journals, logs, or blogs, may be appropriate in courses that involve considerable emotion arousal, such as a course on death and dying or a course on family violence. Fink (2003) advises faculty to read students' reflections and periodically provide feedback. In our view, any faculty feedback should consist of appreciation for the views being shared, with no grades being assigned (see chapter 8 for examples of written reflections and teacher responses included in our descriptions of course teaching by other teachers).

Directly pertinent to every college teacher is our case study professor's practice of *self-reflection*. This practice was formalized by the audio recorded interviews during the case study research project, but we concur with the useful suggestion by Race (2010) that faculty simply use a self-reflective checklist after class. The checklist begins with "What is the thing about this session that is at the top of my mind at the moment?" (p. 239), analogous to our professor's reflection about "what stood out." Another self-reflection item highly relevant to the pedagogy described in our case study is "To what extent did I manage to get the students *learning by doing* during this session?" (p. 240). In addition to evaluating what did, and did not, work well, from the faculty perception, the checklist also includes student-focused items such as "What was the most hurtful comment or grading in students' feedback? Would it be useful for me to do something different next time round to address this particular aspect of critical feedback?" (p. 241). It may be especially important to promptly analyze how the "best-laid plans" for a class went awry, to prevent lengthy ruminating. If the idea of completing a checklist is unappealing, more informal journaling can be done:

> Jotting down your thoughts as reflections on a session can sometimes be a relief! If you've had a session where things didn't go well, and it continues to prey on your mind, making a short, reflective analysis of the session can be a way of "getting it out of your system," helping you to identify particular issues that you can address another time.
>
> (Race, 2010, p. 238)

Conclusion

This rigorous examination of instructional planning practices revealed what is missing from prosaic textbook advice to teachers. Although Weimer (2013), Blumberg (2017), and others have rightly pointed out the critical importance of the instructional design aspects of an educator's role and provided some useful guidance regarding newer teaching techniques, most of the literature of instructional planning has not kept pace with learner-centered trends in 21st-century education. Even the newest books retain reliance on the lecture method. For example, Mackh (2018) writes, "While I'm planning for each week of a course, I create the PowerPoints for my lectures" (p. 101). Textbook advice on planning often emanates from a very behavioral, cognitive, or other philosophical focus on transmission of knowledge, with neglect of the existential dimension of learning. Step-by-step guidance for creating lesson plans may be useful to new teachers, but leaves little room for teacher creativity and imagination. Moreover, the extant literature is not particularly relevant to a phenomenological approach.

We contribute to this literature by offering a fresh look at instructional planning obtained through the data of our case study research project. The extensive planning done by our case study professor, a master teacher,

64 *Preparation for Teaching*

clearly facilitated the level of "deep learning" described by Blumberg (2017), in which students connect their course-related learning to their own lived experiences in a transformational way. Actual *co-creation of knowledge* took place in this professor's classes. Co-creation such as this cannot take place in classrooms where students are passively consuming the teacher's presentations of content—even if the teacher is charismatic and lively. Traditional textbook advice about planning is not germane, in many respects, to a course designed from a phenomenological philosophical orientation in which dialogue is central.

Our case study professor, through his ingenious and diverse strategies, "blew the students away" and facilitated changed lives. Fink (2003) offered a new metaphor for teaching that captures the kind of transformative teaching demonstrated by our case study professor: *helmsman*. Crediting King (1993) for recommending the positive switch from "sage on the stage" to "guide on the side," Fink (2003) still viewed "guide on the side" as a dissatisfying metaphor. Based on his experience in whitewater rafting, he proposed "helmsman," the most experienced of the rafters who works collaboratively with the oarsmen to navigate the stream. Together, helmsman and oarsmen can navigate slower, less challenging waters before moving on toward steeper rivers and highly challenging rapids when they are ready. The helmsman's expertise is vital, but each individual paddler is indispensable to the effort, and it is the interdependent, collective whole that constitutes the transformative teaching/learning gestalt.

4 Teaching as Improvisational Jazz

"To Go Somewhere to Answer a BIG Question"

> Improvisation is about seeking connection. When you work well with others, it is a lot easier than when you are insistent upon doing your own thing. If you listen and copy and build on what everyone else is doing—oh God! I don't know how to explain it. Some kind of magic happens. It's as if you are all one being, sharing each other's minds. It feels safe and exciting at the same time. It's like together, somehow you can open yourselves to the spirit or God or the muses or whatever you want to call it and create work that you could never create on your own in a million years.
>
> (Dillard, 2015)

Dillard is describing his experience as an improvisational jazz musician. But he could have been describing the lifeworld of the classroom where a teacher furthers an intersubjective intertwining of the "network of relations" (Merleau-Ponty, 1945/1962) that comprise the human experience, and launches students and teacher into the world of the course content. As any jazz connoisseur will know, jazz is not just one style. It varies depending upon the degree to which the group of musicians maintains the melody of some familiar song, one musician leads other members of the ensemble, the tendencies of each of the musicians, and more. This is true also of classrooms in which teachers facilitate conversations with a phenomenological attitude, an attitude open to the ambiguity and wonder of the world, that encourages students to join them in considering intuitive assumptions and alternative views by listening to be influenced (Churchill, 2012; Finlay, 2008; Henriksson, 2012).

We found that improvisational jazz is an apt metaphor for describing our case study professor's teaching. A particular episode from a class session stands out in which almost all students joined the professor in conversation to share their thoughts about the meaning of time vs. the institution of time (see Box 4.1).

> **Box 4.1 Class Episode Exploring the Meaning of Time**
>
> The readings in preparation for this class session were focused on human perception of time vs. the institution of time. The professor entered class with audio equipment and, after greeting students, played a version of Leonard Cohen's song "Suzanne." The room filled with the beauty of Judy Collins's voice, the melody, and the words. Silence fell over the room during the performance and for at least a minute afterwards. Everyone seemed connected to a shared sense of awe. The professor paused, then asked, "What stood out for you as you listened?" Students began to share, first about the beauty of the experience but soon about the meaning of the song—they listened, took notes, and built upon each other's experiences. Through careful, subtle guidance, the professor turned the conversation towards exploring the meaning of time. And, together, they opened themselves to a spirit of creating insight that was all the deeper because of their improvisation.
>
> (Class session 10.12, 25-minute episode)

In this chapter, we present a first-person description of the experience of the professor while teaching and illustrate how the professor displayed a phenomenological attitude that was informed by existential phenomenological concepts as discussed in Chapter 1: the primacy of perception within the lifeworld of the classroom (Merleau-Ponty, 1945/1962), including the conditions of sociocultural embeddedness, embodiment, intersubjectivity, and ambiguity, as well as the subjective states of intentionality that provide an attitude of interacting in the world (Searle, 1999). The findings we share below show clearly the consistency the professor displayed from his preparation for class (detailed in Chapter 3) with his actual teaching in the fluid context of the classroom. In this chapter we focus on sharing examples of the classroom interactions of the professor and his students, his experience of teaching, and his reflections after each class session.

Together, Chapters 3 and 4 (case study findings related to the professor's planning and to his experience while teaching), 5, 6, and 7 (case study findings related to student experiences) provide a comprehensive picture of teaching and learning based on our phenomenological approach—situated within an improvisational jazz style of teaching in an advanced graduate seminar. But other styles of teaching can also utilize our approach's guidelines. In Chapter 8 we provide overviews of six course descriptions in which other teachers describe their styles such as *math missionary* and *interpretive dance* when teaching courses to undergraduates or less

Teaching as Improvisational Jazz 67

advanced graduate students. These six styles of teaching also illustrate the attention we give to certain phenomenological concepts in our approach. We discuss these in our conclusions after presenting our research findings and examples.

Next in this chapter, we share more about our research of the case study professor's teaching experience. We begin by describing the context of the case study seminar. Then, we present our findings from two studies.

The Case Study Classroom Context

Class sessions took place in a historical building that sat at the top of a hill, the highest point on the campus. Typically, course participants climbed wide marble stairways with carved wood banisters, worn and indented where generations of others had walked. One door near the end of the rectangular room provided entrance to the classroom. On the two exterior walls, large, old-fashioned windows allowed in natural light. The room was paneled in warm-toned wood where there were no black chalkboards, which covered the two interior walls. Commonly used for mathematics courses, the desks were rearranged by the students into a rectangle at the beginning of each session so that everyone could face each other. The professor and a research assistant sat across the front width of the rectangle (on the same level as the students) with easy access to the blackboards behind them. Students and participating faculty members sat on the other three sides, most choosing the same seat each session. All students had name tents displaying their first names, for use in class, and a research participant number, to identify them in the case study research. Microphones were placed where they could record all conversation.

In every session, one could see a stack of handouts and other items placed near the professor, ready to be used based on the professor's intuitive determination that they would enrich the class. Many times, only a few of these items were used during class, resulting in students expressing curiosity about those not used. Students set up laptops or brought pads of paper for taking notes. They also brought the book or photocopied pages of the often esoteric reading(s) for that session. Rather than feeling a need to remain quiet when they did not understand the reading, the professor invited students to share what stood out for them, whether due to confusion or insight.

On a few occasions, a portion of class time was spent with students working in small groups followed by sharing their ideas or findings with the large group, such as when one student conducted a phenomenological interview of another student while other group members reflected on what was happening. At other times the class might work together on some activity, such as organizing into themes the words students had called out

68   *Teaching as Improvisational Jazz*

about their experience of the body. The professor would often lecture for two to 10 minutes. These brief mini-lectures were mostly in response to student comments or questions, or if not, were opportunities to introduce students to new concepts or constructs related to course content for which he assumed he was the only person present who had knowledge to share.

But in our case study, open conversation dominated almost all class sessions. During these conversations, the professor typically invited students to share their ideas, including alternative perspectives regarding course content. Students chose for themselves when to join the conversation. Seldom did a student raise her hand, nor did the professor arbitrarily call on students. Often, the professor invited students to share what stood out for them rather than asking or telling them to respond to a specific, limited question.

Almost always the professor would begin by either sharing a personal experience (his own or that of an expert in the field) or asking students to share a personal experience related to the content focus of that session. Typically, a conversation would develop first between the professor and one student, with one or two more students joining that conversation by elaborating on what had just been said, sharing their own experience, or asking questions. Sometimes students would share alternative perspectives or ask questions that led the conversation in a different direction. While these conversations seldom involved more than two or three students talking with the professor during a 5- to 15-minute time period, our field notes and student reflections revealed that the vast majority of students appeared to be attending to the conversation and reflecting on it throughout the sessions. And almost all students participated verbally at least once in every class session.

We refer to this kind of verbal interaction as *dialogue*, and by this we mean there was an openness to the outcome of the conversation. The case study dialogues varied significantly from classroom *discussion*, in which the teacher commonly asks questions for which one-right-answers are expected (or responses that agree with the thinking of the teacher) and often one student responds briefly, other students possibly adding more information. Indeed, some teachers intentionally limit discussion to a review of ideas shared by text readings or the teacher herself. We view the metaphor for facilitation of *discussion* as being more like the teacher as a conductor of an orchestra.

The professor carefully monitored the need to change midstream from a dialogue, a class activity, or a mini-lecture. There were times, though rare, when conversation bogged down, he sensed some kind of resistance from students, or he heard sounds of restlessness. While the professor provided one 15-minute break in each 2-hour, 45-minute session, the timing of the break could vary. He avoided stopping a dialogue midstream, as this might result in a loss of momentum when taken up after the break. On other occasions, the break brought new life into the class.

It is important to note the complexity of facilitating classroom dialogue, particularly when the goal of dialogue is to develop a deep understanding of course content. Indeed, many teachers consider the risk of dialogue too great—that students will be unable to participate effectively (Rader & Summerville, n.d.). Too often, social constructivists recommend dialogue as a means to helping students construct their understanding of course content without providing an in-depth exploration of what it entails. We believe the findings from our data presented below provide a clear picture of one way to engage students in dialogue that enacts the phenomenological attitude of openness. Our results demonstrate the professor maintaining control while encouraging improvisation rather than a strict, orchestral style of teaching.

Case Study Research Findings

We provide a detailed picture of the professor's improvisational approach by sharing findings from two studies:

1. Phenomenological analysis of the professor's description of his approach to teaching.
2. Process coding of transcribed excerpts of classroom interaction using descriptors determined by the Transdisciplinary Phenomenology Research Group (TPRG).

We begin with a description of the professor's perspective about his experience in the classroom based upon a phenomenological analysis of a 2-hour interview.

Launching Students Into the World: The Professor's Perspective

We conducted an extensive interview in which we asked our case study professor what stood out as he reflected on his experience while teaching the graduate seminar during class sessions. We then analyzed a transcript of the interview, interpreting his comments using a phenomenological approach to identify themes (Sohn, Thomas, Greenberg, & Pollio, 2017).

Our analysis resulted in four themes that stood out for the professor from a contextual ground. Figure 4.1 illustrates the Gestalt structure of the experience of the professor. We will discuss each theme separately. (Note that quotation marks around all or part of a theme name indicate the use of the professor's actual words.) The themes and contextual ground include:

Ground: *"To go somewhere to answer a BIG question"*
Themes:

1. *Free-flowing journey*
2. *Energized*
3. *Questions within questions*
4. *Traffic control*

70 *Teaching as Improvisational Jazz*

Figure 4.1 The Thematic Structure of the Professor's Perspective on His Approach.

"To Go Somewhere to Answer a BIG Question"

The professor described both physical and psychological aspects of his lived experience, discussing "the physical geography of where I [sat] and where they [sat]. That was always important because of the way [students] perceived this [psychological geography] as [either] being in the way or as a path." His intent was "to go somewhere" which highlights movement through space towards some place. Tuan (1977) described the difference of human experience of these two phenomena. While space is often experienced as freedom to move, place is experienced as safety. The degree to which physical space and/or place can become a barrier depended for the professor, in part, as to whether everyone could see others, as when seated in a circle.

And the professor emphasized that it was the psychological structure of space and place that "led me to exactly where I needed to go [so that] everybody had a right-of-way." In this description, he emphasized the in-the-moment aspects of the lifeworld of the classroom. He described a tension he felt as he led the class: "I want to get someplace and look around in order to be in the familiar environment. [But] you don't look around, you want to be where [the students] are, cause that's where you

Teaching as Improvisational Jazz   71

need to be at that moment." We contend that this fit with his egalitarian perspective as leading an improvisational jazz ensemble.

But despite this tension, he had a guiding principle for finding the ideal "place"—a sense of connection to the lifeworld of the classroom. He saw his job as much more than taking students to some particular place of *his* choosing:

> My intent is *to go somewhere*—where students want to go—[to focus on] what stands out to them. [And, primarily] to find an answer to some BIG question related to the topic of that session. . . . I know certain places that I want to go. We go, and we get there. [But] my job is to show them how they can get themselves there. It's the revelation of self.

In addition, the professor spoke of the ideal response from students to his intent, "I would rather have the student tell me, 'Here, here's what Merleau-Ponty thinks is important. Here's what I think is important. And here's what [other ideas] are important.'" Similar to the words of Churchill (2006), the professor needed to "stand" where he could perceive what students perceived.

The professor described his experience when "going somewhere" was successful: "If [we] all agree, then we smile. I say, 'That's pretty good. We made it.'" He also spoke of his experience of not reaching a place together with students, "And sometimes we don't agree and of course it's what do you do at that point." He knew he needed to improvise based on the lived experience at "those points" in the lifeworld of the classroom.

Out of this lived context, four themes stood out for him. We discuss each of the themes separately to illustrate their contributions to his improvisational jazz style of teaching with a phenomenological attitude in the lifeworld of the classroom.

Free-Flowing Journey

Classroom dialogue for the professor was about a journey, a "free-flowing journey." His descriptions illustrated for the classroom what Smith (2018) wrote about the capabilities of expert jazz musicians, "an affinity for irresolution, missteps, in-between shiftings of weight, the moment not at the apex of a jump but just after." And the professor's descriptions reveal his connoisseurship as a skilled leader of improvisation. For example, he was very aware of the everchanging flow in the lifeworld of the classroom:

> People will let you go no further than they want you to go. [It] always says something important. [There were times when students] just picked it up and kept going, opening up, just wide enough to get it through. They opened up, they pushed me.

72 *Teaching as Improvisational Jazz*

The professor also described his awareness of student needs related to the free-flowing aspects of this journey, "you want to be where they are because that's where you need to be at that moment." This awareness seemed to help open him to a journey in which he did not always know where they would go in conversation. And it revealed his focus on perceptions in the lifeworld, at times on the sociocultural embeddedness of students, or on their embodiment, intersubjectivity, or the ambiguity regarding content in the given moment.

The professor also talked about the importance of intersubjectivity and embodiment as part of the *free-flowing journey*:

> It flows and most everybody's looking at you or toward the person who is talking and they're not talking to anybody else and I think that basically, there is no resistance in the class. It's going better than you would ever hope. You've got someplace where you never expected.

But even with an intent "to answer a BIG question," the professor saw the journey as meandering in directions he could not always predict, allowing freedom within the lifeworld of the classroom. He described the need to trust the process:

> You know, you [actually] hope to God [because] I don't know where we're gonna [go]. We'll end up some place really good and because the class trusted me, and I trusted them. I said "Let's go. Where are we going?"

The professor responded to problems with flow in various ways. Foremost, he believed that there was not one way to respond. As an improvisor, he was always ready to change direction. He stated, "I am not looking for anything—I am looking for everything." He would veer off on another path if students were not following him, if there seemed to be resistance or a negative reaction from students, if there were weak answers to his or others' questions, if a connection was broken, or if there were no clear connections between students and the class topic. He would work to find "an opportunity in a situation." If, for example, a student challenged something he said, the professor would look to see whether the student could be interpreting his comments in a way that makes sense—to explore some ambiguity in ideas about course content. In these circumstances, the professor stated a need for patience:

> I'm really ready to go any way they want to go, and we'll have to draw a lot of different ways they want to go. You really want to see what happens here and you [as professor], you're gonna have to wait.

Teaching as Improvisational Jazz 73

But he also described the need to guide the flow in a different direction; he described his embodied sense of what was happening in the lifeworld of the classroom.

> How do I know [when] to change what I'm doing? Let the class tell me. They're not interested. And . . . they normally become quiet when they don't understand. . . . It doesn't really fall apart but you feel like something is about to happen. . . . You're doing something good when the class keeps talking. You can sense that they really want to know about this and [it would be] doing them a disservice [if] you didn't follow up with them.

These perceptions on the part of the professor illustrate his egalitarian stance of following students' lead.

Energized

This theme highlights the importance to the professor of a "stimulating" lifeworld in the classroom. He spoke of his need to "arouse" feelings in students, or to seek a "singing answer" from students. He watched for times when more energy was needed, such as when students were not following the conversation, when there was resistance, weak answers, or when the conversation broke a connection.

He wanted "to break the ordinary." He would "grab one [disruptive idea] and say 'This is really interesting. I think we're gonna get some place that's really interesting.'" Indeed, he often used a dialectic approach to compare and contrast other perspectives with the course content—displaying his value on ambiguity as part of teaching and learning. He described one of the ways he sought to energize students by watching for some kind of challenge to his ideas.

> You see when a [student] challenges what you say, you [may] suddenly find out that he, he could be interpreting it in a way that makes sense and you're interpreting to where it makes sense. And then [you find] a conflicting situation there and that's going to break the ordinary . . . stuff that's going on in the classroom.

One way he set up a dialectic was by pointing out ideas of some well-known expert that conflicted with his own perspective and that of authors of course readings. For example, he stated, "I think you'll find that Descartes is the one I come back to over and over again [in this course] because he's so smart and so articulate and so *wrong* some of the time."

But he made decisions carefully about what to present as part of a dialectic: "I had to know the [students in order to] do these things. And the

74 *Teaching as Improvisational Jazz*

more outrageous ones . . . have to be done with people that you know." Intersubjectivity clearly stood out to the professor. And yet he was interested in challenging students, in taking them out of their comfort zones. He stated, "I don't care if they feel comfortable or not . . . just [that class is] stimulating."

One might picture a classroom atmosphere that was tense with strongly held views frequently being debated. But the free-flowing, improvised atmosphere that researchers witnessed, and students shared in their reflections, was much more like, as one student put it, "My happy time." And the professor spoke of his actions that contributed to these more positive qualities of an energized class. "I was very interested in what's really more entertaining."

Stories and personal descriptions of some experience were frequently used to energize the lifeworld of the classroom. When the professor shared a personal experience, he described his need to be expressive. When a student was telling a story without much expression, he would join that student by dramatizing some aspect of the story. For example, when a student was describing a very young child's reaction to her mother moving stuffed animals off her bed, where they had "lived" for a long time, the professor yelled out, "Don't do it, Mama!"

Another common element of class conversation was the use of humor. The professor often spontaneously and playfully added comments as he talked that brought the class together with laughter. And he welcomed students when they added humor, often building off their beginnings. See Box 4.2 for an example of a class session where the professor became aware of the need for more energy and improvised with humor and metaphor.

Box 4.2   Class Episode of Teacher and Student Energizing Dialogue with Humor

The BIG question in the class session was, "What can we determine about another person's consciousness, the interior world?" A student shared the phenomenological method of getting the person to talk about what stands out to her about some phenomenon. The professor responded, "That's the royal road to the interior world." Then he stimulated the conversation by adding an alternative perspective, "behavior is a way into that world, too. And we shouldn't throw it away." Another student then jumped in and said, "people don't necessarily act in a way that is in line with their interior world." And the professor quickly replied, "Are you saying we lie with our behavior?" Everyone laughed. The professor then led the students in thinking about a common personal experience of lying in the classroom (such as nodding at the teacher when you don't understand). He asked, "How can you lie with your behavior in the classroom?" He looked at the student with whom he had been talking and said, "Did you ever do that?" The student quickly responded, "I never have." The professor answered just as quickly, "I knew that. That's why I asked you. You're perfectly clean in this particular regard." Laughter ensued throughout this conversation, which went on to explore other examples. And, through his contributions, the lifeworld of the classroom was energized.

(Class session 10.12, 25-minute episode)

The professor's intentional use of humor and a playful manner went far beyond entertainment. He shared his intent to energize the lifeworld of the classroom within the present moment. In a post-class reflection, the professor shared his belief that spontaneous laughter communicates understanding and solidarity of the class members in a nonverbal embodied manner. He stated,

And I thought they needed it that day because it was a very, very serious class. . . . And when everybody laughs at the same thing, it is kind of an indication of group solidarity, and kind of it was there [at] the right moment . . . for most of the class too . . . in a very serious sort of way. I was aware . . . about how important that joke was . . . and it was very good to have it happen in the class. I thought it was funny . . . and [brought about] a sense of community.

In this manner, he could bring students together in a shared awareness of the present moment.

The theme of *energized* also went beyond engaging students. It included his personal need to feel spontaneous and inspire himself "with fresh understanding of related readings including those assigned. I'm bringing [stories, activities] that [are] always gonna appeal to me." But he was aware that what energized him was not always the same for students. When he sensed this in students, he shortened his story or changed the subject, as can be seen in the theme of free-flowing journey. And, very frequently, questions stood out as his preferred method of finding what would cause students to be inspired.

Questions Within the Questions

The use of questions was a dominant theme in the professor's focus on the lifeworld of the classroom. He did not explicitly state his BIG question. Instead, he talked of the need for open-ended questions that were carefully crafted to keep focus on his BIG question. For him, the purpose of a question was "giving direction." This focus furthered the improvisational atmosphere of the lifeworld of the classroom, including his egalitarian stance of being another learner exploring course content. It also helped him avoid a utilitarian attitude in which he might encourage students to spit out facts from readings instead of sharing the meaning the readings had for them.

The professor agreed that he often asked a series of questions: a rhetorical question, followed by a choice (usually yes/no) kind of question, and then a related, open-ended question. What also stood out to him were questions that came to him during class. He described what happened in one class when students began to ask about the relevance of phenomenology to their fields of study, such as clinical or experimental psychology.

> Everybody immediately took [the topic] as a big road into them and that was, they asked 100 questions. I knew I was not gonna get back to my lecture, [but] I didn't know what way to go 'cause it, it wasn't my life. [It wasn't] what we [were talking] about.

The professor also recalled that he tried to help students go deeper into their personal ideas related to course content by *asking back*—asking questions immediately after a student shared a comment or question. He stated, "the answer to the question doesn't matter, the answer to the question is another question. I want the answer and then again, there was this question in the questions." His attention was also drawn to times when students "give you an answer but it's a weak answer. It's not a singing answer." A utilitarian, "factoid" answer was an example to him of an answer that did not "sing."

Another focus for the professor was his attempt to energize by asking *vocative* questions (van Manen, 2014): questions that in some way *call* to students in a manner that brings experience to life. He spoke of avoiding "baby-like questions over here and factoid questions," one-right-answer, fact-oriented questions. He described his response to students asking factoid questions and displayed his egalitarian stance. "When the student asks the question and really wants to know the answer I ask him, 'What do you mean by that? What was that about for you? Where should I pay attention?'"

The professor reported that he often began class by asking an open question related to the assigned reading, such as "Where do we start? What questions do you have? What was Merleau-Ponty talking about? What didn't you understand? What pages did you really like? What pages did you really connect with? What [was Merleau-Ponty] really saying?" Such questions can lead easily into an improvisational style of teaching. But they also can raise the likelihood of furthering a phenomenological attitude in the lifeworld of each class participant.

Traffic Control

Some critiques of this kind of open questioning worry that the teacher is giving up all control—that the free-flowing conversation looks more like chaos. But the professor was clear that he did not lose control. "A question looks like it's giving up a control, and the fact [is] that you're giving direction." Our case study professor shared, "I am always in control, or someone else will be. I am much more in control than [one] would think." Indeed, he reported seeing himself as a traffic controller on the free-flowing road to somewhere, based on the BIG question related to the course topic. And yet his control did not provide roadblocks to what students said and/or how they answered his questions. Determinations about controlling the free-flowing journey included an awareness of what he was looking for. "I'm not looking for anything—I am looking for everything." For the professor displayed a truly egalitarian stance of being "a fellow traveler on life's journey" with his students (Thomas, 2005).

The professor shared how he went about controlling the dialogue, how he was aware of the structure of the class conversation. If he disagreed with a student, he reported telling the student, "I don't agree with that." Or, more frequently, he asked questions to get the student to go deeper. Based on what he sensed was needed in the moment, he would be prepared in advance to improvise, "either have a story or have a question or have mini-lectures." But mini-lectures were not his preferred method of assisting students to go someplace. When asked under what circumstances he would lecture, he responded, "[When] I feel the point must be gotten across, about something really important. And, when they couldn't possibly know [something] directly, for example something that connects the topic to the Hebrew Bible or to the etymology of a word."

He was conscious of how he controlled his sharing stories of personal experience. There were times when the professor felt they were not being well received by students. He shared his intent to not "force his story on them." He said when that happened, "We changed, and then we just moved the topic, moved it away." This is another example of improvisation based on his awareness of the need to pay attention to embodiment and intersubjectivity.

The professor stated that his type of control did not include "[giving] stuff away" or "[dispensing] facts." He said he did not control by taking students where he wanted to go, and yet he did control by showing them how to get to an answer of the BIG question for that class. He directed them by finding an opportunity in a situation by asking, "'What do you do at that point?' . . . I wanted [students] to get somebody's help and be able [to do] this by [themselves]." And he spoke of asking students to help him reach the goals he set for the class, which is, of course, an egalitarian approach. He described how he provided freedom by trusting the process while always directing traffic—always being in control.

78 Teaching as Improvisational Jazz

These four themes illustrate how the professor experienced and facilitated the lifeworld of the classroom. They stood out to him from his ground of "to go somewhere to answer a BIG question," his intent for his teaching. Together, the ground and themes provided the structure—a framework—he perceived in his teaching. Next, we consider his actions during class.

Improvisational Jazz in Action

We wanted to explore the professor's style of teaching in more depth to answer a number of questions: How did he enact the four themes he experienced? What specifically did he do to create a free-flowing journey? What best describes the ways in which he energized students in the lifeworld of the classroom? What kinds of questions did he ask? And how specifically did he control the conversation? Our second study of the professor's teaching explores these questions as we share transcripts of two exemplary episodes of actual classroom interaction.

Research Procedures of Study 2

In order to understand the professor's specific actions during classroom conversations, researcher members of the TPRG analyzed transcripts of numerous recorded classroom interaction episodes. The episodes were determined by members of our research team who reached consensus that they stood out due to several criteria. For example, episodes were selected when, according to field notes, more students entered the dialogue, more students began taking notes, or a major shift occurred in the focus of the dialogue.

During these analysis sessions, the transcripts were read aloud, and TPRG members discussed what stood out to them about the professor's role as facilitator of the seminar. Members of the research group represented many fields of study including educational psychology, education, nursing, child and family studies, psychology, and others. Researchers with a background in teaching and learning pedagogy were challenged by others to check their assumptions and explain their jargon. In turn, the pedagogically oriented researchers helped others look deeply at what was occurring during classroom conversation.

The research group created a long list of descriptors of the professor and his students in action. This list was eventually narrowed as some descriptors became subsumed within others of a similar focus. Table 4.1 presents these descriptors with explanations and categorizes them according to their primary importance in relation to one of the four themes of the professor's experience. Note that context, the ground from which the four themes stood out, is not included in the table. As in most phenomenological analyses, the ground provided the overall structure within which specific descriptors emerged. In order to show the reciprocity between the professor and students who interacted with him, the descriptors listed in Table 4.1 were used to analyze both the professor and the students' actions through process coding (Saldaña, 2016).

To best illustrate the figure and ground of the professor's experience of teaching and to show the aptness of the improvisational jazz metaphor, we chose episodes in which several students joined the professor in dialogue. Tables 4.2 and 4.3 present these transcripts and our process coding of descriptors as they occurred. We separated the conversation by speaker, indicating whether the speaker was the professor or a student (and the number of a student based on when that student joined the conversation). Then, we further separated the utterances of any one speaker into discrete units based on the focus of the utterance. For example, all questions were coded separately, even when two or more questions were uttered in a series by the same speaker. When a participant spoke with more than a brief comment, we separated phrases into units if they included a different focus, such as a playful comment, or elaborated on the previous comment. It should be noted that even within discrete units, several descriptors could occur simultaneously. We present our analyses separately for Episodes 1 and 2.

Study 2 Findings

Process Codes Relation to Themes

The professor consistently enacted his intent to facilitate a free-flowing journey in which students were energized to explore some BIG question related to course content. Although the conversation went in many directions based on what students shared as meaningful to them, the professor was always in control, often directing the conversation towards the BIG question by asking questions within questions. However, he varied what he did based on what occurred in class. For example, sometimes he elaborated more than students. At other times he encouraged students to do so. Some of the time, the professor described an experience rather than having one or more students share a story of their own personal experience. He often dominated the conversation as he talked primarily with one to three students—who together spoke with almost equal frequency with him. Nevertheless, each of the descriptors listed in Table 4.1 occurred frequently and provide insight into the way in which the professor enacted the existential phenomenological framework.

Four descriptors denoted how the professor went about "controlling traffic" during classroom dialogue. The most prominent of these were his actions in *opening* the dialogue to what was of interest to students, including their questions and confusions about course content. He displayed an attitude of acceptance and even enthusiasm regarding what students said. He invited them to share their views, even if in conflict with

80 *Teaching as Improvisational Jazz*

Table 4.1 Descriptors of Classroom Facilitation and Their Relation to Themes

Theme	Descriptors
Traffic Control	*Opening*: To display an attitude that invites others to share alternative ideas, personal experience, confusion, questions, etc.
	Joining: To become another learner in exploring an experience, question, or topic in the conversation; may or may not join as an expert
	Leading: To move others in a particular direction through comment, question, or description; may or may not change the general direction and flow of the conversation focus
	Following: To contribute to the conversation in a manner that maintains the present, general direction and flow of the prior comment, question, or description
Free-flowing Journey	*Describing*: To provide a description of an event, personal experience, features of a construct, examples, or a story
	Elaborating: To clarify, expand, or present an alternative view from the prior comment, question, or description shared by oneself or another person
	Weaving: To connect some aspect of course content with a description, example, or personal experience shared by oneself or another person
Energized	*Entertaining*: To afford playful and spontaneous laughter and surprise
	Dramatizing: To convey excitement or other emotion; use words that are vivid; evoke or provoke others
	Disrupting: To challenge a common worldview or expert/ novice perspective
	Assuring: To agree with another person, point out the importance of something the person said, praise, or reassure the other person
Questions within Questions	*Asking rhetorical question*: To ask a question merely for effect with no answer expected
	Asking choice question: To ask a question in which the responder is given two or more options for the answer
	Asking open-ended question: To ask a question in which the responder is free to answer as chooses

his or another expert such as an author of a reading. At times he **joined** students in learning by revealing his own curiosities and challenges. The professor also controlled traffic by sometimes *leading* and sometimes *following* students. Upon occasion, he led students in a particular direction to explore some aspect of course content. At other times he led students in a new direction by asking a question with a different focus, describing an experience or asking a student to do so, or presenting a new activity.

Sometimes, the professor followed students in the direction they established, controlling the direction they took the conversation through his questions or comments.

Three descriptors stood out to research team members regarding how the professor furthered a "free-flowing" dialogue. The professor *described* his own experiences, or shared other descriptive stories related to course content. When students asked questions, he frequently engaged them in describing a related experience. More often than not, this led students to a deeper understanding without the need for an explicit explanation. Often, he *elaborated* on something he had just shared or the contribution of a student. He did this by clarifying, expanding, or offering an alternative view. Elaborating was frequently accompanied by, or served to, **weave** personal experience with course content. While the journey was free-flowing, course content was not left behind.

We found four descriptors that revealed how the professor energized students during the dialogue. Often, he *entertained* students with light-hearted, humorous, and playful comments. Occasionally, he roleplayed a character in his or a students' story by **dramatizing** what might have been said in the situation. At other times he engaged in *disrupting* the dialogue by challenging a common worldview, something said by a student, or creating a dialectic with some other expert perspective. And, he energized individual students by **assuring** them as he briefly shared his approval or interest in what they contributed to the conversation, or by reassuring a student that it was okay to share confused thoughts or an alternative view. Indeed, these kinds of assurances appeared to energize more students beyond the one making the contribution.

Questions were a very important part of the way in which the professor facilitated the dialogue. We found three types of questions stood out due to their frequent use. As noted in our research on the professor's preparation for class in Chapter 3, he spent considerable time making a list of questions that he might use, as appropriate, to guide the students toward the BIG question. During the dialogue, he often asked questions in a series. First, the professor asked a *rhetorical question*, one he stated for effect and with no expectation for a response. He immediately followed the *rhetorical question* with a *choice question* that guided students in a certain direction or encouraged them to consider a few alternatives. Third, he asked the question that he hoped would lead the dialogue forward, an *open question* for which there were many possibilities for a response.

Process Coding of Classroom Conversation

We present our process coding of each of the two transcripts separately. Episode 1, *Illusion in Illusion* (see Table 4.2), occurred in a class session in which the professor's BIG question for the session was, "What is the role of perceptual 'illusion' in our lives?" This episode from this class session

Table 4.2 Episode 1 of a Transcript from a Graduate Seminar Dialogue with Process Coding Analysis of Descriptors

Episode 1: *Illusion as Illusion*

Context: The professor began the class by reminding students about the last session in which they examined a series of optical illusions in an effort to explore aspects of perception from a Gestalt, figure/ground perspective. Then, he asked them to describe what stood out to them about their experiences inside and outside of class, prior to this session. His BIG question to guide the free-flowing journey was: What is the role of perceptual "illusion" in our lives? (Duration: approximately 3 minutes).

Item	P = Professor, S = Student (1, 2, 3, etc.)	Descriptors
1.	P: Ok, so now . . . go through [the optical illusions] mentally, you know, and think about one you think stands out to you as being the most interesting or whatever.	Leading/Opening
2.	P: Anybody got one yet?	Inviting/Opening
3.	S1: *Yeah. I was driving to Ohio and I just kept thinking about it and thinking about it. I was by myself when it dawned on me that the initial observation I made was the illusion.*	*Following/Describing/ Dramatizing*
4.	P: When in fact, you had no illusion whatsoever!	Elaborating/Following/ Joining/Dramatizing
5.	S1: *I just kept thinking about it, and that's just when it dawned on me that the initial observation I made was the illusion.*	*Following/Describing/ Dramatizing*
6.	P: So, it was a hell of an illusion!	Assuring/Following/Joining/ Dramatizing
7.	S1: *Yeah. It was.*	*Assuring/Following*
8.	S1: *So just the perception of the phenomenon was flipped for me.*	*Elaborating/Weaving*
9.	P: Does anybody want to ask him a question?	Inviting/Leading/Opening/ Asking rhetorical question
10.	S2: *So, just a question or does it have to be a phenomenological question?*	*Following/Entertaining/ Asking choice question*
11.	*[Everyone laughs]*	
12.	P: Any.	Elaborating/Following
13.	S3: *Did you have the radio on or were you just quiet and you were thinking you were . . . ?*	*Leading/Describing/Joining/ Asking choice question*

Item	P = Professor, S = Student (1, 2, 3, etc.)	Descriptors
14.	S1: I was thinking about all my classes and how this is my last fall semester.	Following/Describing
15.	S1: I started thinking about material in the classes.	Elaborating
16.	P: Go on . . . give us a little more detail about that.	Inviting/Leading
17.	P: Where did your thought get to?	Asking open-ended question
18.	S1: That the perception of the phenomena is . . . is not really reliable, may not be reliable.	Following/Weaving
19.	S1: Um, because what I understood the phenomenon to be, based on my perception, turned out to be inaccurate.	Elaborating/Weaving
20.	S1: Um, and then, I thought about that more as I was driving a little over the speed limit and I looked for	Describing/Entertaining
21.	[Everyone laughs]	
22.	S1: Police cars. And, there was this one bend where the guard rail interacted with the hill	Elaborating/Describing
23.	S1: and my stomach went just, it just flipped.	Dramatizing
24.	S1: Because it looked like a police car. But then, it wasn't.	Elaborating/Describing
25.	S1: So then, I just thought, "Wow! My perception failed me again!"	Describing/Dramatizing
26.	S1: But my perception was influenced by what I was expecting to see.	Elaborating/Weaving
27.	P: What does it mean, your perception failed you?	Leading/Weaving/Asking rhetorical question
28.	P: Here is a really strong claim.	Assuring/Dramatizing
29.	P: Because when you think about it, we say, "If you can see something, show it to me and I'll believe it."	Elaborating/Describing
30.	P: And you're saying that perception failed you.	Weaving
31.	P: This is not a confrontational question,	Assuring/Elaborating
32.	P: I think it's a really interesting statement that you said.	Assuring/Elaborating/ Joining/Dramatizing
33.	P: Does everybody see what I'm saying here?	Weaving/Asking rhetorical question

(Continued)

84 *Teaching as Improvisational Jazz*

Table 4.2 (Continued)

Item	P = Professor, S = Student (1, 2, 3, etc.)	Descriptors
34.	P: In the Western world, perception—and in the scientific situation, scientific perception is . . . is what you want.	Elaborating/Leading/Weaving
35.	P: You want everybody to see the phenomenon, to see what's happening.	Elaborating/Weaving
36.	P: And here we have a case . . . where by ordinary standards perception failed you.	Elaborating/Weaving

included here was around three minutes in duration. The professor began by inviting students to describe an optical illusion that stood out to them from the last class session about perception. Student 1 responded to the professor's initial question by describing the context in which he gained deeper meaning about perception. Nevertheless, the professor *followed* the first student into exploring his reflection about what he learned regarding the meaning of perception—including his description of an experience that occurred while driving. Student 1 contributed much more than the other two students. He responded to the professor's initial question by describing the context in which he came to a conclusion about the meaning of illusion he had realized. Students 2 and 3 spoke one time each. Student 2 *followed* the professor's request for students to ask questions of Student 1. But he did so by asking a humorous *choice* question that entertained the class. Student 3 joined the conversation by *leading* Student 1 to respond to her choice question that included a description in the given choices. The professor spoke a bit more than the three students combined. Other than Student 1's *description*, all participants in this short episode primarily *elaborated* on the contributions to the conversation and **wove** course content with Student 1's description.

In episode 1, the professor utilized all aspects of his framework. He *controlled traffic* primarily by *following* students in the direction Student 1 established. The professor furthered a free-flowing journey by *elaborating* on other contributions to the conversation as well as by *weaving* course content with the *description* of personal experience shared by Student 1. Both students and the professor sought to energize others in the dialogue by adding *drama*. Student 2 *entertained* others by sharing a humorous question. The professor also asked several *rhetorical questions* and one **open** question, while students asked **choice** questions.

The second episode we include in this chapter differs in a number of ways from the first episode. Episode 2, *My Time vs. External Time* (see Table 4.3), occurred in a class session where the BIG question was, "What

Table 4.3 Episode 2 of a Transcript from a Graduate Seminar Dialogue with Process Coding Analysis of Descriptors

Episode 2: My Time vs. External Time

Context: The professor just finished sharing a story about a child's perception of time being much longer than adults. His BIG question for this class session was: What is the role of perception in our internal, first person, vs. external, third person, experience of time? (Duration: approximately 5 minutes).

Item	P = Professor, S = Student (1, 2, 3, etc.)	Descriptors
1.	P: What I'm saying is the estimation of time for the child is longer than the estimation of time for the adult.	Elaborating/Weaving
2.	P: Just think of your own life. Think about time from [ages] 4 to 8 and then think about your time when you went to four years of school.	Invites/Describing/Opening
3.	P: In retrospect, the 2nd one went very, very quickly.	Elaborating/Dramatizing
4.	P: You wanted to say something, didn't you?	Invites/Opening/Asking rhetorical question
5.	*S1: Well, I guess when you [asked this] question, I was thinking of the scratching on the face [of a baby].*	*Following/Describing/Joining*
6.	*S1: You know the scratches and the fact that they healed so quickly?*	*Elaborating/Asking choice question*
7.	P: Yeah	Assures/Following
8.	*S1: So, I was thinking about time being more rapid in a, I guess, from a physiological perspective, healing*	*Elaborating/Weaving*
9.	P: Healing is. . . .	Following/Joining
10.	*S1: The body heals itself more quickly in youth than it does in older age*	*Elaborating/Weaving*
11.	P: Yet at the same time you have the paradox of it heals itself quickly, but the time seems to go by more slowly psychologically.	Following/Elaborating/Weaving/Disrupting
12.	P: That that's a very interesting sort of thing	Assuring/Dramatizing

(Continued)

Table 4.3 (Continued)

Item	P = Professor, S = Student (1, 2, 3, etc.)	Descriptors
13.	P: but again, these are all violations on the clock being the standard of, of time	Elaborating/Weaving/Disrupting
14.	*S2: And you know it seems that I, I just keep thinking about my experience when I had little kids. There was this constant conflict between, you know, the clock time*	*Following/Describing/Weaving*
15.	P: Uh huh	Assuring
16.	*S2: And their experience of time*	*Weaving*
17.	*S2: and that and I always felt bad. I mean I felt bad about it. I felt guilty about it*	*Describing/Dramatizing*
18.	*S2: that you know, they would be engaged in some activity that was great. And I would have like, because it was such and such a time and we had to get some place, I'd say, you know, stop that activity and um, you know, interrupt their experience, whatever, you know to get them some place.*	*Describing/Dramatizing*
19.	*S2: So, I mean I as a mom, I'm sure you know, lots of mom, all moms experience this. But it's this constant conflict or confrontation of this external time and, um, their experience or even getting . . .*	*Elaborating/Dramatizing/Weaving*
20.	*S2: I remember getting my 2-year-old, you know, to her two mornings a week school . . . You know, she was always really slow so, you know, we'd be taking breakfast in the in the car and I'd be thinking, "this is so stupid."*	*Describing/Dramatizing*
21.	*S2: you know?*	*Asking rhetorical question*
22.	P: I think we've all experienced that. And I think this relates to what I said before	Assuring/Weaving
23.	P: about, why does the school have like a 50-minute class?	Leading/Asking rhetorical question
24.	P: Sometimes, you only need 30 minutes and sometimes you need 2 hours to do what you're doing.	Elaborating/Describing

Item	P = Professor, S = Student (1, 2, 3, etc.)	Descriptors
25.	P: And that's kind of like where the clock coerces the hell [out] of you and you've got to be places on time.	Elaborating/Dramatizing
26.	P: It's coercive and limiting	Dramatizing
27.	P: and stuff like that.	Describing
28.	P: But, she said something really extraordinarily interesting just now.	Assuring/Leading/Dramatizing
29.	P: She used the word "external."	Elaborating/Weaving
30.	P: That is external to me, right?	Asking rhetorical question
31.	P: The clock, the clock on the wall back there and then it and then the watch is external to me and the sense of time that we're talking about accidents, mementos, all of those sorts of things [are] sort of my time that . . . belong to me.	Elaborating/Describing/Weaving
32.	P: So, what we've got is a time that runs by, external to us and seems indifferent to us, the clock and calendar, and the time that's really our time which is not indifferent to us at all.	Elaborating/Describing/Weaving/Disrupting
33.	P: It's incredibly, incredibly important.	Dramatizing
34.	P: It has to do with power. It has to do with ah, an excitement. It has to do with memory, it has to do with relationship, it has to do with all kinds of things so that we have two types of time. The time of the clock which, I said that.	Elaborating/Describing/Weaving
35.	P: I like that phrase, "it's external" to you.	Assuring/Joining/Weaving
36.	P: And, and the time of our, of our experiences which is certainly ours uniquely.	Elaborating/Dramatizing/Weaving
37.	P: Ok, so what can we say about time?	Inviting/Weaving/Asking open-ended question
38.	P: I, I'm confused now.	Disrupting
39.	P: Hmm	Joining
40.	P: What can we say about time?	Inviting/Weaving/Asking open-ended question

(Continued)

Table 4.3 (Continued)

Item	P = Professor, S = Student (1, 2, 3, etc.)	Descriptors
41.	S3: *It is a complex, multi-layered, multi-faceted concept*	*Following/Weaving*
42.	P: Now, you sound like a psychologist now	Entertaining
43.	*[Everyone laughs]*	
44.	P: So, what we can we?	Inviting/Weaving/Asking open-ended question
45.	P: Yes, all of that is true	Assuring
46.	P: but everything we talk about is like that.	Elaborating
47.	P: Isn't it?	Weaving/Asking rhetorical question
48.	P: Ah, my job is	Leading
49.	S2: *No, I don't think so*	Following/Disrupting
50.	P: You think the body was any better?	Following/Weaving/ Asking choice question
51.	P: When we talked about the body?	Elaborating/Weaving/ Asking choice question
52.	S3: *I, I think that culturally, our perception of the body is listed from my perspective, from my health perspective that it's a complex multi-level, multi ya da ya da*	*Following/Elaborating/ Weaving*
53.	S3: *but time culturally, we generally don't think of it as a complex multi-layered, multi-faceted concept*	*Elaborating/Weaving*
54.	P: [laughing]	
55.	P: Say that once more?	Entertaining
56.	P: That's really cool	Assuring/Dramatizing
57.	S3: *I just wrote this stupid-assed paper and I used that term over and over again. It's*	*Elaborating/Disrupting/ Entertaining*
58.	*[Everyone laughs]*	
59.	P: Yes, what, what, what do you think about when we talk about other people?	Following/Weaving/ Asking rhetorical question
60.	P: You think they're not going to turn out to be a complex, multi-faceted, whatever the thing was that you said before	Elaborating/Weaving
61.	S3: *Multi-layered*	*Following/Weaving/ Entertaining*

Item	P = Professor, S = Student (1, 2, 3, etc.)	Descriptors
62.	[Everyone laughs]	
63.	P: multi-layered, multi-faceted, ah, ah sna snowball	Elaborating
64.	S3: Huh?	Asking rhetorical question
65.	P: Our job, our job is in this class is continuously to ask the question;	Leading/Weaving
66.	P: What is the 3rd person experience?	Weaving/Asking rhetorical question
67.	P: The cultured one?	Elaborating/Weaving/ Asking rhetorical question
68.	P: The measured one?	Elaborating/Weaving/ Asking rhetorical question
69.	P: And what is the 1st person one?	Elaborating/Weaving/ Asking rhetorical question
70.	P: Which is our experience of that in the situation?	Elaborating/Weaving/ Asking rhetorical question
71.	P: And when do they agree with each other?	Elaborating/Weaving/ Asking rhetorical question
72.	P: And when don't they agree with each other?	Elaborating/Weaving/ Asking rhetorical question
73.	P: And what should we do when they don't agree?	Elaborating/Weaving/ Asking rhetorical question

is the role of perception in our internal (first person) vs. external (third person) experience of time?" This episode was longer than the first: a total of 5 minutes. Further, the professor dominated the conversation in Episode 2. In part this occurred because of the many times the professor *wove* course content into the conversation as he *elaborated* on course content in relation to personal experience. In addition, he asked numerous *rhetorical questions* as the focus of a mini-lecture at the conclusion of the episode. Though much less frequently than the professor, students also contributed by *elaborating*. And they provided almost as many *descriptions* as the professor provided. Although considerably less frequently than the professor, students did **weave** course content into the conversation.

90   *Teaching as Improvisational Jazz*

In Episode 2, the professor again enacted all four aspects of his framework. He primarily controlled the dialogue by *inviting* students to share through comments displaying his *open* attitude. He also **led** and **followed** students to the same degree. And he energized student interest in the dialogue primarily by *assuring* students and by *dramatizing* as he shared strong feelings in his personal descriptions.

Conclusions

Fundamental to all phenomenological approaches is the concept of the lifeworld, "the world of lived experience inhabited by us as conscious beings and incorporating the way in which phenomena (events, objects, emotions) appear to us in our conscious experience or everyday life" (Brooks, 2015, p. 642). Because of the case study professor's improvisational style, the findings we present in this chapter provide a clear illustration of focus on the lifeworld of the classroom—the dynamic process that takes place *in the present moment*. Course content is not left behind, but it is addressed through focus on real *living* experience rather than mastery of content as demonstrated through regurgitation of the ideas shared in readings or by the professor. The improvisational jazz metaphor highlights the idea of focusing on how teacher and/or students can co-create an experience of teaching and learning intertwined with course content—how personal experience relates to abstract knowledge. Indeed, according to Merleau-Ponty (1945/1962), our perceptions provide our only link to abstract knowledge. And an improvisational jazz approach nurtures awareness of our perceptions through our lived experiences in the classroom, contributing to the adoption of a phenomenological attitude.

As discussed in Chapter 1, teachers often overlook the primacy of perception. We focus in our approach on four concepts that stand out to us as being of particular importance in teaching and learning because of the ways they influence perception and intentionality of teacher and students. First, every participant perceives the lifeworld of the classroom through their personal sociocultural embeddedness—their own lens for viewing the world, developed over time, based on their personal experiences in a given family and society. But, especially in the case of the teacher, this embeddedness includes the culture of the field of study in which the teacher is engaged. Second, the atmosphere in the lifeworld of the classroom affects the embodiment of each participant individually, the way that person's senses intertwine with, indeed are a part of, thinking. Third, intersubjectivity amongst students and teachers affects perceptions occurring in the lived experience of the classroom: the tendency for the atmosphere to be open and safe or closed and anxiety-producing. And fourth, the ambiguity of our understanding of any aspect of the world, including course content, is either acknowledged in the lifeworld of the classroom or it is ignored, leaving students less or more able to find personal meaning related to course content.

Along with the concepts detailed in Chapter 1, a phenomenological approach to teaching includes two other aspects of the lived experience as discussed by Merleau-Ponty. It avoids what is commonly dominant in higher education: the utilitarian attitude, with its emphasis on training students so they develop knowledge and skills needed in some career—often with little connection to lived experience of the world (Cuseo, 2007; Henriksson, 2012; Willis, 2012; see Chapter 7 for a more in-depth discussion). And an improvisational approach to teaching nurtures the lifeworld of the classroom through an egalitarian approach to intersubjectivity, viewing students as "fellow travelers in life's journey" (Thomas, 2005, p. 71). Indeed, teachers who share Merleau-Ponty's perspective on the phenomenological attitude interact quite differently with students than those who perceive themselves as authority figures who always have the one-right-answer. Dialogue can occur when the teacher facilitates conversation in which everyone is encouraged to listen to be influenced by alternative ideas, to ask back to ensure understanding, and to seek relationships among differing perspectives—while feeling free to *mess about* (Hawkins, 1974) and play with ideas.

Finally, the professor's improvisational jazz approach to teaching provides a comfortable means for weaving personal experience with course content. Description is of prime importance to all phenomenological schools of thought. In the process of describing a phenomenon by giving a detailed account of salient aspects of an experience, teachers can avoid detached, utilitarian, analytical language and reflection. The idea is to delay analysis and explanation and, instead, focus first on what stands out in an unreflected manner, within our gestalt of lived experience related to some phenomenon, some course content.

When we compared findings of a study of the professor's preparation for class to our findings of his experience of teaching, we discovered a clear consistency. As discussed in Chapter 3 and here as well, his framework for designing instruction and for facilitating conversation in class were based on his in-depth experience in existential phenomenological philosophy. In the planning study, he talked about his desire to "open up the world" of first-person experiences for his students (Franklin, 2013). The context guiding him while in the classroom was "to go somewhere" related to course content, again focused on first-person experience. At the same time, his openness to where they would go and what would be shared reflected his desire to bring out his students' sociocultural perspectives and join them as another learner in exploring course content. While the professor prepared for class in a fairly typical fashion of most teachers—selecting activities, thinking about key questions he might ask—we found, he was always ready to go *with the flow* of the experience, omitting some activities, re-sequencing the order of others during the session, following students in new directions as the class evolved. He was clearly in tune with the lifeworld of the classroom, in all its intersubjectivity—in a very similar manner to improvisational jazz musicians.

Our synthesis of the findings from these studies provides a clear picture of the ways in which the professor's style was consistent across *his* planning, *student* descriptions of their learning in the course, and the *existential phenomenological framework* of our approach presented in Chapters 1 and 9. Our research on the lived experience of this professor helped us understand how describing experiences relevant to course content prior to explaining it allowed both him and his students to explore their living perceptions and meaning at a deeper level. Assumptions were questioned, alternative ideas discussed, and realizations often took place.

Our findings support the frequent occurrence of dialogue in the professor's classroom. His intent and the interactions that took place were distinctly different from what typically occurs in class discussion. They demonstrate how dialogue can keep course content as the central focus, similar to the ideas expressed by Parker Palmer (2007) in *The Courage to Teach*, but also bring attention to the existential phenomenological dimensions of perception necessary in order to develop a deep understanding of course content.

Our case study revealed that a teacher can facilitate transformative learning without knowing the perspective of each student individually, without engaging in conversation with all students frequently, and without giving up the opportunity to do most of the talking in class. But certainly, the professor and his students went to the heart of teaching and learning when the class was taught as improvisational jazz where students could add their own melodic sounds. He was far removed from acting as a conductor of a symphony where musicians play exactly as told. His elaboration of content was weaved into ideas that stood out to students, rather than as part of a scripted lecture. And the sharing of students often involved, at his invitation, class reflection on detailed descriptions of some personal experience—that was woven with course content. But as the professor made explicit, he did not open a class conversation, lean back, and passively watch where it went. He was always in control, guiding students through openness towards exploration of some BIG question he had in mind. They explored course content by seeing if, together, they could find insight.

In other words, the case study professor launched students into the world of course content by making space for the alternative percepts implicit in the several dimensions of perception. In this manner, he facilitated students' exploration of *how they stood so they saw what they saw* (Churchill, 2006)—a holistic gestalt of the context from which certain aspects became figural. Further, his framework honored the lifeworld of the classroom—that place within the present moment where we are most aware that we exist. And this context was defined by the kind of conversations that took place.

A concern of many reading this chapter may be, "What about my teaching? I have a much larger class size, I can't possibly know the personal experience of each student. I am required and expected to cover specific subject matter. I can't meander through the experiences of students. And, I have an ultimatum and belief in grading my students, giving assignments where I can determine their mastery of content. I am not a humorist or talented conversationalist as the case study professor may be [indeed is]. This is all interesting, but it doesn't apply to my lifeworld as a teacher." We respond that there are many ways to adapt a phenomenological approach—and a great need to do so. For through an existential phenomenological approach, we can help students overcome assumptions and judgments that exist due to confirmation bias and other fallacious thinking. If left to simmer out of reach, these assumptions interfere with learning. In Chapter 9, we discuss how other higher education pedagogies that readers may already use or espouse enact some aspects of these principles and may be enriched by incorporation of more of a phenomenological approach.

In Chapter 8, we provide numerous examples of teaching that, along with a phenomenological attitude, apply existential phenomenological principles, open the intentionality within our minds to enact these principles, and go to the heart of teaching and learning. But that chapter also reports findings of student experiences in which teachers mess up. Our main response here is to say that we, as teachers, ignore the lifeworld of the classroom at our peril.

5 Free to Learn
A Radical Aspect of Our Approach

Lois: I didn't feel like a student, I felt like a learner.

Brian: The atmosphere of the classroom was open, engaging . . . [with] people sharing their stories to bring a richer experience to the classroom. It was like a relief, so I would come in and relax.

Kari Ann: I'm always happy to come to class . . . in the midst of a crazy busy day, it's my happy part of Tuesday . . . where I can . . . breathe and listen and engage and not be completely stressed about the next step of my day.

Sonia: It [was] an exploration . . . you're in there and you're kind of almost getting your hands into something and molding it and playing with it and working through it and trying to figure out how it works, what it looks like, what it feels like.

Barbara: There's less . . . trying to outdo each other and come across as the brightest student in the class . . . it feels a lot more free—a free place to exchange ideas and it's a genuine exchange of ideas rather than vying to establish oneself as the top dog in the classroom.

Lisa: This beautiful . . . group of people . . . go with [the] flow and think deeper and put themselves out there and [are] available to put out ideas and flounder . . . and mess around with it and get messy . . . and nobody's afraid of doing that . . . You can put an idea out there and get muddy and it's, it's ok. It's good. It's all good.

The quotes above illustrate aspects of the *student experience* of learning in the case study course. What stands out across the student participant data, from post-class reflections to focus groups to individual interviews, was that the course was a place that was open, safe for mistakes, and comfortable. Unlike in many other courses they had taken, students felt *free to learn*.

In Chapter 1, we shared what stands out for our research team regarding a phenomenological attitude based primarily on the writings of Merleau-Ponty (1945/1962). In Chapters 3 and 4, we shared details about the professor's experience of preparing to teach and while teaching in the lifeworld of the classroom. In this chapter, we focus less on characterizing the phenomenological approach taken by the professor and more on illustrating the meaning of "free to learn" for participants in our case study course and in other studies. (Note that quotation marks around all or part of a theme name indicate the use of a student participant's actual words.)

Through phenomenological analysis (Sohn, Thomas, Greenberg, & Pollio, 2017) of data from the case study course, we interpreted a thematic structure. This structure is based in part on prior analysis (Sohn et al., 2016) but is expanded to include data from all our case study data sources (see Chapter 1 for an overview of our research participants, data sources, and analysis of data). The ground of participants' experience was other college courses. The figural themes included the following:

a. the course was *"different"*
b. the atmosphere of the course was *"free"* and *"open"*
c. they felt *"safe"* and *"comfortable"*
d. participants were *"collaborative"* and *"connected"* with other students
e. the course was *"personally"* and *"professionally relevant"* to their lives

Students felt different because the institutional role of student, with its technical features (such as the grades and assignments) and its deeper structures (such as competition and knowing the "right answer") had been removed. The atmosphere of the course, influenced heavily by the instructor's planning and facilitation, was experienced as free, open, safe, comfortable, and collaborative. What they learned was personally and professionally relevant. There was freedom to read or not, to attend class or not, to speak in class or not, to agree with the professor or not.

Themes

In the following section, we share quotes from participants with the intent to provide readers with a seat at the table in the classroom. We begin with the theme of "different" and the ground from which it stood out. We then share the other themes of the case study that focus on what it was like to be a learner in the course. As with many phenomenological studies, the themes are not exclusive of each other—quotes that illustrate one theme often illustrate another. What we present as themes are "natural lines of fracture" that together illuminate the gestalt of student experience (Thomas & Pollio, 2002).

Different From Other Courses

For the case study participants, their experience as learners in the course was different. As Sonia put it, "it was a lot different than I thought it was

96   *Free to Learn*

going be . . . I feel more a part of the experience than sitting outside of it, which unfortunately a lot of educational experiences are like that now." Students referred to the course as "unorthodox" in approach (Alexander) and having an "unstructured structure" (Lois). It was different in the level of commitment students perceived in their classmates: George noted that in most graduate courses, students just "take notes and leave," but not in the case study course, where participants described their peers as invested and engaged.

The context of a university provides a frame for the ways in which students felt free to learn: they could not strip off their clothes or set off firecrackers—it was still a classroom with conventions and unwritten sociocultural rules. But it was different enough from other courses that the vast majority of the participants made a comment suggesting it was unique. And what made the course unique was the experience of being free to learn.

Free to Learn

The freedom students experienced in the course was expressed both in terms of freedom *from* particular constraints and freedom *to* pursue the course in the ways they saw fit. Here we illustrate subthemes of participant experiences with their words.

"Free and Open"

Participants were able to co-opt course objectives for their own purposes in the diverse fields within which they studied. They described the course as having "an openness that most lack" (Brian). For example, Barbara described the course as "a free place to exchange ideas." These and other literal expressions of openness and freedom were coupled with many statements implying freedom and openness—students described the learning experience as "playing," "exploring," "messing around," and "getting dirty." Lois described her experience of the openness to ideas:

> I think that by surrounding the environment with this ability to bring out ideas—not just from the person in charge but from *all* of the people involved in the class was a huge learning experience. I didn't feel like a student. I felt like a learner . . . I was energized when I left. . . . In *this* class, [the professor] would start a conversation and give us a starting point but then the real learning came as a collaboration among all of the participants in the class.

"The person in charge," the professor, opened the classroom space for discussion and depth. Lisa remarked that in many courses, time is not taken to delve deeply into critical concepts, but in the case study course,

"We played with [concepts]. We moved them around and manipulated them . . . and used 'em and . . . shifted 'em and worked with 'em and handled them and . . . grappled." There is a sense in the data that participants took this work, this play, with good humor but also seriously. Course participants laughed together over absurd or ironic anecdotes but also listened respectfully to stories of anger or familial deaths, all with the intent to "grapple" with course content.

There were many times when students, working and grappling with the ideas, went in their own direction. As Kari Ann put it,

> We just all got caught up in telling our stories about something or we really just connected sort of emotionally with some topic and so we were talking about it and we [were] getting away from—poor Merleau-Ponty's been left behind or something and . . . no one was ever shot down or chastised for that. It was ok to take that, you know, to express those feelings on the topic or something and then come back to the theory train and where we were headed for that class.

Here Kari Ann expresses a feeling that she and her classmates *should* have stuck closer to the topic at hand. Part of feeling free, in this case, was perhaps a sense of bucking professorial authority. But in many activities, such as when practicing how to conduct phenomenological interviews, the professor wanted participants to speak about whatever they were interested in (see Chapter 4).

In the focus group interviews, which ostensibly had the goal to elicit participant stories of learning in the course, students veered into a discussion about the lamentable, divided nature of the disciplines at the university. While the discussion began in relation to course content, these participants created a dialogue in entirely their own direction, far from the intent of the focus group. While this may have frustrated a traditionally trained focus group interviewer, as phenomenologists, we took this as a genuine sign that participants felt free to seek their own directions and learning goals with the course as a base. That participants were willing to go their own direction also spoke to their experience of the course as safe and comfortable.

"Safe and Comfortable"

Like with freedom and openness, there were literal statements regarding safety and comfort, such as when James or George referred to the atmosphere of the course as safe. Course observers noted other behaviors that can be associated with safety and comfort such as laughter, smiles, and looks of concentration. The quotes we share here give a deeper portrait of what it was like to feel safe and comfortable in the case study classroom environment.

98 Free to Learn

George felt safe and comfortable from day one to the end of the course. In the first post-class reflection, he noted, "The class environment was relaxing, and I felt freedom to share in a safe place without being judged." After the course's conclusion, he added, "I feel free [pause] without any pressure to perform . . . that the grade isn't there, that just releases me to really put more into it. It's the only course I've ever had like that ever!" Several participants connected the lack of a formal grading procedure with a lack of pressure to perform. But the comfort to share deeply personal stories, such as those of birthing children, dealing with familial deaths, or managing insomnia could not be solely attributable to the instructor's assurance that all students would receive an A.

The sharing of such stories was attributed by some students to the "intimate" nature of the questions of existential phenomenology. Sonia, who in an interview activity and in whole-group discussion shared her experiences with insomnia, remarked, "it's a joy, it's an enjoyable thing that you finally get a chance to speak about something that has been there for so long and it gives it some type of validation, appreciation, and no judgment."

For Sonia, the lack of judgment and intimacy made for a joyous opportunity to share. For others it meant that coming to class was "a relief" (Brian, see above), "relaxing" (Thomas), and the "happy part" of the day (Kari Ann, see above). There was one participant that expressed *dis*comfort because of some of the sharing—Alexander remarked that when hearing the experience of a classmate's father's death, he felt like a voyeur. Yet he attributed the lack of judgment and "unorthodox" course structure with a *genuineness* among participants and a willingness to delve deeply into and understand what would for many students be intimidating philosophical content.

The philosophical content of the course focused on existence, disrupting normal patterns of perception, and valuing the first-person perspective. Seven of the student participants described moments of the course or the course generally as therapeutic—an extension of comfort and safety. In the following quote from Phil, we share his account of a moment during a class session focused on the ten-year anniversary of the September 11, 2001, terrorist attacks in the United States.

> There was definitely a *healing* aspect to how we . . . collectively held the tenth anniversary [of the 9–11 attacks]. One of the ways in which I benefited a lot from that [was] just being able to tolerate my own ambivalence around 9–11. I've thought . . . a lot about it, and how America reacted to it. I always felt that I understood the two sides of it. I think that we were perhaps justified in our, our *wrath* over what happened. At the same time, putting myself perhaps in the position of . . . someone else, in another part of the world, I can understand where perhaps intense hatred against America led to what it led to . . . Being

able to consciously bring [the two perspectives] together and kind of let them coexist at the same moment . . . was therapeutic.

Those that discussed the course or moments of it as therapeutic achieved some individual sense of greater wholeness or peace regarding a troubling situation. Yet these comments were always in the context of the group setting. Participants reflected frequently on the connections they made with their classmates and their contributions to building understanding of themselves and course content.

"Collaborative and Connected"

The theme of collaborative and connected represents the experiences students had of working together to develop their understanding and working towards changes in being—such as becoming better listeners. We detail the student experience of other students (SEOS) more extensively in the next chapter, but as an essential element of the student experience of the course, here we share general reflections and descriptions of feelings of collaboration and connection.

Students in the course described connecting with each other beginning in the first class session. They said they missed others when they were absent. They asked each other questions from week to week and took them as signs of care. Along with their social connections, as one participant-observer put it, students were united in their pursuit of "the art of being better." This common existential project will be discussed further in the next chapter. There was one contradiction in the data—Thomas, after one of the final class sessions, contrasted himself with other students noting that he did not take "much of a relational stance" to the course. However, Thomas appeared to grow close with two classmates. Other students, like George, were "surprised" at how close they became with their peers.

Three participants connected the lack of grades with a lack of competition. But simply removing grades cannot so easily remove the tendency of students to hide their confusion or demonstrate *just* how well they understand (while others do not). Students felt connected and exhibited a willingness to share what they understood, however incomplete it might have been. We remind the reader here that, as we described in Chapter 4, the instructor never chastised or shot down student ideas. Sonia echoed Barbara's quote from the beginning of this chapter:

This class gives you an opportunity almost to kind of express yourself without feeling like you're competing for things . . . I'm not fighting for a grade or trying to prove that I know more than you do or any of that. I'm just trying to understand it better. You know and by talking it out loud, that helps, especially getting through some of the [laughing] *readings and things*.

100 *Free to Learn*

Sonia, with good humor, indicates the difficulty of the material and the need for help from others to understand it. She was not alone in this sentiment. Only one student had a formal background in philosophy and many of the course texts referred frequently to well-known philosophers such as Descartes, Kant, Husserl, Heidegger, Sartre, and others. Yet the collaborative nature of their learning and the perspectives provided by others were often mentioned as part of reflections in which students described ways course content was relevant and applicable to their lives.

"Relevant and Applicable"

Across all our sources of data, the relevance and applicability of the course was documented by participants and observed by researchers. Post-class reflections included ways the participants could use or had used course content in professional and personal contexts. George sorted through the death of his father in relation to class discussions on time. Sonia managed new insight and progress with her insomnia after class sessions regarding human experience of the body. Thomas, a clinical psychologist, applied a course topic, the centrality of first-person perception, to his work with clients. Lois and Brian, educators, borrowed from the instructor's teaching methods. Participants saw the relevance of the course content—as Thomas said, "It's such a broad approach to understanding people" (see Chapter 7).

The instructor often asked students questions that blended course content with who they were and what they did for work, but he never explicitly asked anyone what they might *do* with their newfound knowledge. As we have discussed, the instructor did not ask students to do much. As James put it, "there are no assignments—JUST READ & LEARN!" (original emphasis). But they did much more than "just" read and learn, in a traditional sense. They did "acquire knowledge"—many students commented with surprise at how much easier it was to understand the preface of *The Phenomenology of Perception* (Merleau-Ponty, 1945/1962) on the final day of the course as compared to when they first read it at the beginning. But more interestingly for us (and many of the participants, as well), students spontaneously transcended the classroom environment; they integrated course content through imagination and direct action into their lives. They developed or honed a phenomenological attitude. We devote Chapter 7 to a thorough examination of the learning reported by case study course participants.

Theme Summary

The major themes of the course as described above can be written in narrative form using primarily the language of participants. Readers should understand it as a synthesis of all the student participants and how they would describe the experience of being a learner in the case study course:

> I experienced this class as *different* from the way in which I have experienced other classes. In this course, I found that what I learned was *relevant* to me *personally* and *professionally*. I experienced the classroom atmosphere to be *comfortable, freeing, open* and *safe*. I also developed a new set of connections with what I was learning and with my peers. These connections left me *free to learn* with them in a different and collaborative, rather than competitive, mode. During class time there was a great deal of laughter and excitement that seemed related to the sense of freedom and discovery we shared.
>
> (Sohn et al., 2016, p. 191)

Free to Learn

It was the voices of these students that sparked our dive into a phenomenological approach to teaching and learning. Amid educational trends such as mobile phone clickers and "active learning" strategies and higher education horror stories of forced participation and abusive teachers, in our data we saw an uncommon combination of powerful learning, active engagement, and openness that is rare in any educational setting. In this section we sketch out the connections between the phenomenological approach of the professor and his students' experience of being free to learn. There is no one-to-one correspondence between the gestalt experience of learning of the students and the aspects of the phenomenological approach: we leave cause and effect to the instrumentalists. But here we discuss the most direct links between the student experience of learning and four concepts inspired by Merleau-Ponty's (1945/1962) perspective on phenomenology that influence perception and intentionality: ambiguity, intersubjectivity, sociocultural embeddedness, and embodiment. Then we bridge these connections to other literature including our other phenomenological studies. Along the way, we consider what students were free from and what they were free to do (see Table 5.1).

Implications of "Different" (From Other Courses)

It is the gestalt of all the themes that helps in understanding why participants described the course as different. But the aspect of the phenomenological approach we highlight with the theme "different" is ambiguity. The professor infused ambiguity throughout his facilitation as Chapters 3 and 4 illustrate, through his phenomenological attitude.

Rather than ambiguity, the desire for certainty and explanation pervades most academic endeavors. A part-time appreciation of ambiguity no

102 *Free to Learn*

Table 5.1 Themes and Concepts of Phenomenology in Relation to the Student Experience of Learning

Theme	Aspect	Freedom from/to
Different	Ambiguity	From institutional constraints/to open up . . .
Free and Open	Ambiguity	From assignments and judgment/to explore, but exploration requires a foundation . . .
Safe and Comfortable	Embodiment, Intersubjectivity	From judgment, grades/to explore, be wrong, learn from each other . . .
Collaborative and Connected	Embodiment, Intersubjectivity	From competition/to collaborate across disciplines . . .
Relevant and Applicable	Sociocultural Embeddedness	From specific objectives/to co-opt content

doubt exists in the arts and humanities, but even in these fields, *teaching* still emphasizes theory, explanation, and certainty. Many theories of education call for cognitive dissonance, disruptions, or discomfort. Scholars frequently cite Meno's description of being "stung" by Socrates' questions (e.g., Mayo, 2010) as evidence of the efficacy of knocking learners out of their comfort zones. But there is a difference between planning specific disruptions and accepting the fundamental nature of ambiguity in perception.

For example, in Langan, Sheese, and Davidson (2009) and Macdonald (2013), the intent of disruptions such as bringing a sex worker in as guest speaker in a sociology class (Langan et al., 2009) or confronting a student visiting South Africa from the United States with an accusation of savior complex (Macdonald, 2013) was to shock and discomfort students in order to instill in them an understanding of critical theories of race, class, and gender. Such theories are contested and evolving, yet they are presented as enlightened, whole, and certain. We find our case study illustrates the need for a phenomenological attitude that authentically opens to ambiguity.

And such theories and explanations push subtle and ever-present ambiguity aside. As Merleau-Ponty (1945/1962) says, "I am not the outcome or the meeting-point of numerous causal agencies which determine my bodily or psychological make-up" (p. ix). With post-structural theories, human experiences in their particularities are replaced by worldviews that exist high above the daily lives of students. With a phenomenological approach, it is the particularity of subjective lived descriptions that allows ambiguity to help illustrate the meaning of course content for students, and this is radically different from what is typical.

Ambiguity is hindered by institutional norms. Universities create tracks, programs, majors, certificates, and badges: a clear path to follow. The sequence of courses, requirements, and hour counting can be taken up by students with a kind of checklist mentality (Johansson & Felten, 2014). Checking boxes in a linear progression canalizes what could be learning experiences that meander or pool. Attempting to reduce ambiguity ignores the potential provided by tangents that turn into epiphanies. Programs in their rigidity can push the student to fulfill a role in which they sacrifice freedom for the certitude of doing what is expected.

Yet when students are reminded to stay alert to the constraints and supports that pervade their academic world and to the varieties of descriptions or interpretations of peers, they are freer to be authentic. It was novel (or disrupting) to experience a teacher who practiced authentically, who enacted his values, who freed students to examine carefully their role, face ambiguity, and make choices they usually did not. With typical course features such as papers and exams missing, it was up to them to choose how to spend their time and what to learn.

Ambiguity was highlighted through frequent experiential accounts from students and the professor, and in findings from prior phenomenological studies. *It is not normal in an academic setting* to hear first-person perspectives of the existential grounds of time, body, others, and world. They are inevitably particular, inevitably ambiguous. Hearing stories of when those grounds disrupt projects brings them from background to figure: time can oppress us, or we can lose track of it; our bodies fail or perform beautifully; other people are barriers, helpers, or lovers; our context rears up, the world falls apart or transforms. It is freeing and powerful for learning to integrate the very basis for our lived experience into course content. Certitude is a closed system. An embrace of ambiguity necessarily calls for openness.

Implications of "Free and Open"

Ambiguity allows for multiple perspectives and exploration. The professor's guidance through a series of visual exercises during the first two class sessions of the course led students away from explanation and towards description. He encouraged a kind of playing with perception to free it from the tyranny of corrals. The sediments of experience pile up in layers, they calcify. Just as an institution can be a supporting structure for personal progress and a limiting and oppressive structure, the layered, calcified set of individual experiences supports and limits as well.

The limits of experience come into play with *categorization*. With that kind of analysis, perception is robbed of its potential. It is confined to Piaget's (2003) assimilation or accommodation. Piaget's (2003) schemas, already in existence or ready to be created, rob experience of its existential power and create an illusion of separation between the seen and the seer. In a classroom, the drawbacks of quick categorization can be seen today in the superficially savvy students who, having read a headline on social media related to a course topic, "already know it."

104   *Free to Learn*

A phenomenological approach *delays* the quick rush to categorize. It calls for a suspension, a setting aside, an acknowledgment of what is known. Through the intensive use of description, students can be freed from what they know to see with new eyes.

But to see with new eyes and express it while surrounded by a master teacher and classmates requires either a special kind of courage or a general sense of freedom from judgment. This is one of the principal features of a "safe" classroom (Holley & Steiner, 2005) mentioned explicitly by our case study course participants and discussed further in the next chapter. Without the weight of potential embarrassment that comes in a social situation, sociocultural norms such as "being cool" can be left behind to explore, play, and be present with and in the course.

The freedom from judgment, coupled with the course emphasis on description, opened up students to the ambiguity of everyday life. When examining their lives through the phenomenological lens, students found new universal meaning in simple actions like driving a car or looking at pictures. One may argue that the content of existential phenomenology was particularly suited to this kind of discovery of new worlds within the known world: Taylor (2009) has argued that existential course content sets students up for transformative learning. But we believe that a phenomenological approach with any subject area could do the same (see Chapter 8 for examples).

But a foundationless freedom is terrifying; there must be a place from which to venture out. Ambiguity of one sort can be more easily tolerated when other elements of a classroom experience are certain, and participants in our case study course balanced their exploration and doubt of what is and can be known with a sense of safety and comfort that derived principally from the collaborative and connected nature of the course.

Implications of "Safe and Comfortable, Collaborative and Connected"

In our case study course, genuineness and authenticity was possible *as a group*. That participants shared in the rediscovery of ambiguity and uncertainty was one of the ways in which they built intersubjectivity. Play was an important element in the creation of the course atmosphere, and students attributed their embodied sense of safety and comfort with one another to activities in which perception was challenged. For Greene (1988), an intersubjectivity rich with relatedness, communication, and disclosure is the context in which freedom can be felt in an embodied sense (p. 121). She envisions classrooms where students come together to create freedom and "possibilize different futures":

> The aim is to find (or create) an authentic public space, that is, one in which diverse human beings can appear before one another as, to

Free to Learn   105

quote Hannah Arendt, "the best they know how to be." Such a space requires the provision of opportunities for the articulation of multiple perspectives in multiple idioms, out of which something common can be brought into being. . . . In contexts of this kind, open contexts where persons attend to another with interest, regard, and care, there is a place for the appearance of freedom, the achievement of freedom by people in search of themselves.

(Greene, 1988, p. xi)

The case study course participants envisioned new practices, new ways of being, and a new university, one in which the traditional academic silos were torn down in favor of interdisciplinary projects where quantitative and qualitative research would work to advance knowledge and understanding of the world. Students in our case study course collaborated towards those ends with care and regard for one another. They felt safe and comfortable despite the sometimes quite intimate explorations of self and existence.

When students are freed from various kinds of competition—who can look the smartest, who can perform the best on exams and make an A, who can be the most favored student of the teacher—they can feel freer to collaborate. Bodily feelings of comfort and safety with each other can increase a sense of intersubjectivity. We discuss this intersubjectivity and its implications to a fuller extent in the next chapter, where we focus on the student experience of other students.

The sources of competition for students come primarily from two sources: performance in relation to their peers on a regular basis and performance in a course overall, which is most commonly represented by a grade. Grades are multi-dimensional measures (Brookhart et al., 2016): they are often fuzzy in that they mix demonstrated performances and non-cognitive factors such as effort. While many professors believe they do not suffer from the same lack of reliability found in K–12 environments, Brookhart et al.'s (2016) literature review found otherwise. This lack of reliability creates an uncertainty among many students and can cause their focus to move away from learning course material and toward performing well on assessments (Pollio & Beck, 2000). Clarification of how grades are tallied removes some of the typically felt uncertainty and so helps students work together. For our case study professor, his goal of giving every student a grade of "A"—a move he made after extensive study into college grading (see Milton, Pollio, & Eison, 1986)—was to help students "stop worrying about the rent" (see Chapter 8 for Kathy's course description and student reaction when told that no grades would be given by the teacher).

As collaborators, students overcome many of the hurdles commonly associated with group work such as accountability. As we discuss in the next chapter, the freedom from competition in part opened up the ability

106 *Free to Learn*

of students to hear each other and find deeper meaning in course content through the multiplication of their own perspective through the perspectives of others (Garrison, 2010).

Implications of "Relevant and Applicable"

Students in the case study course felt free to apply the learning from the course that they found relevant. Part of Merleau-Ponty's (1945/1962) understanding of freedom hinged on the situated, historical nature of the individual in a society. Rather than seeing situations simply as obstacles to freedom, he described them as the background through which freedom could be understood:

> The world is already constituted, but also never completely constituted; in the first case we are acted upon, in the second we are open to an infinite number of possibilities. But this analysis is still abstract, for we exist in both ways at once. There is, therefore, never determinism and never absolute choice, I am never a thing and never bare consciousness. In fact, even our own pieces of initiative, even the situations which we have chosen, bear us on, once they have been entered upon by virtue of a state rather than an act. The generality of the "role" and of the situation comes to the aid of decision, and in this exchange between the situation and the person who takes it up, it is impossible to determine precisely the "share contributed by the situation" and the "share contributed by freedom."
>
> (Merleau-Ponty, 1945/1962, p. 453)

In other words, freedom isn't free. Embedded in worlds and cultures, individual situations bear on people, in life and in the classroom. Our situations precede us; as Garrison (2010) says, "Culture has you before you have it" (p. 39). Our participants were in a classroom situation as graduate students: their freedom was relative within the world of education—*their* world of education.

Each student came to the course with an embodied history and layers of sociocultural embeddedness. The nurse, the teacher, the counselor, and the sports psychologist all brought their own biases and the assumptions from their fields. These fields were also embedded in a larger sociocultural context of Western academia. But they were not forced to reproduce particular conceptual knowledge through assignments, learning objectives were not overly specific, and students developed an understanding of the course content as it related to and *enhanced* their academic field.

The case study students, with one exception, were adults with careers. One could argue that course relevance is easy to find when you have a job, particularly when content included such broad topics as "playing a role." But a phenomenological approach is not limited in usefulness by the age of the student (see Box 5.1).

Box 5.1   Reflection, *Brian Sohn*

With course content related to "motivation" in my teacher education courses, I prompt students with the following: "Think of a time in school in which you were motivated or unmotivated." I model phenomenological interviewing with a volunteer student. I proceed with few questions and try to have them focus on description rather than explanation. I then ask students to pair up and interview each other. Students proceed from these interviews to compare and contrast what they heard and felt in three interviews: the model interview, their own, and those of their partners. Sharing similarities and differences can assist in *contextualizing* the stories in the broader context of experiences of schooling. The varying student identities tend to multiply perspectives: what is figural for one may be unacknowledged by another, depending on different histories, cultures, and bodies. These descriptions give students lived, contextualized examples of motivation. Since many theories of motivation were developed in laboratory settings or settings outside of schools, through stories we make these theories real. For some students, this helps them bind their formal and informal knowledge more rigorously to further a personal theory of motivation they can use as future teachers.

The relevance of the case study course to students' personal lives may have its most dramatic manifestation in the description of the course as therapeutic. Their embodied knowledge and ways of knowing were flipped upside down by the phenomenological emphasis on description. Yet like with their academic embeddedness, the bodies, cultures, and experiences of students in their personal lives were brought to bear on the course content and shared in a forum ripe for the development of insight. Examples from our other research shows that students can develop insight into themselves, the wider world, and their role within it whether or not topics such as being and existence appear explicitly on the syllabus (see Chapter 8).

A phenomenological pedagogy explicitly values first-person perspectives and therefore aids in the development of relevance and applicability. The ways in which students are embedded provide them a perspective through which to explore, reach out, and feel free. With open-ended, experience-focused questions, students can narrate their way to an unexpected understanding of how a particular concept exists meaningfully in their lives. The professor's objectives were broad enough that, rather than being impeded by individual worldviews and goals, they were enhanced. The sociocultural perspectives and practices of the students provided structures with which they could build and transform their ways of knowing and being in response to the course content.

Conclusion

With a phenomenological approach, there are enough constraints to hold people together: the institution, the syllabus, the classmates. But there is also sufficient freedom to learn transformatively. But to put a phenomenological approach into practice there must be trust.

Carl Rogers (1969) in his book *Freedom to Learn* writes specifically on the importance of trust for freedom in the classroom. He describes three attitudes a teacher must have in order to facilitate learning: "realness," "prizing, acceptance, and trust," and "empathic understanding" (pp. 106–112), which he details with the idea of understanding where students are coming from. He goes on to emphasize trust, a quality that runs as a thread through the themes presented above:

> It would be most unlikely that one could hold the three attitudes I have described, or could commit himself to being a facilitator of learning, unless he has come to have a profound trust in the human organism and its potentialities. If I distrust the human being then I *must* cram him with information of my own choosing, lest he go his own mistaken way. But if I trust the capacity of the human individual for developing his own potentiality, then I can provide him with many opportunities and permit him to choose his own way and his own direction in his learning.
>
> (Rogers, 1969, p. 114)

Trust can be a foundation for developing a phenomenological approach. It requires a phenomenological attitude, one that seeps into the lives of students as well as teacher. And in the next chapter, we examine in greater detail the manifestation of trust and other qualities in the case study student experiences of other students.

6 Student Experiences of Other Students

"All Together in This Space"

> One of the things I got . . . from the class the most, is I never expected the connection . . . I think we're so used to going in and taking notes and then leaving . . . [~1 minute later] I was just drawn, drawn to these intelligent people, some just sharp people. Probably much sharper than I am . . . and that was ok and yet I felt free to share and I didn't feel judged, but I felt connected in there. . . . There was like a couple people like, Oh if I need to understand (said while laughing) Merleau-Ponty. I'd call on Blake or somebody.
>
> (George)

In the excerpt above, taken from an individual interview conducted at the end of the case study course, George's emotional connection to his classmates and feelings of freedom to share without judgment are representative of the 20 other student participants. In their words, they were "all together in [one] space," saw each other as "genuinely invested," and "completely caught up" in class discussions and activities. As the course progressed, they "came to appreciate" their diversity. Through their appreciation, they were able to take advantage of differences for the sake of learning and growth, rather than be divided by them.

In Chapter 5 we examined the experience of being a learner in the case study course. In this chapter we focus in on the student experience of other students (SEOS) and contrast it with the predominantly alienating experiences that, unfortunately, are common in higher education, particularly for students of color and nontraditional students (e.g., Smith, 2016; Thomas et al., 2007). We begin by discussing research regarding facilitation for student interaction.

Student Interaction

Student interaction in the world of higher education research often falls under the larger umbrella of learning environment studies or group work. The topics of such studies include participation, "safety" and "risk," and

110 *Student Experiences of Other Students*

collaborative or cooperative learning. Many studies over the years have shown that only a small percentage of students tend to actively participate in class (Karp & Yoels, 1976; Fritschner, 2000; Allan & Madden, 2006). In 1982, the landmark Hall and Sandler (1982) "chilly climate" study revealed that women spoke less than men and identified some of the factors, such as microaggressions, that may contribute to what Karp and Yoels (1976) called the "consolidation of responsibility." Hall and Sandler's (1982) study led to other studies of more granular factors in participation and the ways in which safety and participation were connected for women and other traditionally under-represented groups of college students.

A concern for classroom safety, which seems to have reached a critical mass in the 1990s (Boostrom, 1998), sparked some pushback against the idea of making classrooms "safe": ideas from Plato to Piaget show the need for discomfort, not safety, if significant learning is to occur. But many studies have shown the attempts at safety tend to fail for under-represented student populations (e.g., Booker, 2007). Our studies (Davis et al., 2004; Smith, 2016; Thomas et al., 2007) confirm the elusiveness of a kind of sense of belonging, or safety *for* academic risk-taking seen as ideal for finding the balance between the comfort of the familiar and the challenge of new learning (see Chapter 8 for a discussion of these studies).

In higher education, peer-reviewed studies on safe classroom climate rarely answer what, according to students, are its attributes, and they often ignore the existential experience of students. Holley and Steiner (2005) surveyed graduate and undergraduate students in order to develop an emic perspective on safe classrooms, unsafe classrooms, and how they relate to learning. Teachers were "unbiased and nonjudgmental" in safe classrooms (p. 56), and "critical and 'shot down' student ideas" in unsafe classrooms (p. 58). Other students were "respectful, . . . honestly shared thoughts, . . . nonjudgmental, . . . and friendly or supportive" in safe classrooms (p. 56) and "did not speak" or were "afraid to speak" in unsafe classrooms (p. 58). In safe classrooms, students learned from "others' ideas, perspectives, and thoughts" or "others' experiences" (p. 55). Students reported that they learned more and felt challenged in classrooms that were safe (p. 56).

Participants in Holley and Steiner's (2005) study placed the responsibility for classroom safety on the professor, but in an interesting survey study that sought to disentangle student interaction from teacher-student interaction, Sidelinger and Booth-Butterfield (2010) found that student connection had greater influence on student preparation and participation than "confirming" teacher behaviors, which included practices such as using student names and providing positive feedback. They concluded that "using a participatory teaching style in a classroom lowers the potentially adversarial nature of teacher-student interaction, fosters a sense of linkage among students, and can generate a comfortable, supportive communication environment" (p. 178). Rather than encourage student

Student Experiences of Other Students 111

interaction, professors often simply use group work activities without attending to the difficulties of its implementation.

The benefits of cooperative and collaborative learning are well documented. Although much of the research on group work comes from the K-12 arena (e.g., Johnson, Johnson, & Smith, 1998), some scholars have extended this work to higher education. In Weimer's (2013) meta-review of reviews of literature on specific forms of group work in higher education, she found support for problem-based learning approaches that can lead to greater retention of knowledge and improved problem-solving abilities. With one particular approach, Process-Oriented Guided Inquiry, peer learning is specifically implied: "students sa[id] that working through materials with other students help[ed] them understand the content better" (p. 45). But most of the study results she mentions do not focus on learning, rather their proxies like grades, and they tell us little about how learners may or may not appropriate course content such that it affects their lives beyond the classroom. Group work approaches, particularly the cooperative learning espoused by Johnson and Johnson (n.d.), are highly controlled by the teacher, offering little freedom for students.

This may be why so many students still complain about group work—they can't find a time to meet, one did all the work and the others coasted, a partner didn't let one student do anything. Rather than designing an efficacious group structure, many teachers instead reduce the role of group learning. Even in whole-class discussions students can find their peers irritating. Studies show frustration with peers who dominate class discussions, speak off topic, or stand out for achievement (Attenborough & Stokoe, 2012; Fritschner, 2000; Galanes & Carmack, 2013). But many of these concerns seem petty in relation to the general experience of students of color and traditionally underachieving students (see details in Chapter 8).

In some circumstances, participants in our studies of black, international, and underachieving students share positive experiences about their connections with other students. With these stories we can begin to walk a path towards the kind of powerful whole-class intersubjectivity we saw in our case study course.

The Power of Connection

In the case study course, George and his classmates experienced a kind of safety, a connection, a "solidarity" that was rare in their time in higher education. Their experience of other students helped create a classroom climate that they said contributed strongly to their growth and transformative learning. When we asked students after each class session to share what stood out to them, we were surprised that the charismatic professor was mentioned only rarely (excluding the first and final class sessions). They spoke much more often of their experiences of each other. In the next section we share results from Sohn's (2016) dissertation study on the SEOS of students in the case study course. We believe that a phenomenological approach to teaching and learning can help students have similarly positive experiences of each other in other contexts and avoid having a classroom in which students "go in, take notes, and leave."

Methodology and Results

The procedures for forming Sohn's (2016) research question, bracketing, analyzing data, and writing the report were similar to those described in Sohn, Thomas, Greenberg, and Pollio (2017). The difference for Sohn's (2016) study was the specific focus on SEOS. Sohn (2016) re-read the data from the second year of the case study, looking for statements by participants that referred to another student or students. At times, for example, participants mentioned another student by name. At other times they would refer to a "discussion." In this case Sohn (2016) listened to class audio recordings to see if another student was involved. With these delimitations, analysis proceeded (as in Sohn et al., 2017) and resulted in the following thematic structure, shown in Figure 6.1, and discussion. (Note that quotation marks around all or part of a theme name indicate the use of a student participant's actual words.)

The ground, or context, of the themes was *"all together in this space,"* which represents the importance students placed on each other for support and connection. From the ground, three panels that represent the figural themes rise to meet at a peak. The triangular panels rest on the ground, indicating the necessity of all the pieces to make the whole figure.

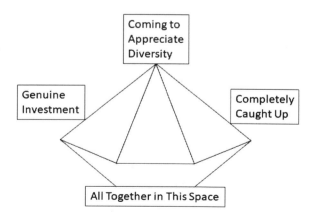

Figure 6.1 The Thematic Structure of the Student Experience of Other Students.

There is *"genuine investment,"* a theme that represents the efforts of other students. In their words, participants noted other students' willingness to "mess about" or "explore" the content and the ways in which they took "responsibility" for each other and for learning. Participants also described themselves as *"completely caught up."* This theme describes the experience of being swept up emotionally in each other and the content of the course, for example in the activities they did together or their peers' stories. The third major theme, *"coming to appreciate diversity,"* represents a progression of learning through each other (Sohn, n.d.). From the beginning of the course, participants noted the "**diversity**" of other students. They then related differences in student origin or field of study to differences in perception—participants began *"seeing variations."* Students reflected on and applied course content, *realizing* it in their lives. Finally, participants described *changes in being*, which involved becoming better listeners, for example. Details on what "variations" were seen and what changed in student ways of being are shared in Chapter 7. Below we discuss findings regarding the SEOS and illustrate them with data from our case study.

Ground: "All Together in This Space"

In the SEOS, the ground was "All together in this space." Participants expressed a general feeling of being together in a collegial atmosphere in which they worked collaboratively to develop new understandings. As Kari Ann said in her individual interview, there were many times when "we really just connected sort of emotionally with some topic. . . . We're all working together to try and understand these things." Donna remarked after the final class:

> I have greatly enjoyed the experience of this class & I almost feel emotional about our time together coming to an end. As we reflected on what we have learned, I feel fulfilled & satisfied. I hope to have similar experiences in future classes but I know that this experience can never be re-created; we will never all be together in this space.
> (post-class reflection, Class 15)

Other participants wrote statements such as, "we're all friends here" (Brian, Class 5) or used "we" extensively in their reflections or interviews. They talked of feelings of validation, safety, or comfort with and through their classmates.

Participants noted that others in the course revealed vulnerability and attributed the personal disclosures to the safety of the group. Participants were together, present in a classroom, and as part of this presentness, participants noticed the "genuine investments" their classmates made in the course.

114 *Student Experiences of Other Students*

"Genuine Investment"

With the participants' experience of togetherness in the background, they experienced each other's particular contributions as figural. Rather than seeing their classmates as going through the motions, participants considered the students around them to be genuine. Some participants remarked that the non-competitive atmosphere of the course, created in part by the professor's assurance that everyone would receive an A, allowed them to act as *learners* pursuing understanding together as opposed to *students* "fighting for a grade" (Sonia, individual interview).

Participants described personal and academic contributions in this theme. After the third class session, Whitney noted the following in regard to a discussion: "Students really . . . tried to actively engage in different tasks like challenging perception. This ultimately challenges the beliefs of truths. The engagement of students was truly phenomenal" (post-class reflection). In Whitney's case, engagement is related to taking on difficult tasks, spurred by a sense of responsibility to learning.

During a group activity that carried over from the fourth to the fifth class session, Donna "fel[t] like [she] let [her] group down by not bringing . . . notes" (post-class reflection, Class 5) from the previous class session, indicating her sense of responsibility to her peers. Jackie showed responsibility when taking on certain roles in class activities, in her case as an interviewer:

> During the interview activity my role was to be the interviewer. I found myself wanting to engage in regular conversation but could not [because] I didn't want to ask leading questions. I felt a sense of responsibility as the interviewer to keep the engagement going until completion and while the participant was speaking, I was constantly trying to think of my next question.

The interview activities were often mentioned in SEOS data. Sonia wrote, "During the interviews, I felt an intimacy caused by the type of questions asked—the subject matter—real experience/perception [because] we aren't always asked these questions" (post-class reflection, Class 7). She shared this observation aloud the tenth class session:

> [In phenomenology] you are asking people questions that nobody asks . . . you have to reflect on thoughts in a way you normally never do, so suddenly, [the professor is] asking me things and I'm making connections going, "Wow, why hadn't I thought of that before?" . . . because I had never taken the time to think about it.

Sonia noted that certain explorations of the self do not usually happen, despite dealing for many years with, in her case, insomnia. She said that people do not make such connections on their own, "But with people

Student Experiences of Other Students 115

asking me the questions, it was suddenly like, 'Oh yeah! Okay.'" Through the other students she explored and got "a deeper understanding" into her insomnia and the interview activity "led [her] into areas that [she] would *never* had gone before this [interview]" (focus group 1). In Sonia's quote she highlights the connection between investment in the form of taking time, asking intimate questions, and the ground: without the intimacy of the group, students may not have disclosed such "deep stuff" (Phil).

There were few times when participants remarked on other students *not* being invested. After the 14th class session, in regard to a discussion of assigned readings by William James, both Phil and George suspected that others had not done the reading or had not given it sufficient effort. An expectation had been established regarding student involvement, and it stood out to Phil and George when that expectation was not met. But by and large participants experienced each other as genuinely invested, and this contributed to another facet of the SEOS, "completely caught up."

"Completely Caught Up"

Students were wrapped up in what they heard and saw during class sessions. They were engaged emotionally, as expressed by Kari Ann after a class session in which classmates shared flashbulb memories from September 11, 2001:

> I was so moved, nearly to tears, as people began sharing their experiences. I felt completely caught up in Lois' story of watching it all unfold with her boys. I was on edge as if I didn't know what was going to happen next, and reflecting on what it would have been like to go through that with my child. I say "completely caught up" but I was also aware of the woman who lost her brother on 9/11, wondering what she was making of all of our secondary experiences of her more personal tragedy.
>
> (post-class reflection, Class 11)

Ingrid had a similar experience that class session, if less specific: "Many of the experiences people shared today brought tears to my eyes. I'm not sure why my reaction was so emotional" (post-class reflection, Class 11).

Along with emotional engagement in each other's stories, some participants noticed when classmates were "completely caught up" in an activity. "The big awareness today was the silence during our experiment with grouping items. I don't think we have had so much silence ever before in the class. I looked up and around and everyone was diligently categorizing" (Brian, post-class reflection, Class 8). What was expected by the eighth class for Brian was students being vocal, and here another way to be "caught up" is in silence. Barbara often made

116   *Student Experiences of Other Students*

similar observations of the class as a whole, as in the following quote from after class session 5:

> As George and Brian read the interview like a play, the students reacted like a Greek chorus—making sure the audience understood what was being said, drawing attention to bits and pieces that stand out or are related to each other. Class members became more animated during the process and very interactive. People smiled at each other frequently and nodded.
>
> (Barbara, post-class reflection, Class 5)

Here Barbara described the ways in which other students were "completely caught up" in the reading of an interview transcript about a time the participant traveled. In this quote the ground "all together in this space" can be seen in the nonverbal cues described by Barbara.

Being "completely caught up" often resulted in a "spilling out" of course content into domains beyond the case study course. There were times in which participants could not contain their learning or involvement in the conventionally allotted time and space. As Alexander said, "My learning experience won't stop when the class stops" (individual interview).

The spilling over could be content-driven or social, as described by Kari Ann:

> I was really struck by how much more friendly chatter went on after our focus group. . . . I had been crocheting during the focus group, and everyone seemed interested to know what I was making that led to an extended conversation regarding crafting, store locations, family relationships, etc. that I hadn't expected.
>
> (post-class reflection, Class 13)

The "spilling out" was often attributed to what other students had said in a class discussion. These instances lead to the final theme, "coming to appreciate diversity," which describes the ways in which participants learned from each other over the length of the course.

"Coming to Appreciate Diversity"

"Coming to appreciate diversity" is a theme that shows a progression in student experience of other students as time went on and captures a mode of learning through the SEOS (see Sohn, n.d.). During a focus group, Barbara talked about how she had been "coming to appreciate diversity." After describing her learning in the course as "growing" as a result of people "bringing their own background" or "experience," she remarked on the class's diversity:

> Not only in terms of our different disciplines and academic backgrounds, but . . . we have a wide variety . . . of ages, all sorts of

different, I don't know, it seems as if we have a pretty diverse range of . . . personal philosophical standpoints and religious standpoints and so forth and I have really *come to appreciate* [emphasis added] it because in all of the other classes I'm taking, everybody's a clinical psychology student, so it's like everybody kind of comes to the class with very similar perspectives on things.

The subthemes are divided by level of depth on a spectrum from superficial to profound. The subthemes are *"diversity," "seeing variations,"* and *"changes in being."*

"Diversity"

Diversity was salient to the majority of the participants after the first class session, in which everyone introduced themselves. George was most exhaustive in sharing what diversity meant to him: "I was appreciative of the diversity (age, gender, religion, experience, education) that our class has and what I can learn about others (and share about myself)" (post-class reflection, Class 1). An element of comparison or categorization was evident in many statements in this subtheme. After the first class session, for example, Thomas and Brian noted student religious differences and Phil observed that no student was studying the natural sciences. These statements, around two thirds of which appeared in the first third of the course, were all relatively superficial in comparison to those garnered in subsequent post-class reflections and statements in the focus groups and individual interviews.

After the fourth class session, Phil connected the diversity of perspectives and the perceivers: "In our group, different members had very different interpretations of certain passages. . . . Seemed related to individual interests and backgrounds" (post-class reflection). What began as diversity based on categories like age transitioned to diversity of perspectives based on the experiences and backgrounds of other participants. "Seeing variations" was the next step in the progression of "coming to appreciate diversity."

"Seeing Variations"

A variation in the phenomenological sense is a kind of example. After the seventh class session, Barbara made a statement evincing a deeper engagement with the differences and similarities of "diversity":

I liked hearing so many interpretations of the poem. I had a sense of trying each one on (like a hat) to see if I can relate this particular view point to my own experiences. I especially like it that I can accept a completely opposite point of view as being true. I have experienced both points of view. So, I see no conflict. And a-ha! I am seeing "variations"!

(post-class reflection)

118   *Student Experiences of Other Students*

Lisa remarked on the same activity that she could see the different interpretations of the poem in a similar way to how the Rubin figure (the vases and faces illusion) pops back and forth between what is figure and what is ground. The quotation marks around variations likely refer to a course reading, Ihde's (1986) description of Husserl's imaginative variation, in which variations, or perspectives, are equalized in order to find the essence of the phenomenon. Her a-ha moment is an expression of progress towards seeing phenomenologically.

The vast majority (18 out of 21) of participants "saw variations." Many participants in each focus group mentioned this theme. Donna not only "saw variations," but the knowledge she gained helped motivate her to engage more deeply with the next week's readings: "others sharing their experiences . . . shapes my understanding in a new way . . . and gives me things to digest and think about and it compels me to be more interested in the readings next week" (focus group 1).

For James, too, "seeing variations" was critical to "digesting" the difficult course texts. Reading Merleau-Ponty was frustrating: he reported, "I don't even know what I just read." But he looked forward to class, where others' perspectives gave him a "wealth of knowledge." And students gained more than knowledge through each other in the course; they experienced changes in being.

Changes in Being

In the most profound level of learning through others, participants experienced changes in being: this dispositional learning was expressed generally as new openness to experiences and others in the world. Notable in this theme is that participants reflected on course content, but the ways they were engaging with each other to learn the content became so personal that they noticed changes in the ways they interacted with others in their lives.

George described learning as growing and used the term healing to describe what happened for him through other participants' perspectives during focus group 2:

> I found because of my peers, because of all of you, [prolonged pause] I saw a lot of different ways of being, some similar ways of being that made me feel okay with who *I* am. And, I really wanted to . . . I developed a desire to really want to grow and change.

George noted that he began to "value things that [he] did not value before." After the final class session, Blake wrote, "I realized just how much my understanding of phenomenology has changed, and how I have changed from my understanding of phenomenology." He said he had gained an appreciation for art and poetry, as did James, who said in his individual interview that he wanted to start going to art museums with his wife.

It was at times difficult to distinguish between deep learning of content and changes in being. Phil reflected after the final class session that "everyone learned a lot, and not just about philosophy/psychology." He noted that he "became a much better listener at times when I strongly disagreed or wasn't interested. This led me to be able to appreciate other points of view much more than before" (post-class reflection). In the first focus group, Jackie and Barbara discussed the ways their new tendency to "stop and listen" and "engage [others] in dialogue" could help them be better citizens and foster greater understanding. Listening was one of the key skills that was taught as a phenomenological interviewing technique, but six participants directly attributed their change in disposition to other students in the course.

Summary of Themes

With these participant quotes, "coming to appreciate diversity" can be seen as a progression from social comparison with others to learning from others to integrating and becoming with others. The ground of togetherness expressed in being "all together in this space," the "genuine investment" of participants, being "completely caught up" in each other's stories and ideas, and "coming to appreciate diversity" were all part of the gestalt of the SEOS. Without one of these themes, all the others would have been different. We do not suggest a causal relationship between the themes, but note that these themes exist together and can be interpreted to draw conclusions about classroom climate and the role of others in the classroom. In the next section, we will discuss the findings and their implications.

Discussion: Creating Positive Intersubjectivity

It is not difficult to see that a more didactic, lecture-based teaching approach would preclude the kind of SEOS portrayed in the preceding results. But in many ways the case study professor fulfilled his traditional role: he planned with particular learning objectives in mind, selected materials, designed activities, and lectured—although mostly in brief mini-lectures (see Chapters 3 and 4). Perhaps not completely atypical, at one point he noted, "the students are paying for my knowledge."

Nonetheless, we believe that the professor's phenomenological approach and phenomenological attitude supported the kinds of SEOS and *intersubjectivity* expressed by our case study participants. The professor shared personal stories—so did the students. The professor used humor—so did the students. The professor was deeply interested and respectful—so were students. Students followed the lead of the professor and in turn the lead of the other students, taking responsibility for their own and others' learning.

120 *Student Experiences of Other Students*

As Lois said, the professor "would . . . give us a starting point, but then the real learning came as a collaboration among all of the participants in the class." But if a starting point for content is all that teachers provide, students sometimes struggle to take it from there. We believe that in order for students to be active, take responsibility, and be emotionally engaged, the teacher must help them form relational connections that provide a kind of structure for the classroom climate. And this happened best when these students developed or adopted the phenomenological attitude displayed by the professor through what he said and did.

The case study professor never put down or rejected a student idea. The students seemed to follow the professor's lead in this regard as well. They were exceptionally non-judgmental—only four of the 992 post-class reflection comments included language that was indicative of students appraising other students negatively. Lisa, in an individual interview, said, "You can put an idea out there and . . . get muddy and it's, it's ok. It's good. It's all good."

Through humor, intimacy, and openness, intersubjectivity was strengthened and grew, starting in the first class session and continuing throughout the length of the course. Based on the data shared above, in the next section we discuss ways the phenomenological approach influenced the intersubjectivity of the students in the case study course.

Play and Intimacy: Sitting Around the Fire

An appropriate analogy for building intersubjectivity may be drawn to the experience of sitting around a fire with others. When class participants are staring at something surprising, when everyone can open up to the wonder of course content together, the shared experience of witnessing and participating can create strong intersubjectivity. For here is where a phenomenological attitude thrives. Borrowing a phrase from Merleau-Ponty (1945/1962), "Reflection does not withdraw from the world towards the unity of consciousness as the world's basis; it steps back to *watch the forms of transcendence fly up like sparks from a fire*" (p. xiii, emphasis added). Participants in the case study course watched the sparks fly up together.

Lisa characterized class demonstrations and visual activities as toys; Sonia noted activities that created an intimate atmosphere: "We talked about [things] that, you know, you should talk about all the time, but no one ever asks those questions." The questions she referred to focused on experience and sparked deep personal explorations and discovery. These explorations were shared in experiences both playful and intimate, and sharing experience created a sense of a shared classroom space. For example, after the students spent some time in small groups, rather than ask about, for example, what students learned from each other, the professor asked students to talk about the group work process. This prompt, and others like it, focused students on the processes of learning together and the intellectual and emotional engagement of their classmates. With the kind of engagement participants noted, typical issues with group work were never an issue.

As noted in Chapter 4, on the first day of class the professor used humor and expressed great interest in the students as they introduced themselves; he asked follow-up questions and made personal connections with student research interests or backgrounds. His interest was so keen that Eloise, who worked as a college teacher herself, remarked that she wanted to learn to emulate the teacher's "intensity of interest in others and their experiences." From the first class the professor exhibited his wonder and curiosity, a part of his ontology (see Chapters 3 and 4). Through his questions he respectfully highlighted the subjectivity and ambiguity that each student brought to the course.

Of course teachers *want* students to share goals and feel connected. Some data from the case study course and other studies suggest *how* to make that happen. The case study professor did more than what is often suggested in the literature, for example, knowing student names and validating student comments (Ellis, 2004). Along with his humor, knowledge, storytelling, and expression of interest in students, the teacher of the case study course gave space to students to share their own humor, knowledge, and stories. The personal stories and playful activities helped create what Kasl and Yorks (2016) would describe as *empathic space*. In an empathic space, students present their knowledge through nontraditional means such as narrative or art. In the formal setting of a classroom such displays of knowledge are seen as vulnerability, and vulnerability creates trust.

But there is potential for students to splinter, rather than unify, as they get to know each other better. Superficial chit chat is easier to keep civil than discussions of religion, politics, or worldviews. But when students are asked to adopt a phenomenological attitude of wonder, when they are tasked with seeing with new eyes, even controversial, deeply held personal values can be just more sparks flying up from the fire. When students acknowledge embodiment and sociocultural embeddedness, they are able to see variations as a *shared* condition of humanity. So even activities that reveal great differences can contribute to intersubjectivity.

Intersubjectivity is also enhanced through identification of a common "enemy." According to Haidt (2012), a social psychologist, the *hive mentality* is a tendency of humans that arose evolutionarily to protect group survival. He says leaders can activate a "hive switch" by highlighting in-group similarities, downplaying in-group differences, and encouraging extra-group competition. In the case study course, the teacher united students with appeals to humanism and encouraged thought experiments in which together they explored ways in which perspectives contrary to those of the course content were destructive in the world. Descartes's influence, for example, was a commonly cited "enemy" of a holistic treatment of humans and human systems.

122 Student Experiences of Other Students

Seeing and Appreciating Diversity

Students engaged together in what could be called academic team-building exercises. Students learned through activities intentionally designed to highlight their sociocultural embeddedness and experience as they related to course objectives. One of the most difficult barriers to learning, according to Greene (1973), is the comfort that comes from assurance or the presuppositions that "fix [a] vision of the world" (p. 11). To learn more, to begin to bring unity to a fragmented or undifferentiated view of course content, learners must set aside what they presume to know. And when a novel vision eludes an individual, multiple voices can spur the creativity needed to see anew.

In the professor's words, the intent of activities and discussions was to "*blow them away*" and inspire in students a vision of how the world of the content was enhanced by and expanded their own lifeworlds. When students were launched into the world, their contributions to course dialogue were interpreted by their classmates as genuine and authentic. This authenticity contributed to getting "caught up" in classmates' "diverse" worlds. Barbara's remarks on the class's diversity and its role in her learning highlight the importance of learning through the perspectives of others. By some measures, the course *lacked* diversity. There were only two students of color. But there were 10 males and 11 females, and because students were encouraged to become aware of the power of personal, bodily experience in learning, they could experience diversity. For example, there was great variety among students' personal and professional experiences. The students of color and the women made no remarks about microaggressions—their data was not remarkably different than those of the male students.

In their roles as counselors, teachers, nurses, and philosophers, students were able to share their unique perspectives as a result of the open nature of activities that launched their worlds. During one class session, 14 of the 19 students present discussed interpretations of a poem by Mark Strand, "Keeping Things Whole." For context, this poem is a first-person account of moving through a field and stating that by moving out of the field, the field becomes whole. Below, we share a transcript from the discussion between a few of the students and the professor:

George:	Yeah, [quoting the poem] "wherever I am, I am what is missing." I'm interested in hearing what others in here think about that sentence, or that last part.
Sonia:	But when—
George:	Did some feel like Meg and I heard, or did y'all hear something else?
Whitney:	Or could it be the opposite though, because, "wherever I am, I am what is missing," so it's again, going back to,

Student Experiences of Other Students   123

here's the field, and I'm standing in the field, so I'm taking up that part of the field, that's missing, so I am the part that—of the field, that is missing. So then, at the bottom, when, [quoting the poem] "we all have reasons for moving, I move to keep things whole" because the minute I move out of the field, the field is whole again.

Professor: Or the opening that I was, is closed.

[three talking at once: Professor, Lisa, George]

Lisa: So I am missing in the field, and I moved, and now it's whole again.

George: The old field is whole, or the new field is whole?

Brian: The old field is whole.

Lisa: The field, well, I don't know if it's old or new, but it's whole because I'm not in it, I'm not taking up space any more.

George: I heard it the other way. [laughter]

Lisa: It's like the vase, and the faces.

George: I agree with that.

Lisa: Ooo, it is like it's that. [laughter]

Sonia: I think it goes back to the whole thing of us being embedded in our space, uh, it's not, I don't necessarily see it as a negative poem, because, this, this is what I create, this is, this space, this perception is what I create, so it has to have me in order to be created. So [quoting the poem] "in the field I am the absence of field" because I am I am the originator, I create this, this is all about what I perceive and what I, what is me, extended into space, so it has to have me in order to exist. [pause] That's what I thought.

This excerpt of a class discussion illustrates the potential of a phenomenological approach. Here the professor provided an artifact, the poem, which was challenging and relevant to the learning objectives for the class session. He asked students an open question: "What stands out to you in this poem?" He provided more structure with follow-up questions yet gave students freedom in how they responded. The connections students had formed were strong enough that the conflict between Lisa and George was accompanied by humor rather than tension. And this conversation was a key for many students in learning to be better listeners. They saw that two conflicting interpretations of a poem could be equally plausible.

Parker Palmer (2007) writes, "competition is the antithesis of community, an acid that can dissolve the fabric of relationships. Conflict is the dynamic by which we test ideas in the open, in a communal effort to stretch each other and make better sense of the world" (p. 106). In sources as diverse as Plato's story of Meno, Piaget's discussions on socio-cognitive conflict, and in DEEP ecological processes (see Chapter 2), the necessity of conflict for learning seems clear. But the conflict must come with some common ground, and most powerful in a classroom is a common existential project in "the art of being better." Rather than hammering square pegs into round holes, the case study professor's approach fostered a broad enough shared goal that individual students were still able to co-opt the course goals for their own purposes.

Many scholars discuss the importance of students being actively engaged in a community of learners or collaborative group work, but the contribution of our approach is how teachers can encourage students to not only participate in order to provide each other with alternative perspectives on course content, but to engage in a common educational pursuit, a common existential project, through which they can connect in surprising ways and realize course content in their lives. As George said, "Every single person in that class contributed to my growth. Every one." In the next chapter, we focus specifically on what that growth looked like.

7 Transcending the Classroom
Student Reports of Personal and Professional Change

> And for me, not having a philosophy or a psychology background other than my own studies . . . it's introduced me to a whole wide world of, of new thought and understanding but yet it tapped into thoughts and ideas that I've had over the course of my lifetime.
>
> (Lois)

In this chapter, we highlight the learning of students described in the case study data with a focus on the ways in which they realized course content in their personal and professional lives. These stories provide us with evidence of personal and professional change, such as one participant's approach to clinical psychological counseling, another's redesign of his approach to teaching, and another coming to terms with the death of his father. Participants discussed changes in their ways of seeing the world and changes in how they related to others. We discuss implications of these changes as evidence determining whether the goals of a transformational phenomenological approach have occurred. We begin by exploring the inadequacy of the predominant methods for defining and measuring student success.

How can the outcomes from a phenomenological approach to teaching and learning be determined in the current assessment-driven milieu noted in Chapter 3? An ever-growing number of education stakeholders demand *measurable outcomes* and evidence of *mastered competencies* (Biggs & Tang, 2011; Donnison & Penn-Edwards, 2012; Muller, 2018; Neem, 2013). Test scores, rates of student retention, grade point averages (GPA), and degree or certificate attainment are emphasized. As described in Chapter 3, these measures of success have produced students adept at surface learning and passing exams, while avoiding deep and durable learning. Characteristics of surface learning include memorization techniques associated with rote learning, and the desire to avoid failure with the least amount of effort (Floyd, Harrington, & Santiago, 2009). In a college mathematics classroom, for example, surface learners

126 *Transcending the Classroom*

are able to quickly and efficiently compute algorithmic solutions, what some cognitive psychologists refer to as fluency or procedural fluency, but cannot engage in dialogue concerning problem contexts or interpretation of results.

Higher education is also undergoing the immense external pressure of corporatization, requiring a focus on specialized preparation for the nebulous *21st century workforce*, at the expense of preparation for citizenship or implanting a commitment to society's *common good* (Dorn, 2017). Sixty years ago in *Existentialism and Education*, Kneller (1958) provided prophetic advice:

> Something should be done to counteract the ever-increasing emphasis on vocationalism, applied arts, professionalism, and other types of training which have had a detrimental effect on education as a personal, aesthetic, academic experience, valuable in its own rights and liberating in its effects.
>
> (pp. 40–41)

In a 1958 interview, Merleau-Ponty (1958/2007), in a defense of the rationale for the need for continued study of philosophy, referenced Balzac in describing the need for "*profound people* [emphasis added] not merely those who calculate; radical minds and not merely technicians. Thus, we will need people trained through doubt and examination" (p. 385). He continued with a comment that parallels the social and political climate of our current era: "The havoc caused by routine politics and political improvisation is clear enough today" (p. 385). We believe that learning rooted in an environment that fosters transformative experiences is essential to the development of the "profound people" desperately needed by the world's polarized societies of today.

We join the chorus of voices citing the need for an approach to teaching and learning with goals beyond student acquisition of knowledge and skills as evidenced by traditional classroom assessment (Henriksson, 2012; Willis, 2012). Quality higher education demands a pedagogy that goes beyond a narrow view of success to include the holistic development of the student, resulting in the growth of the whole person, intellectually, emotionally, socially, ethically, physically, and spiritually (Cuseo, 2007). With the following excerpts from our case study course and other studies, we argue that a phenomenological approach offers just such a broad view of success. In accord with Henriksson (2012), we affirm that teachers confront "aspects of pedagogical practice that do not lend themselves to quantification, intellectual reasoning, or theorizing" (p. 121). Phenomenology, as a philosophical approach that "champions a holistic, nondualistic approach to life" (Finlay, 2011, p. 29), provides us with a way of knowing, a phenomenological attitude, that is "relevant for pedagogical practice and classroom interaction" (Henriksson, 2012, p. 121). We contend that not only does phenomenology inform a quality approach to teaching and learning, but also provides the appropriate approach for exploring the outcomes of teaching and learning in the lives of students. A description of surface learning has been provided. Now we turn to a clarification of the attributes of deep learning—learning that lasts.

Learning That Lasts

Mentkowski and associates (2000) define *learning that lasts* as an integration of learning, development, and performance. They contend that learning that lasts contributes to the development of the person. It is "realized through effective performance in work, personal and civic life," through "learning outcomes that become part of the individual" (p. 1). Learning that lasts is "mindful and emotional, intellectual and committed" (p. 1) and is accompanied by the transformative experience of the integration of course content into knowing and doing combined with reflective awareness. Transformative learning experiences trigger a restructuring of the self that goes beyond classroom learning experiences and vocational choices to encompass civic and personal relationships. Transformative learners recognize their inseparable link with the web of relations that comprise the human community. In Mentkowski et al. (2000) a transformative learner is described as a "lucid interpreter of life consonant with his or her own experiential background" (p. 238).

Integration, as we describe it, results is an intertwining of course content with the learner's individual experience. Taylor (2009) describes individual experience as "the primary medium of transformative learning" (p. 5). It is through the interdependent relationships of individual experience, critical reflection, and dialogue that the learner challenges his or her attitudes, values, and beliefs. Through these challenges, transformative learning occurs. Taylor (2009) presents dialogue as relational and trustful classroom communication that clears the way for critical reflection to be put into action. Our phenomenological approach promotes transformative outcomes that transcend the classroom through the students' integration of course content into personal and professional lives, thus becoming part of their identity. In other words, learning that lasts. A phenomenological approach promotes teaching for transformation, allowing students "to transcend mastery" through the *realization* of course content. In this manner, learners find "deep, personal meaning in their learning experiences and lives" (Sohn et al., 2016, p. 6). A multi-layered exploration of deep and transformative learning has been explored through the lenses of ethology, biology, and cognitive science in Chapter 2. An understanding of *realizing course content* allows one to hear in student voices whether transformative learning has occurred.

Realizing Course Content

In the foreword to the reprint of his 1966 work, *Existentialism in Education: What It Means*, Morris (1966/1990) notes "what is conspicuously absent from the pantheon of educational strategies is one which focuses on and celebrates the personal self, the individual growing into his or her idiosyncratic place in the world" (p. vii). Sohn et al. (2016) asserted that although teachers in higher education begin with the goal of the student mastering course content, many share the view of a need for a pedagogy that transcends mere acquisition of knowledge and skills. High quality learning involves *realizing*, which goes beyond knowing course content "to a transformative understanding of the world and the indiviual's place within it" (p. 2). These authors also state:

> Such understanding enables creative enlargement and application of the course content. This transformation is manifest in students realizing the relevance of course content in their personal and professional lives—in an aesthetic sense of gratification that imparts confidence in one's understanding or insight—an intuitive sense of its truth and worth.
>
> (Sohn et al., 2016, p. 2)

The idea of integration is at the core of the hoped-for outcomes of a phenomenological approach to teaching and learning. From our own personal experience as phenomenological researchers and educational practitioners, we have noticed changes in our own ways of seeing and being in the world. We authors approach our everyday lives differently. The phenomenological attitude has become a positive transformation permanently ingrained into our identities.

As stated in Chapter 1, student mastery of course content as evidenced by test scores and GPAs is not sufficient evidence that the realization of course content has occurred. Case study participant Sonia remarked that she was transcending the classroom when she stated the course was "seeping into a lot of other areas of my life." The deeper understandings and resulting perspective transformations seeping into students' personal and professional lives are best evidenced in their voices. Selected excerpts that fit with our definition of outcomes have been phenomenologically analyzed. These passages were selected from student interview transcripts, focus group transcripts, and post-class reflections from the case study course. The student voices reveal life-changing perspectives that have positively affected both their personal and professional lives.

Results: A Life-Changing Experience

> But just, you get a whole essence of learning and you come away from it changed. I feel I've really had a life changing experience through this course. And I don't always walk away from coursework feeling that way.
>
> (Lisa)

What does a life-changing experience that transcends the classroom look like from a student point of view? Here we share the case study course participants' descriptions of their learning. As previously noted, the professor was deeply committed to a phenomenological approach. His approach exemplifies the phenomenological attitude (see Chapters 3 and 4). The life-changing theme is prevalent throughout course participant interviews and reflections. Sonia described both initial misgivings regarding taking the course and changed perspectives as a result of being a learner in the course:

> I didn't look forward to taking this class at all, but I'm extremely happy that I took it and I think I would recommend it to anyone. What I get most of, I think, it challenges the way that I look at things and it's allowed me to make connections between things that I never would have made before, and also, see those connections on a deeper level. It just never occurred to me.

The qualities of the phenomenological attitude became part of their lives through a new way of seeing, increased openness, and greater awareness of the interconnectedness of everything. Case study students spoke of a greater sense of empathy and compassion, increased ability to critically reflect, greater awareness of their biases, willingness to continually question the taken for granted, and willingness to change. Students noted a greater appreciation for aesthetics as found in art, poetry, or music, increased reflexivity, and a better understanding of sociocultural context. In their focus on becoming more open, students described becoming better listeners, having a greater appreciation of differing perspectives and diversity, and of valuing multiple ways of knowing. Students also described an understanding of and appreciation for the interconnectedness of everything, with a special emphasis on the importance of the connections between people. They contrasted this interconnectedness with a frustration with the compartmentalization of the university, visible in the separate silos of the different departments. In the following sections, students' own words are used to elucidate these themes.

A New Way of Seeing

Participants described changes in the way they went about their day to day lives consistent with the sense of wonder inherent in the phenomenological attitude. This new way of seeing featured a greater awareness of everyday life, an increased appreciation for the aesthetic, and a better understanding of sociocultural context. James explained, "I think there's a challenge to be more engaged with everything, of little things throughout your day even and just kind of like seeing those things in your life."

130   *Transcending the Classroom*

Greater Awareness of Everyday Life

Lois in describing her new way of seeing the world said the "smallest things in life may be trivialized as a rule [but] there is nothing really trivial about any part of any person's life." Sonia agreed:

> I try and pay attention a little closer now. Now as I give myself a little more credit for things and also time to kind of go beneath the superficial level that we all kind of use day to day.

In addition to describing greater awareness, other participants, like George, described finding increased value in becoming more reflective:

> Reflection was valuable. It's a good skill to be a reflective practitioner. If I'm gonna be a therapist or even if I'm going to train the counselors in mental health to be able to talk to them about it, but [also] be able to do it myself. So, I like the reflection. I could have written a lot more.
>
> (laughing)

Whitney, as well, reported increased reflexivity as an outcome of her experience in the case study course.

> I think that makes, at least in my own experience, has made me really reflective, kind of analytical on my own sort of being, which I think is nice. And it's healthy to appreciate that. It's almost like therapy.

A change in perception, characterized by a greater awareness as an outcome, is a common theme voiced by the case study participants. Merleau-Ponty's (1945/2012) description of the role of the "perpetual beginner" features the continual questioning of assumptions allowing one to approach the phenomena of everyday life with both wonder and openness (p. lxxviii). Continual questioning allows a space to explore the ambiguity of everyday life with a sense of excitement and discovery. Participants express this embrace of ambiguity in a greater appreciation for the aesthetic.

Increased Appreciation for the Aesthetic

As part of this greater awareness many of the case study participants expressed an increased appreciation for the aesthetic, especially in regard to poetry, paintings, and music. This appreciation was grounded in the idea that art provided a different way of knowing. Participants stated that their increased appreciation for art provided a new way to interpret the world and a greater understanding of the interpretations of others. Blake described his newfound appreciation:

> Before this course, poetry and paintings and artwork in general, to me, were really abstract. I didn't really care too much for it, just because I know there's a great deal of interpretation. But I realized that human nature really is pervasive in all of those things, and for me to deny that, not to see that, is a shame.

Students described a growing appreciation for the interpretations of others through exploring works of art together. Thomas said that he "found it amazing to hear how similar and different my thoughts were from others." He expressed his appreciation for art as an experience for eliciting "great insight, creativity, and conversation." Two of the participants said they intended to take their wives to art shows. James described reflecting on song lyrics as a way to appreciate another's point of view:

> I enjoyed listening to (and) reflecting on the song "Suzanne." It was one I was unfamiliar with and did not necessarily enjoy myself, however, I love it when others find meaning in things. I am always interested in listening to music, whether I like it or not, when someone else has found meaning in it. Sometimes hearing it from a different point of view brings new light and possible enjoyment to the song. Plus, it really made me think!

James also described the enjoyment he found from the opportunity to challenge himself through art and poetry, which he described as not "relevant to me before." As the students discussed their perspectives, connections were revealed with the qualities of the phenomenological attitude and Merleau-Ponty's (1945/2012) concepts regarding perception.

Better Understanding of Sociocultural Context

Connected with an increased appreciation for differing perspectives and diversity, was a greater awareness of the language, culture, and historical contextual factors through which we all interpret the world. This awareness of context is rooted in the concept of social embeddedness.

George talked about his increased awareness:

> I was much more aware of all of the contextual factors and variables that exist. Social context in particular is important in my interpretation of the world as it relates to clients'/patients' thoughts, feelings, motivations, behavior, etc. I also realize that who I am is determined by the contextual field, and by my perception and history. The

132   *Transcending the Classroom*

example of the mother cleaning and rearranging the room made me more aware of how ambiguity, change, and chaos can affect me and others.

Kelly described becoming more aware of a potential for ignorance in regards to contextual factors:

It made me aware that there are those that are completely blind to contextual factors and there is an ignorance with all of us to some of the factors. Some things we don't perceive as stereotypical and may never get to bring to light. Not in a negative way per se, but there are many layers to each situation.

Openness

The phenomenological attitude is marked by both openness to others and a critical reflexivity. Case study participant Barbara attests to this change:

(My) viewpoint [my] way of looking at the world. I think, coming out of this class, I'll have more openness to the experiences. To people that I might encounter in the future. And I hope that I would be able to engage them in dialogue better, such that both of us could learn from each other.

Sonia explains that openness allows for "deeper connections, better understanding, and a lot more cohesiveness." Associated with their increased openness, case study participants reported better listening, greater awareness of differing perspectives, and valuing multiple ways of knowing.

Better Listening

Phil explained that he became "a much better listener at times when I strongly disagreed or wasn't interested. This led me to be able to appreciate other points of view much more than before." Participants noted that becoming better listeners positively affected their personal and professional relationships. George, a counselor, describes this on his approach to his practice:

It's important for me not to put my perception over a client's or the person speaking. And I could share mine if they ask me "What do you think?" So, it helped me to be a little more open to letting others describe and think. I'm pretty open anyways, which reminded me of how important that is to listen and let people describe what they're going through. And not do too much explaining or [said while

Transcending the Classroom   133

laughing] analysis or, just let 'em talk, kind of let 'em be. The importance of being, of non-directive kind of therapy.

Lois stated something similar:

> I think it made me more critically aware of really listening to what they were saying. Um, and it [is] sort of like, what you're doing here is. I would follow up with questions and relate to them in a different way than I would have before. It's hard for me not to talk, but I found myself forcing myself to ask a question and stop and really listen to what they [students] were saying. And when I did I—I really feel that that's made a huge difference.

Thomas, a clinical psychologist, also described the impact of better listening on his professional practice:

> There's a lot of learning that happens outside of the class, embedded in my other [pause] work or my current experience. This is the first semester I've been seeing patients, clinically, in the program here. Which has been really incredible. I've learned a lot in how to talk with patients. Listening to patients, not behind the patients all the time. Coming from a psychoanalytic background, a lot of listening is behind patients, like triangulating meaning, that might not be conscious for that person and themselves. But, really valuing that first-person experience has been [pause] a way I've learned. And I think that points to my experience of learning in the course. It's just how it goes into other domains. It's such a broad approach to understanding people.

Jackie described the positive effects on other students in the seminar:

> I think it's very therapeutic for them to talk about their experiences. And just talk about it to someone who is not judging, just listening. I don't think a lot of people listen very well, and so I've had a couple of participants walk away and just say, "Oh, man. I feel like that was a therapy session or something." But [they said it] in a positive way.

A phenomenological attitude is accompanied by an increased sense of empathy and compassion. Lois describes the course experience as causing "me to think in a different way than I often think of, it's made me very hopeful because of the empathy and the compassion that the members of the group show for one another." Brian expressed his discomfort when classmates discussed issues such as pregnancy and nursing; however, when he thought about this in terms of future experience with his wife, he found the discussion to be "empathy building."

134   *Transcending the Classroom*

Greater Appreciation of Differing Perspectives

Connected to the increased openness, participants expressed a greater appreciation of differing perspectives and a greater willingness to listen to differing points of view. Whitney described this as an awareness:

> I think I really enjoy, just the awareness of self, the awareness of others' perspectives. Just getting a new perspective to your positionality within the world, and your own world, and how it relates to other people. Just tying in that awareness [of] you with all the different backgrounds we've had, and different experiences. It's just been really interesting.

Lois described how the greater awareness of different perspectives has resulted in a change in her teaching. "I'm relating differently to my students because of it, factoring perspectives that I never would have factored before." Stephen described finding value in the personal stories of others and how this would be useful in other learning contexts:

> I was aware of how the many personal stories created a rich field to see themes. It was an experimental learning process, rather than solely an intellectual exercise. For me the learning was deeper and served as an example I could use in other education environments.

Jackie explained how this was fostered during the learning process and how it extends beyond the class to their roles as citizens:

> So there's like this democracy in the learning process that we've engaged in over the course of the semester. And I think there's a bigger message that we've learnt from this class, hearing everybody else's differences in perceptions on the same picture, or piece of art, or poem, or what have you. And it teaches us to respect other people's opinions and to stop and listen, and to learn from somebody else's perception, even when it's so different than ours. And I think that helps us not only as students, but as, you know, as just citizens of our community.

Mark echoed this idea, explaining there are "different ways of looking at the world and one isn't necessarily better than the other." Lois portrayed diversity as not just something to be accepted but something that is essential, using her daughter's experience as an opera singer:

> I thought about opera . . . because my daughter is an opera singer and my husband was the technical director of the Opera Company. I know what it is like in the audience and backstage. How everyone has prepared to this point. Everyone is at a different point in their

Transcending the Classroom   135

career, education, and experience, and brings a different perspective. How dreadful opera would be if everyone was a tenor or a lighting designer. Each person is critical to the success of the opera.

Lois stated seeing "things from a very different perspective really changed my perspective on a lot of different issues." She championed the value of being willing to change based on the consideration of different perspectives with this powerful claim. "If we as a whole society could, could have that perspective, then we would all be so much better off [. . .] that the world would be so much better off."

Valuing Multiple Ways of Knowing

Included with the increased appreciation for differing perspectives and diversity is a greater awareness of the importance of multiple ways of knowing. Although this may not be a surprising finding with students taking a seminar in phenomenology, their arguments for valuing multiple ways of knowing, particularly for understanding the human condition, are compelling. Phil explained:

> An interest I came into the course with, and one that this course has intensified. And I have a similar [methods course], my research stats, and [with] this course. There does seem to always be this tension between qualitative approaches, which are largely marginalized or disregarded, and the quantitative approach, which is generally considered more rigorous and more credible. But what has been intensified for me is an interest in understanding how the qualitative emphasis on subjective description, and the quantitative analysis of objective data can complement one another. As we discover things in the descriptions, whether it be from clinical patients or whether it be from participants at a given market. Why can't that lead to whatever sort of data analysis to perhaps verify or understand better, how generalizable those descriptions are? And then, in turn, I see it as kind of a circular process in which the, whatever generalities are reached, those can be further explored or perhaps reaffirmed or [the researcher can] discover variations within those generalizations based on further, more detailed qualitative explorations.

In agreement with Phil, Sonia viewed the utility of qualitative and quantitative methods used to complement one another in the development of deep understandings. This was in opposition to the dualistic, either-or thinking that has fueled the long-running research paradigm wars:

> I think our struggle between the research methods kind of speaks to our reluctance to kind [of] get up close and personal, giving some

136 *Transcending the Classroom*

validation to perception. And how people really feel in that moment. And I think that speaks to us not wanting to get messy with the human experience. But in breaking it down like we have been talking about, how this is ethical . . . across subjects and disciplines. And you break it all down and you wind up with people. And, I think by giving us validation, you get a deeper understanding of just about any subject, if you start there. Or at least build it into the quantitative analysis. But you have to understand it at the root of any type of data. People were experiencing what you're trying to measure. Getting that first experience, it helps you give different, give deeper meaning to whatever it is that you are studying.

Kari Ann spoke of admonishing her students regarding the perils of solely relying on the numbers:

even what I tell my one-on-one students as they're writing their papers. I'm like, "You can throw numbers at me all day long, but unless you put a face on your argument unless you know, give it that human quality of the story of someone actually experiencing what you're talking about, you're probably not going to convince me or many other people that this is really an issue."

Interconnectedness of All Things

Merleau-Ponty (1968) contended that all phenomena and meanings are interconnected. The holistic concept of the interconnectedness of all things is a key understanding within the phenomenological attitude. Sonia described her growing understanding of interconnectedness:

So, I mean . . . it comes up in my conversations now when I'm talking to people about any kind of subject. Now, I'm making connections between that and something that I've read about, or something that I've started thinking about, just because of this course.

Case study participants described developing an increased understanding of interconnectedness through the following three subthemes: everything is connected, breaking down silos, and the interconnectedness of people.

Everything Is Connected

Much of the discussion centered on the connection between academic disciplines. Mark talked about these connections:

We had discussions about music. It really has helped to integrate all these things for me and helped me realize that even with things like biology or physics, they can all be tied together in some way, even the basis of psychology and physics and biology and geography, and the words that all of those things are rooted in. When you go back and look at those things. Everything was integrated before and we've separated them all. Coming back and trying to, to bring them all together, is a good thing. And that's what I try to do, is integrate knowledge. And I think this class has helped me with that.

Lisa expressed the importance of being able to communicate across disciplines:

So, I see it as inter-disciplinary and trans-disciplinary in that you can have conversations with people from other disciplines. And you can understand what they're talking about so it crosses disciplines. And I think with the way our world now works, we work . . . across disciplines. So, I feel that through phenomenology, I would be able to engage with nursing, with medicine, with other disciplines that would enhance my work that it would be [a] really great way to engage in my practice.

Sonia continued this theme:

Well, academically it's helping me to kind of make connections between things at a level that either I just didn't know of or did not know how to articulate maybe. I'm taking classes in Social Ed and um Cultural Studies and just some of the issues about society and social construction and all these things that are coming up in my other classes. I'm able to sit in phenomenology and make it real for me. Bring the people, bring the personal view into it and see how it works on the day to day level. It's allowing me to really tie a lot of elements together which is fantastic.

Breaking Down Silos

Case study students expressed frustration with the silos inherent in the university system. An interesting comparison is that first-year community college students used similar language in describing their difficulties upon arrival in higher education (Smith, 2016). We have described a phenomenological approach as a holistic approach to teaching and learning, but the compartmentalization prevalent in colleges and universities makes this difficult (Sherman, 2014). During a focus group Mark expressed this frustration, shared by his classmates:

I can build off that and say, one of the things that universities do, is they silo the knowledge. [murmurs of agreement] Here's this

138   *Transcending the Classroom*

department and that department. Well, every day we have this class and I walk out of it. It's mentally tearing down the walls between all these disciplines.

Barbara continued with the same kind of thoughts:

I struggle with the way that the university does put different departments in different silos and it's very difficult to reach across and get an understanding. I really appreciated the perspective of people in the field of nursing. I think that's been really beneficial for me and for the whole group. So, every time that someone brings their own background, their own experience into it, I grow from hearing them.

Here, Barbara reinforced the value of exposure to different perspectives and used another word, *grow*, that was uttered by many of the case study participants. Donna described how the case study class allowed her to make connections:

To build off of what Whitney said a little bit, I think that this class for me has definitely affected the other class I'm taking this semester. I don't know if others in this class have had that experience. I'm taking [another] seminar, but the seminar is grounded in reflective practice and learning theories and teaching. For me, what I learn in this class and the readings from this class shape my experience. [This seminar and the other], my Monday night class, [creates] a cycle that builds upon each other. I find myself in our reflective practice class. We journal, write reflections. And most of my reflections deal with readings from phenomenology. They're different disciplines, but it's kind of interesting to see the way that I found that connection of the silos, in between.

Connecting With Others Through Authentic Relationships

A phenomenological attitude rooted in the philosophical concepts of Merleau-Ponty champions the benefits of connecting with other people; life is spent in a "network of relations" (Thomas, 2005, p. 71). Case study participants demonstrated this awareness in their descriptions of relationships with significant others and the strong bonds created with classmates during the case study course. Alexander described the impact of the class for him as a future professor:

And so, this class got me thinking about the way, the role of perception in general, and the relationship of student and professor and how those two interact. To me, those are very, very crucial ideas in terms of

Transcending the Classroom 139

like learning the educational environment, and what I would like as a future professor and my [own] educational environment to look like.

George described the importance of the authentic relationships he developed with his classmates in relationship to the growth he experienced:

I found because of my peers, because of all of you, [prolonged pause, approximately 6 seconds] I saw a lot of different ways of being, some similar ways of being that made me feel okay with who I am. I developed a desire to really want to grow and change. And, I didn't expect to do a lot of reflection, personally, in the class. I just thought I'd learn about phenomenology and how to do qualitative research. That's kind of what I went in desiring, and I got a little bit of that and I guess I'm more pleased that I got the growth and the reflection out of it. I have changed a lot this semester and been able to apply some things into some interpersonal relationships. And that's because of my choice to want to do it. But it really is because of classmates and [our professor] and everybody in there.

George's willingness to share reflected the safety students felt in the class. Kari Ann described being validated by classmates sharing similar difficult experiences:

The example of divorce stood out to me because I was thinking of sharing the same one. I was hesitant, however, because I felt like I had already been talking a lot and also didn't want to bring the class down with my personal woes. I was grateful, therefore, when someone else mentioned a similar scenario, both because the example was out there and because I felt validated in my own experience.

As the class came near an end, George provided the following description:

It will be, it'll be disappointing for the class to end. [pause] I almost got emotional there, but I guess I'll miss the safety of the class to be who I am, and miss the opportunity to grow further with some of these folks.

Kari Ann continued with another positive description:

That's my positive experience of it. Just, and that goes back to my whole being treated like a human being, not being competitive. And you know we're all working together to try and understand these things. And everybody's story matters. And we want to hear it. And you know all of those things just really [pause] went a long ways towards making it a memorable class that I'll look back on fondly.

Conclusion: Growth

Many would argue that the purpose of higher education is to create a space for growth through personal transformation. The personal transformations described by the students in our case study seminar were impressive. As illustrated by the students' own words, they developed a new way of seeing, better understanding of sociocultural context, greater appreciation of differing perspectives, and increased understanding of the connectedness of all things. It could be said that the students developed *self-actualizing personalities*, as proposed by Cangemi (2001). Based on a study of administration, faculty, and student perceptions of the purpose of higher education, Cangemi (2001) summarized this purpose as *developing self-actualizing personalities*, succinctly defined as "the highest form of psychological health; the development of one's true self, the development of one's existing or latent potential" (p. 151). Findings of our case study support the assertion of Selvi (2008) that the application of a phenomenological approach in education provides students with the opportunity for self-actualization.

Beyond self-actualization, stories of the students in this graduate seminar demonstrated the transformational power of genuine connection with others in authentic relationship, each student able to grasp and deeply appreciate the perspectives of others very different from themselves.

8 Messing Up and Messing About

Student Needs and Teachers' Adaptation of Our Phenomenological Approach

> I was exploring the inner landscape of *this* teacher's life, hoping to clarify the intellectual, emotional, and spiritual dynamics that form or deform our work from the inside out.
>
> (Parker Palmer, 2007)

We believe in the value of phenomenological research to spur readers to consider the case study participants' experiences in relation to their own, which we did in the preceding chapters. In this chapter, we want to go beyond our case study to explore what Palmer (2007) calls the inner landscape of teachers, to explore their *messing about* (somewhat like Hawkins', 1974 view, but here focused on careful yet imaginative exploration of different ways to teach and engage students in learning). The teachers whose descriptions we share later in the chapter are members of our Transdisciplinary Phenomenology Research Group (TPRG). They describe the meaning of their experience in designing courses that embrace the phenomenological heart of teaching and learning, one that balances the utilitarian goal of much of higher education today (Muller, 2018; Neem, 2013; see Chapter 7 for a discussion). Their examples demonstrate how a phenomenological approach can be used by teachers in a variety of fields and settings with differing levels of students.

But we will first explore the inner landscape of students reported in research studies conducted by various members of the TPRG as well as others. The findings from these studies provided valuable insight about students' experiences, suggesting that their teachers were unaware of *messing up* in their approaches to such learners.

Student Experiences of a Messed-Up Learning Environment

We include studies of African American students on a predominately white campus, international student experience in American higher education, and low socioeconomic status (LSES) and first-generation students

142   *Messing Up and Messing About*

in community college and university settings. We conclude by discussing how messing about with a phenomenological approach can avoid or overcome a messed-up learning environment.

African American Student Experiences

Painful and alienating experiences reported by black graduates of the university's nursing program (Thomas & Davis, 2000) prompted a decision to expand the study to include students in other undergraduate majors. Over a five-year period, several of the authors of this book, along with other members of an interdisciplinary, interracial research team, conducted phenomenological studies of the lived experience of black undergraduate students at a large, predominantly white southeastern university. To obtain the first-person perspective of students, unconstrained by a structured interview protocol, students were asked, "Please describe what stands out to you about your college experiences here at University X."

In the first phase of the study (Davis et al., 2004), we chose to interview successful senior students who had completed degree requirements and were about to graduate, so that descriptions of their experience would not be contaminated by fear of academic probation or failure. The metaphor "Fly in the Buttermilk," used by one of the students, captured the students' perceptions of being the lone black student, isolated and out of place in a class with so many white students. A theme of *invisibility/supervisibility* depicted both the situation of sometimes being overlooked by professors and the equally distressing situation of being called upon to represent the entire black race. The following verbatim quotes are illustrative of the two extreme polarities of this theme. One student stated, "And I can remember some of my classes . . . not really being recognized because I would raise my hand and it would be like I wasn't there." Another shared, "They would ask questions about black people in general you know, and expect you to have the answers . . . you know, do all black people like chicken?" And yet a third reported, "[Professor X had] been picking on me all semester because I'm the only black person. I mean she asked me to sing the Black National Anthem. And I was like, 'no, I can't sing, I'm sorry.' I mean, she would use words like 'you people' and [it was] just horrible."

Deeply troubling to our research team were the descriptions of daily racist treatment both inside and outside the classroom, including incidents of unfairness, sabotage, and condescension. The black students felt they had to prove they were worthy to be at the university, adopting specific strategies to demonstrate to professors (and peers) that they were capable. One student summarized by stating, "I feel like I have to work harder, study more, answer more questions, ask more questions, to prove to both my teachers and to my fellow classmates that, you know, I am worthy to be here . . . Don't automatically doubt my academic capabilities just because I am black." Another student described her strategy:

> I have to work ten times harder to make an A . . . due definitely to the teacher's teaching techniques in the classroom. [In] most of my classrooms . . . the teacher tends to teach toward another area in the classroom. So what I have to do . . . I have to call upon the teacher, get her attention, and ask whatever problem that I have to see if she can help me solve it. I kind of feel neglected.

Findings of this study prompted a new research question: If the experiences of *successful* black students are so difficult, what are the experiences of *struggling* students like? In our subsequent study of struggling black freshmen and sophomores, we heard fresh examples of racist treatment (Thomas et al., 2007). Unpleasant experiences of invisibility and supervisibility echoed those described by the seniors in the previous study. The need to constantly prove oneself was present in the new data as well:

> They're going to look at my work 10 times harder, because they think I speak Ebonics, which I don't. That's something I'm trying to break, the stereotypical mold people have. Just because I'm black does not mean that I cannot speak well and eloquently . . . I'm just like, "Wait, give me a chance."

Most relevant to this book on a phenomenological approach to teaching, we also heard many disturbing stories about faculty who neither taught well nor seemed to care about the students. These struggling black students, despite being well qualified for college by their high school GPA and ACT scores, were shocked to find themselves on academic probation because of low grades. In phenomenological interviews and focus groups that began with the same question used in the previous study, professors were often described as "aloof, arrogant, and uninterested in relating to students or even in learning their names" (Thomas et al., 2007, p. 7). Lecturers seemed hurried and unwilling to stop and answer questions, simply "jumping from one PowerPoint to the next." When the students mustered courage to ask teachers for help, they received *unhelpful help*, consisting of advice to "read the book," "study harder," or "drop the course" (Thomas et al., 2007, p. 9).

Black students' perceptions regarding poor teaching and apparent lack of caring described these mess-ups clearly. One student stated, "My professors, well some of them, seem just to want to throw out information, like write it on the board, have you write it down, and then just get out of there, 'cause they just seem like they don't want to be there." Another shared, "I know professor [X] had tenure so he didn't care about the evaluation or whatever. He's like 'I've got my money.' That's just the mentality." A third described the uncaring attitude of a calculus professor, "He was like, 'I'm not surprised that half of you failed the first test.' And I'm here thinking, 'Don't you care about the students passing?'"

In contrast to these accounts of disappointing faculty behavior, the study data included a few examples of good teaching that avoided mess-ups. One student shared, "My psychology teacher sits down with you, talks to you to see what you're doing wrong and what you can correct . . . that's what he did [to help me prepare for] my last exam." Another described a biology teacher: "My biology teacher is awesome. He takes things and makes them in creative ways, like we took his test yesterday, he gave us three bags of candy and each had the question of the exam in there, and it made you think—and made you loosen up." Yet a third student talked about how an English teacher helped build a relationship with students, stating "[My English professor] sat in class sometimes and talked about when he was growing up, not all the time but little stories here and there, so I can relate to him more."

The findings of these student participants' experiences focus on the need to build relationships, arouse student interest, and share personal stories, ideas that are a part of our phenomenological approach. Spinney (2014) reviewed research on prejudice that goes to the heart of the problem. She summarized,

> In the past decade psychologists have come to realize that the tendency to consider others to be less human than ourselves is universal. This form of prejudice isn't only applied along ethnic lines; it can extend to anyone we fail to relate to. . . .
>
> (para. 2)

But Spinney (2014) discusses additional research demonstrating that although bias increases against those outside a group, it can dramatically change when a person becomes a part of a group, regardless of ethnicity or other difference. This has obvious and hopeful implications for teaching that builds learning communities within the classroom.

Experiences of Low Socioeconomic Status Students

Relationship and a sense of belonging were a common refrain heard in the interviews with black students (Davis et al., 2004; Thomas et al., 2007). And low socioeconomic status (LSES) students, who are often first-generation students, appear to share a similar experience. Based on studies of these students, a concomitant problem was their limited awareness of the academic culture and discourse of higher education (e.g., Lawrence, 2002; McKay & Devlin, 2014; O'Gara, Karp, & Hughes, 2009), as well as "non-academic and non-cognitive factors such as social integration, comfort with the cultural and institutional norms of college, and student motivation and confidence" (Bickerstaff, Barragan, & Rucks-Ahidiana,

Messing Up and Messing About 145

2012, p. 1). For the LSES student this cultural incongruity, as described by Devlin (2013), resulted in feelings of being out of place or not belonging. As one student recalled, "I knew nothing, and I had a lot to learn real fast" (Bickerstaff et al., p. 7). Success for LSES students appears to hinge not only on their understanding the unspoken requirements, or hidden curriculum of higher education (Benn, 2000; Lawrence, 2005; McKay & Devlin, 2014), but also on teachers who avoid messing up.

And teachers messed-up attitudes are evident. Boud (as cited in Lawrence, 2005) argues that some instructors in higher education "have expectations, but fail to articulate them and then make judgments about students who fail to demonstrate them" (p. 248). Lawrence (2005) decries the "sink or swim" approach, evidenced by some faculty and staff who believe they have "little role in, and therefore little responsibility for, students' engagement and perseverance" (p. 205). Regarding his students, a colleague of one of our authors recently stated at a faculty meeting, "It is not my job to get to know them." Perhaps students' first-person descriptions of helpful and nonhelpful teachers bring clearer insight.

Smith (2016), a community college faculty member of many years, explored the transformative learning, first-person experiences of previously unsuccessful (LSES) community college students. For example, research participant Lillian described her perspective of a messed-up teacher attitude when she initially failed at a community college.

> Wow [that community college was], not helpful at all. Looking back today, I can look and honestly say, those teachers, they did not have a passion to say, "Hey, we're going to get you through this, it's gonna be alright. What can I help you with?" "I'm here, these are my hours," et cetera, et cetera. I didn't feel like they made themselves available . . . it was more like, you're in college, I'm going to throw this information at you, what you get, you get, what you don't, you don't . . . I worked third shift and I came to school as soon as I got off from work . . . I just was not retaining anything . . . I didn't have a desire because I didn't feel like I had any support from the teachers . . . you know . . . it was more of . . . throw 'em to the wolves . . .
> (personal communication, May 16, 2014)

Indeed, in Smith's (2016) study, the necessity of communicating was identified by all of the student participants as one of the essential ingredients in establishing positive relationships with other students, faculty, and support staff. These students described how they thrived when authentic relationships were established. Emma provided a description of the support she experienced from faculty and other community college staff:

> Nobody in here is like "Oh well, I'm just here to teach to you. That's it," . . . everybody is in your business. Not in a bad way but . . . they

146 *Messing Up and Messing About*

care about you and actually what you're doing and if you're gonna succeed or not . . . they're actually here to help you . . . that's one thing I love.

(p. 132)

Another student participant in Smith's (2016) study, Rachel, brought this down to the classroom level when describing her teacher's influence when she earned an A in a calculus class after failing with another teacher:

He's got like all this energy and spunk and he would like jump around the classroom and learning is fun and that was fun and like literally doing cartwheels in his classroom . . . for some reason . . . he was very intelligent but that energy, relayed somehow . . . it made it fun to learn it and fun to figure it out . . . but he would also be able to explain things . . . he would give incentive for understanding . . . with the enthusiasm I guess and the energy and "Yeah, you got it right!" and just so excited.

(p. 124)

Researchers have consistently provided evidence demonstrating the connection between strong relationships and LSES student achievement (Goddard, 2003). Relationships with faculty, staff, and peers are the instrumental connections for LSES students to feel a sense of belonging to the academic community (Engstrom & Tinto, 2008; Karp & Hughes, 2008). Engstrom and Tinto (2008) recommended the establishment of learning communities within the college as safe, supporting places to learn and where a sense of belonging is cultivated. Karp (2016) presented a holistic conception of non-academic support that would ensure the existence of an environment for creating social relationships. And we contend that a phenomenological approach to teaching and learning can further healthy relationships and a sense of belonging in the lifeworld of the classroom. The impact of authentic, trusting, supportive, relationships rooted in a phenomenological approach for fostering transformative learning experiences cannot be underestimated.

International Student Experiences

A sense of belonging stood out to international students who came to universities in America and did not speak/write English as their native language. Consider the findings reported by Halic, Greenberg, and Paulus (2009). One student stated, "after a while it's frustrating . . . when you try to communicate in terms of academics . . . and people think you don't know the topic just because you don't know the words" (Josh, p. 82). He further described his frustration:

I had the impression that the people were kinda looking down on me saying, "This guy is not as smart as he looked in his application."

On my application I was really good, I had several published articles, book chapters. . . . So, I guess my professors . . . expected this genius guy . . . and they didn't see it 'cause I didn't have the words to show them. So, it's kind of frustrating.

(Josh, p. 88)

A third student described his feelings under similar circumstances:

It's bad because when you have such a feeling—that you're a stupid person—it is just incredibly reduces your angle and you really feel like a small person, like a mouse in the church . . . Well, that's really embarrassing.

(Michael, p. 82)

Some readers may see these issues as something international students need to address for themselves, rather than having anything to do with messing up on the part of teachers. But studies indicate that the university and its teachers can help to overcome these problems. Paulus, Bichelmeyer, Malopinsky, Pereira, and Rastogi (2005)—as reported by Halic et al. (2009)—found that international students felt far more cohesion when working with other international students. They reported that Americans "were not patient enough to listen to [their] contribution," "go through materials too quickly, making it difficult to keep up" and "assume leadership and hold decision-making power by default of being Americans" (Halic et al., 2009, p. 91). While these students may have been describing their perceived treatment by American students, we certainly can see how these issues apply to teachers who play a considerable role in establishing an atmosphere of positive intersubjectivity amongst students and striving to form positive relations with students themselves. Student participants' experiences as reported in other chapters indicate they were aware of this atmosphere in the case study course. In the Paulus et al. case study, however, the international students developed a learning community amongst themselves that helped them overcome these issues. And other researchers have found similar results using a particular kind of pedagogy, intergroup dialogue.

Intergroup dialogue (IGD) is a practice that brings together people from different nationalities, races, or cultural groups to promote greater understanding and build positive relationships (Zuniga, Nagda, & Cytron-Walker, 2007). A recent University of Tennessee study brought foreign-born and US-born college students together for seven weeks of facilitated small group dialogue (Muller, 2015). The foreign-born students felt branded by their nationalities, reporting continual questions by fellow students about where they were from—rather than being seen in their full humanity (as expressed by one student, "I'm stuck with my nationality"). Not finding where they could comfortably "fit in," the international students described sticking with other foreign students rather than interacting

148 *Messing Up and Messing About*

with American students. One international participant actually described trying to stay invisible, "Usually, when I'm in a class I . . . don't try to make contact with anybody. I just try to stay as invisible as possible."

Participants kept reflective journals throughout the seven weeks of the IGD, and Muller interviewed them after the group concluded. Findings supported the transformative power of dialogue, which took place in the very same conditions of safety and comfort that our case study professor had created in his class. For example, a participant pointed out that the group facilitators—like our case study professor—"were sitting there with us and speaking with us on the same plane as us rather than this top-down teaching at us thing. They were learning with us . . . they were willing to share with us." Later, once she became comfortable in the dialogue group, the international student who had once strived to be invisible said:

> We could just come in and be in that circle and look each other in the eyes right across from each other. . . . You didn't have barriers. You didn't have a desk. You don't have paper, pencils. You just had what you had there with you and a discussion.

Also consistent with our case study research was the theme "Taking It Outside," which described the students' aim to transfer their new dialogical skills outside the IGD after the group concluded, to real-world interactions with their peers, families, and strangers. As articulated by one student,

> A goal after this is taking myself . . . into the real world where it's not as safe and cozy . . . approaching the people who don't have the same ideas as me but also . . . are the people where the organic conversation that we really need, needs to happen.

Some students articulated specific future plans to engage in organizing and activism to combat societal injustices and promote international understanding. One participant phrased her aim this way: "It takes a long time to change the world, but it is not impossible if there are some people who keep trying to open minds and reach people." And this may be no more important than when working to change the messing up on the part of higher education teachers as reported in the experiences of African American students.

The experiences of international, African American, and LSES students suggest similar implications for higher education teachers. In some cases, the issues that troubled students might be overcome by fine tuning current approaches to teaching. In other cases, it may take much more. In all of these cases, messing about with one's approach may well lead to much better learning.

Messing About With a Phenomenological Approach to Teaching

Our case study professor described in detail his experience of preparing for and teaching the seminar using a phenomenological approach (see Chapters 3 and 4). And, the majority of the case study student participants reported a transformative learning experience (see Chapters 5–7). Nevertheless, the question many readers may have is whether other teachers in different types of settings can provide similar learning experiences for students using their own style yet still go to the phenomenological heart of teaching and learning and avoid or overcome the mess-ups experienced by some students.

Each of the course descriptions below includes a metaphor that best represents that person's teaching style. Other styles can allow a teacher to also weave personal experience with course content in a manner that helps students understand themselves and the curriculum better. Other teachers can bring about a clearer awareness of perception, sociocultural embeddedness, embodiment, intersubjectivity, and ambiguity in their teaching. They can also position themselves as a fellow traveler in learning. And they can display a utilitarian approach to teaching specific knowledge and skills without deemphasizing engagement in the lifeworld of the classroom. We believe these qualities of existential phenomenology best influence pedagogy when teachers are open to messing about. We include six teachers and their experiences.

Teaching as Interpretative Dance: Kathy's Synchronous Online Master's Course

I like thinking of my teaching as a form of interpretive dance. Martha Graham, in a letter to Agnes de Mille (as cited in Hava-Robbins, 2002), described the meaning of interpretative dance to her, "There is a vitality, a life force, a quickening that is translated through you into action. . . . Only keep open and aware directly to the urges that motivate you. . . ."

I see myself as a choreographer who uses specific methods to create a dance in which I participate with my students. And this dance that is interpretive based on what my students bring to the course: their background, their beliefs, their relation to learning, their expectations and assumptions in relation to course content, and their emotional engagement with others in the learning community we form together. I tell my students that I don't know how to teach the course until I know what they are thinking. From my perspective, teaching isn't teaching unless it is in sync with student needs within the context of the course.

For many years, I taught master's and doctoral students in educational psychology by assigning readings, asking students to work on individual and group projects, and as we sat where everyone could see the others'

150   *Messing Up and Messing About*

faces, leading class dialogues into which I would weave mini-lectures. I joined students in striving to *listen to be influenced*, to transcend our own, narrower perspectives. I felt I could go deeper into the lifeworld of the classroom. Much of the time, we experienced synergy.

Everything changed when my colleagues and I developed an online master's program. I had the option of teaching my courses in a synchronous or asynchronous format. I found it impossible to dance with my students unless we met together as a learning community—synchronously. I adapted three features of my teaching to this format.

Each class session begins with *check-ins* from all of us. Briefly, we share something going on in our lives that might otherwise distract us from being present in the lifeworld of the class session just beginning. We also become a closer community as we get to know each other beyond our roles as student or teacher, as we learn about our work responsibilities, our families, our values.

After each class session, I ask students to submit *post-class reflections* based on five questions about what they know and want to know now, what helped or hindered their learning, and questions they wanted answered. All students can read and respond to each other's reflections and my replies online. Because I can't clearly read their facial or body cues online, I strive to build relationships as I respond to their reflections. To me this means I must work hard to read between the lines, to ask back, so I can better understand each student's thinking. In the next class, I share a few student quotes from the reflections that provide unique insight into the course and may prove valuable to other students. I elaborate and answer questions. I feel I am dancing with my students.

At the beginning of a course, I create *autonomous small groups* that meet between class sessions to prepare a report for the next class. I give detailed assignments, at times requiring individuals to describe personal experiences that their group will weave with course content when they meet between classes. As groups report during class, I share my insights using a chat feature online. Because of the spontaneous conversations afforded by small groups online, students tell me they feel close to their group members and learn from each other. They also report how their learning is enhanced as they consider the alternative ideas and style used by other small groups when reports are given in class.

While I used these structures in other online courses, I became intrigued by the approach of our case study professor, especially due to the powerful findings of students' experiences of being *free to learn* (see Chapter 5). Hence, I decided to mess about with increasing the free to learn aspect of my approach as I prepared to teach a course about meeting the needs of nontraditional and underachieving learners. I designed the course to engage students in experiencing their own learning needs so they could personally experience learning challenges that might well occur for marginalized learners. I began to mess about as I asked myself: What if I *unassigned* projects? This would mean I would still describe projects that I used to assign, but in this course, everyone would have a choice as to whether they did the projects. Would I lose control? Would class become chaotic and omit important course concepts? Would small groups decide to meet and learn from each other?

To be sure, because of who I am and the program of study for students enrolled in this course, I offered more structure than our case study professor. I gave a survey to help my students understand their own learning needs and to set personal goals for learning course content. I provided suggestions for assignments and small group projects—without requiring students to complete them. I told my students I would provide feedback—as a guide from the side (King, 1993)—based on their requests, but I would not grade their work. Instead, at the conclusion of the course, I asked them to submit a self-assessment and tell me the grade they believed they had earned. I continued the check-ins, small group reports, and post-class reflections. Initially, I felt I might have gone too far as some students expressed anxiety. And it did take time for most students to trust me and sense the freedom to learn. But all participated actively and provided end of course reflections similar to Donna's:

> [Initially] this class put me ill at ease. . . . I was afraid. I didn't get [it]. "Oh, for god sake, please just spoon feed me, I am tired". . . . Then I heard a word, *creative*. . . . Did I hear you correctly, we can be creative? . . . Wow, night after night, it surfaced in my mind. . . . Could I learn my way, at my speed, and pick out what resonated with me, and still pass this class? . . . Intrigued, I trusted, just a bit. I posted a reflection, one that honestly reflected me. And holy cow, it was received, warmly. I was even thanked for contributing. Little by little, I came out of my shell. I began to trust, not just the process, but I started trusting my process. . . . I needed a reminder that learning is freeing. Learning isn't capturing thoughts, and then repeating them. Learning is thinking and creating new ideas that grow into the stories we tell [in order] to mentor others. Learning isn't stagnant. It is a vine that grows . . . up, and sideways, and blossoming blooms that scent the world.

I was amazed as I read final reflections from each student, all sharing in their own words what the course had meant to them—all similar to Donna's reflection, if slightly less poetic. As I reflected, I realized that almost all students completed my "unassigned" small group and individual projects and readings, even though some students/groups changed them to better meet their needs, mostly by enlarging them or doing "extra" work. This experience truly gave me pause in considering the freedom to learn more seriously. For these were not advanced graduate students. Some would have done poorly on the GRE if required for entrance into the

152 *Messing Up and Messing About*

program—and yet almost all have completed the program's rigorous master's requirements and graduated. Most of the other courses in this program are more traditional. But students still tell me this course changed their lives, their understanding of what learning truly means.

Teaching as a Cyberspace Salon: Sandra's Asynchronous Online Doctoral Course

I have been teaching graduate students for 35 years. Over the years, students have described their negative graduate school experiences with vivid figures of speech. Being a phenomenologist, I have been attentive to the metaphors and similes they used to describe their experience: "playing the game," "plowing through," even "slavery" and "torture." They have talked about professors tearing their papers apart, rejecting their ideas, and making them jump through hoops. They have described times of being overwhelmed ("the work never ends . . . more of it coming at me faster and faster"), becoming physically exhausted ("running on fumes"), and actually struggling to survive. *I do not believe graduate school has to be this way* [emphasis added].

I am determined to create a learning environment in my course in which students have a much different, more positive, experience. My challenge is that I must create this learning environment *online*, because I teach in a PhD program that is largely delivered online, *asynchronously*. This mode of course delivery is necessary because my students are working professionals who live all across the USA. When the PhD program transitioned from traditional on-campus seminar classes to online delivery, I was uneasy about my ability to teach well. Gone were the trusty nonverbal clues that students in a classroom are puzzled, bored, or attentively engaged. Yet I learned how to create a "salon" in which rich dialogue among learners takes place via Discussion Board, an open forum for expressing understandings (and misunderstandings) of course content, opinions about assigned readings, and reactions to postings by classmates. In a spirit of sharing, students often post articles, podcasts, links to web sites, or videos that they have discovered. In contrast to some faculty of my acquaintance, I assign no grades to students' posts, so that the climate is entirely safe for free expression, with no onus to post more often (or more loquaciously) to earn points.

Although a seasoned teacher, I simultaneously see myself as a perpetual learner. I take a non-hierarchical stance of humility and openness to what the *students* contribute to our semester together. Influenced both by Merleau-Ponty and by the case study professor, I understand that the students and I are co-creating this course, and all of us will be changed in some way by our interactions.

My course is about qualitative research, but the students know that I am not an evangelist about this type of research. Students are exposed to many qualitative research methodologies through a variety of hands-on experiential activities (e.g., observations, interviews, discourse analysis of a poem). I share my love of phenomenology with them but make it clear that they do not have to like it. I choose a plethora of reading materials, but students are completely free to agree or disagree with the authors of any of the papers (and with me). I hope I exemplify what Paulo Freire said, "I am open, absolutely open, every time to be taught by the students" (as cited in Horton & Freire, 1990, p. 194). My expectation each semester is that students will "teach me something . . . surprise [me] . . . and allow a transformation in both of us" (Merleau-Ponty, as cited in Switzer, 2001, p. 263).

Teaching as Abstract Art: Neil's Undergraduate and Graduate Interdisciplinary Seminar

"Art and Organism" (A&O) is a seminar about the "biology of art and aesthetic experience." In this course, I make extensive use of abstraction in its central sense of selective emphasis on what is most important, often penetrating below the surface of raw stimuli to progressively deeper layers of meaning. For I agree with Gorky, "Abstraction . . . is the emancipation of the mind, it liberates us from the slavery of facts" (as cited in Barcio, 2016).

I believe that the more deeply one goes, the more likely shared meaning can be found, and when that sense is shared in class we can reexamine older ideas and share our understanding of new ones as a group. The depth I seek for us all is emotional as well as scholarly. I believe learning in such an environment is more enduring and ultimately transformative. In this way, new content becomes part of our personal fabric, and all subsequent things are seen in its light.

We begin this journey when I introduce myself by creating a personal mind-map (a spontaneous and intuitive graphic organizer) on the board. I then ask students to create their own during that first class. They are to represent themselves graphically—key turning points in life, interests, family background, etc. I collect them and return them later with brief comments to let them know I am interested in them.

During class I can see myself transitioning from *sage on the stage* to *guide from the side*-like interactions with students (King, 1993). Disciplinary content often includes obscure but highly relevant terms and ideas that are deployed in the service of course content and student-centered concerns. It is intended that the novelty of the terms avoids traditional baggage of meaning and could enable new frameworks for familiar experiences. Much like Coleridge said of Wordsworth, I wanted to arouse them from the lethargy of customary approaches to the world. I seek to push student understanding of the *connectedness* of knowledge and ideas from platitude to living reality.

154 *Messing Up and Messing About*

Student responsibilities are straightforward. At the beginning of each class session, I ask students to orally check in with anything that is on their minds they are willing to share. The focus on course content begins each session with students creating mind-maps related to a key concept that will be of focus during that session (e.g., science or brain). Arguably this is each student's personal definition of that topic and it becomes quickly clear that the same idea means something different to each of us. And, especially when the key concept is a familiar construct, the mind-maps often surprise students. They find layers of meaning and begin to appreciate that different levels have different values for meeting our needs.

The most important assignments are written post-class reflections in which they are to emphasize what they consider stood out from that session. These reflections are handed in, and I respond to each student via email as soon as possible after class. In my response, I request further elaboration, including how their comments might be connected to something else that I suggest they explore, such as a short reading or TED talk or podcast. Often, they initiate a brief discussion related to what they learned during their subsequent check-ins. If someone does not share, I question them about the connections they discovered.

My assessment of student performance is shared by personal, narrative feedback. It occurs in an egalitarian context: when I identify an idea, I urge them to help me find more resources that speak to it, *just as I will provide new resources* to them to help enlarge or extend ideas. While listening to check-ins and assessing responses to my suggested additional resources, I note the level of attention that students are investing. I try to give written feedback at all times (almost always positive) but do not assign a specific letter grade for students' work. Term papers are evaluated but not graded.

After our first experiences with mind-maps, I urge students to tentatively select a personally meaningful idea or experiences or concern that could be the nucleus of a term project. These projects are to be presented as a summary of their explorations and discoveries prior to the end of the semester. On one occasion, I asked each student what theme of several discussed might provide them with a general direction. One woman said in an indifferent manner, "nothing!" My response was, "okay—nothing it is!" She was embarrassed but then I pointed out the critical position of "nothing" in art (e.g., negative space) and science (e.g., vacuum). My point was that every idea is connected if only we have the patience to follow some very circuitous paths, but that the unexpected things we learn along the way may well be worth it.

Teaching as a Balancing Act: Brian's Teacher Education Course

I apply a phenomenological approach to introductory teacher education courses in which I must balance the technical, utilitarian needs of the teacher education program with a desire to instill in students the joys of teaching and learning. Like many higher education programs that provide licensure, teacher education programs are under great scrutiny. But in my course, I attempt to bring students together into the lifeworld of the classroom as they focus on their future as professional educators.

To help bring focus to the lifeworld of the classroom, I model joy: I love sharing my experiences, hearing my students' experiences, stumbling into revelations and unknown worlds that may rest just underneath our everyday awarenesses. Phenomenology has helped me learn to take advantage of potential disruptions that ambiguity, mystery, and contradictions provide. Thanks to the complexity of life, thanks to my students' different bodies and histories, such disruptions are available for teachable moments any time I can take the airplane of the classroom off autopilot. Like good art, everyday classroom moments can inspire reorientations and new ways of seeing because life is taking place as we share within the protection of four walls and a closed door. My students, young people discovering and creating and faking till they're making identities, engage and disengage—they dive deep into concepts like care (Noddings, 1992) and call (Palmer, 2003) but also check their social media. I must see the ways students take on (and fail to take on) the course's typical and atypical essays, projects, and reflections with wide-ranging topics like love in teaching or the official state rubric for teacher evaluation.

I get to know my students through these assignments and activities that highlight student experiences in schools, like prompts that encourage them to discuss a particular classroom or classmate they recall (Rousmaniere, 2000). As they share details with each other about classrooms, assignments, or moments of motivation (or lack thereof), they find our commonalities and build a shared identity as future professional educators who want the schooling experiences of their students to be better than the ones we had.

To build professionalism from where they are, I start with them—the critical moments they remember from an observation of a practicing teacher are the starting points for reaching back into their pasts and connecting to current theories of educational psychology or philosophies that will be their backbone when state policies change throughout their careers.

Students appreciate my enthusiasm, and say as much on course evaluations, but they also frequently wish I provided more direction for them. Long ago Dewey (1935) suggested that teachers in general want to be told what to do, but this is not a problem isolated to teacher education. Asking students to dwell in the classroom, in a concept, with each other, can spark impatience. For every student that deeply appreciates the safe classroom environment, there is another who wishes I lectured more and gave more specific directions. This is an issue I continue to wrestle with as requirements in teacher education change. But I continue to strive for balance, rather than compartmentalization, of utility and the lifeworld of the classroom.

156 *Messing Up and Messing About*

Teaching as a Math Missionary: John's Remedial and Introductory Mathematics and Statistics Courses

I approach my teaching as a math missionary preaching the gospels of learning and mathematics. I refuse to teach as many teach mathematics and statistics. For I agree wholeheartedly with Stephen Strogatz, professor of applied mathematics at Cornell University, who stated, "What we are doing—and the way we are doing it—results in an enormous sector of the population that hates mathematics" (as cited in Lathey, 2014).

Once a math-hater, my recovery has included a changed learning disposition, characterized by a passion for mathematics and learning. As a community college mathematics professor of remedial and introductory non-STEM mathematics and statistics students, it is essential that my enthusiasm for learning and passion for mathematics is evident. Many students arrive anxious and resistant, just like I was. For many if not most of the students their previous, frequently unsuccessful, mathematics experiences were limited to surface learning, memorizing a series of abstract symbols and formulas presented without relevance to everyday life. For the non-math major, it is essential mathematics be made relevant through interdisciplinary connections.

Hoping to spark a desire to learn, I reach back into my own life experience, taking on multiple roles of cruise director, preacher, storyteller, comedian, silent observer, questioner, student, coach, therapist, advocate, and mentor. With a desire to learn, a vast space is opened for empowering a new way of thinking, allowing for the exploration of the world through the beauty and utility of mathematics.

My college, an open-access, commuter, community college, serves urban, suburban, and rural students in southern Appalachia. Although our students are more likely to arrive under-prepared, under-served, and under-supported, they bring a wealth of life experience just waiting to be tapped. Our campus encompasses a wide range of economic statuses. Approximately 60% of entering freshman will need remediation. Class sizes range from 20 to 35. Many students arrive with negative learning dispositions, especially towards mathematics. They believe they do not belong.

My first goal, inspired by a phenomenological attitude, is for students to know they have arrived in a safe and welcoming place where they do belong. Initially, there is an online discussion assignment where students share their mathematics autobiographies, their expectations of their professor, their personal, academic, and professional aspirations, and describe something they are passionate about. As part of the assignment they are to respond to at least two of their classmates, facilitating online student-to-student dialogue. During our initial meeting, I describe my own past, with frequent use of self-deprecating humor, about failing at college three times, and a little about the 26 years in the *school of life* between my third and ultimately successful fourth college attempt. Students begin laughing and gradually anxiety dissipates. One student provided this description of the intersubjectivity of our shared experiences in the course evaluation, "he is able to be empathetic while pushing us at the same time. He urges for us to do well because of his experiences in school."

In keeping with Merleau-Ponty's (1948/2004) concept of embodiment, I remain keenly aware of the relationship between emotions and learning. Goldin (2002) emphasizes that the cognitive demands of mathematical learning cannot be addressed independently of the affective demands. Several students have stated in their course evaluation that they came in expecting to struggle. Here a student describes how the presentation of course content resulted in a changed mathematical disposition.

> I loved hearing all of his personal examples relating to problems worked in class. I don't like math, but he made it enjoyable and made it to where I wanted to come to class and not miss. He was very encouraging throughout the semester and it was obvious he cared for the success of students.

During the first class, I deputize all students as co-teachers, explaining they will learn more from each other than from me. I position myself as another learner among learners. A student describes his role as a co-teacher this way: "I have become so confident in math since taking a course with Dr. Smith! I rarely have to ask questions anymore and when other students need help I jump in. Something I never would have done before."

In my statistics courses, I begin with an online discussion prompt, "What does it mean to be an informed consumer of statistics?" The students have many different perspectives on this question, which allows for critical reflection regarding preconceived notions, prejudices, and biases resulting from their varied sociocultural backgrounds. This recognition opens a space to explore the ambiguity that is always present in the torrent of information and misinformation bombarding today's students. Watt (1957) reminds us not to put our "faith in what statistics say until you have carefully considered what they do not say" (p. 382). From this opening concept, our exploration of statistics as one way of knowing, among multiple ways of knowing, begins.

Teaching as Getting Comfortable in the Discomfort: Lauren's Doctoral Required Research Course

My course is an introduction to qualitative research (Moret, 2018). I am able to limit class size to 15. We meet for 3 hours over a 15-week semester. As a former K-12 teacher from a large, metropolitan, public school system, I have practiced several techniques to engage learners at

158 *Messing Up and Messing About*

varying levels of background knowledge within the same classroom setting, including scaffolding of content using game playing, varying pedagogical and media methods, etc. I have found the tools that work for K-12 students also work for adult learners!

I believe adult learners need support and a little excitement to sustain and thrive in their doctoral studies. When considering qualitative research concepts like positionality or data coding, I ask myself, "How might I engage PhD students to learn more about these aspects of qualitative research?" While I could share definitions and peer-reviewed reading sources, I find I can engage with my students more deeply by having them consider their own subjectivities as results of their life experiences. We use music and poetry, create art and collage, and consider the ways in which personal experiences from life have influenced how and why we are sitting in the room with one another on this day. Activities culminate in a formal paper that becomes a living document, meant to be updated by the student throughout their time as a doctoral student, ultimately making its way to the dissertation document as a PhD candidate. This assignment is meaningful and directly connected to the student personally, while also serving practically as an early draft for a section of the student's dissertation.

Dialogue is paramount in our classroom. The semester begins with students responding to a questionnaire about their prior experience with related content, special interest in theorists and dissertation focus, and anything about how they learn that they want me to know. This leads us next into answering some simple questions about the work we do. I ask students: "What interests you about your work/content area? Tell me about a time when you had an experience with . . . (blank). What do you know to be true about . . . (blank)? What has influenced you in your life to make you want to know more about . . . (blank)?" These questions provide an entryway for students to examine their own subjectivities and onto-epistemological leanings. I believe it is important to have the students understand where they are and examine how they got here before moving forward.

At this point, things usually get a little uncomfortable for students. I've been asked in the past, "What do you mean I have to think about my personal past in order to professionally move ahead?" I tell them, when we understand our foundation, we can begin to uncover more about what we think we see in our studies ahead, including any presuppositions and assumptions we hold about the work and anyone else involved in the research context.

As a result of participating in the class, students transform how they see their content of interest and the ways in which they may approach understanding it further. One student shared:

> You made me constantly question my decisions, until the point I feel comfortable enough to defend them. And even then, humble enough

to doubt them. If I cannot defend my coding choices, most likely, I need to give them more thought and go back step by step, until I can defend the entire road.

For some students, the class helped them to work through notions of uncertainty common when taking on qualitative research. Another student offered, "This course has been one of the most important courses I took through my academic journey and for sure it made me a much better qualitative researcher and a much more reflexive person." For yet another student, the class contributed positively to their research learning and their personal life.

> And your class, especially, has provided me continuous opportunities for growth. Besides making me fall even more in love with QUAL work and philosophies, I have learned even more about the value in the practice of reflexivity, both professionally and personally. Through our personal correspondences, your lectures, readings and assignments (including the weekly journal), I have been better able to process, make connections, and seek balance, which then helps me to stay focused . . . even when overwhelmed. It's a beautiful mess I'm in.

The semester brings them to a place where they understand that it is okay not to know the answer to every question; it is okay to say "I don't know," or "it depends"; it is important to be mindful of assumptions and try to keep them in check throughout the duration of a project by continually bracketing or bridling beliefs. And finally, it is important to have fun.

Some Conclusions From a Phenomenological Perspective

Based on the experiences of students and teachers shared in this chapter, we gained more insight about the phenomenological heart of teaching and learning. In the studies of African American, International, and LSES/first-generation students, our findings revealed that the lifeworld of the classroom was the ground from which aspects of perception stood out to these students. Although asked open-ended questions about their experience, they chose to focus on *being* students rather than their success or failure in mastering specific course content. And it seems when teachers are on autopilot, as Brian put it in his description, there is much more likelihood of messing up. To go to the heart of teaching and learning there has to be an authentic connection between teacher and students.

Our six teachers have explored existential phenomenology in-depth. The majority of us took the case study professor's course, analyzed our extensive data, and/or are authors of this book. But not one of us attempts to clone the professor's improvisational jazz approach. Rather, our intentions as we teach are influenced by our own awareness of our inner landscapes, our own sociocultural embeddedness—of our personal and professional lives and, our own intentionality related to a phenomenological attitude. Likewise, our understanding of existential phenomenology has increased our awareness of the lifeworld of the classroom in all its fluidity and situated context. We have become more sensitive to the primacy of perception for ourselves and our students as we naturally seek to find meaning in this world, especially that of our course content. Our descriptions serve as examples of the variety of ways a teacher can use this approach in multiple types of courses with widely varying students, including graduate and undergraduate courses, face to face and online, and in fields such as teacher education, educational psychology, mathematics and statistics, and interdisciplinary upper level courses. Our experiences lead us to believe a phenomenological approach has and could be used in all kinds of settings with all kinds of learners.

Research findings of our case study as well as those included in this chapter consistently revealed that intersubjectivity stands out to students. Sadly, the findings we reported in this chapter illustrated the dominance of students' struggles with teachers who messed up by not striving to establish positive intersubjectivity with their students. All of the first-person descriptions included in this chapter demonstrate student participants' need for community, a need for a sense of belonging with their teachers and other students. Indeed, a need for attention to the lifeworld of the classroom.

Our six teachers highlighted the ways in which they intentionally strived to build positive relationships with and among students. For example, Brian and Sandra described how they work to form a learning community in the classroom. John focused on his need to connect with students through sharing in a humorous manner his own academic struggles. When teachers' and students' intentionality regarding intersubjectivity is strong, the lifeworld of the classroom is full of teachable moments.

To be sure, some teachers, especially in higher education, even including some teaching preparatory courses in community colleges, believe that their role does not include attention to the lifeworld of the classroom. We wholeheartedly disagree—for intersubjectivity influences all teaching and learning. We believe the case study professor as well as the six teachers in this chapter clearly display their skill in developing positive relations with and across students.

All student participants shared their experiences through their sociocultural embeddedness and embodiment. As with all humans, it is difficult to reflect on these influences because they determine who we are. In the case of these research participants, however, they stood out in the lifeworld of their classrooms because they were marginalized—as African American, non-native speakers, or LSES college students. They all too well recognized how they did not meet the sociocultural embeddedness expectations of their teachers and of other students.

Our six teachers shared how they attempted to overcome their own and students' embeddedness. For example, Kathy and Neil described their use of check-ins to help break down stereotypes and help all class participants get to know each other beyond their roles as student or teacher. Lauren described her clear focus on students grappling with their epistemologies as researchers. And Sandra described how her students used Discussion Board for sharing of knowledge and resources as well as confusion.

Embodiment was also figural for student research participants. International students described their discomfort when unable to express their thoughts clearly in English. LSES/first-generation students described frustration in not knowing the hidden rules of higher education. African American students felt invisible or hyper-visible in the classroom. These embodied feelings appeared to interfere with their learning or at least influenced their sense of intersubjectivity in a negative manner.

Our teachers described their own and their students' sense of embodiment in relation to their teaching. For example, Neil described his responses to students intended to provoke them to move through a challenge to realization. Sandra shared metaphors of negative experiences her students shared about graduate school. Lauren and John both spoke of the need to make class fun in order to overcome negative embodiment of students uncomfortable with course content. And yet, when teachers feel committed or forced to focus on the utilitarian aspects of the course content, then embodiment can be ignored. The focus, instead, can be solely on getting students to memorize and use abstract knowledge or related skills.

Donna, a student in Kathy's course, described her initial desire to be told what to do, what to learn (or memorize). Brian and Lauren discussed the impatience some students expressed when asked to reflect on their personal experience in relation to course content, rather than attempt to absorb concepts and complete assignments with minimal exploration of their own thinking. This is a common reaction in students primarily exposed to a traditional lecture, test, and/or projects approach to higher education. Students are often indoctrinated with an attitude to learn the one-right-answer to course content, which may include even in more ambiguous fields an assumption of the teacher that students should accept their sole opinion. This approach ignores the ambiguity of humans' experience of the world. How much better would it be to help students enjoy the mystery in our experience of the world? How much better to learn from the multiple perspectives of experts as well as all participants in the classroom? Kathy noted this in her description of students enjoying the different perspectives across group reports—and the learning that came from broadening their perspectives. And Neil noted the surprise students felt when their intuitive mind-maps revealed multiple meanings across class participants.

Our teachers spoke of their reliance on description in their teaching. John described the stories he tells students about his own experiences as a learner. Kathy shared her request for student descriptions of their personal use or struggle with specific learning strategies. Neil talked of his use of post-class reflections to encourage students to describe connections to related resources he assigned them.

162 *Messing Up and Messing About*

Underneath the descriptions provided by each of our teachers is a quality of messing about to acknowledge and encompass a phenomenological approach—realizing that mess-ups may occur but can be better identified when paying attention to teaching and learning from a phenomenological perspective. And messing about includes a fluid approach to the lifeworld of the classroom. John, Lauren, and Brian described this is in the manner in which they interact with their students. Kathy shared her in-depth, personal response to every student's post-class reflections. These are examples of the connoisseurship of teaching—of the art of teaching that is just as important as the science. And, they reflect the phenomenological heart of teaching and learning.

Readers of this book may find their approach to teaching confirmed, at least in some respects. We believe a more explicit understanding of implications of existential phenomenology for teaching and learning can stimulate an attitude to mess about, to go further in honoring the lifeworld of the classroom. In Chapter 9, we discuss in detail these implications and provide a framework that teachers can use to explore and perhaps refine their own, individualized approach. We compare and contrast our phenomenological approach with other pedagogy recommended for higher education.

9 Contributions of Our Existential Phenomenological Approach to Higher Education Pedagogy

Implications for Theory, Research, and Practice

> To know psychology, therefore, is absolutely no guarantee that we shall be good teachers. To advance that result, we must have an additional endowment altogether, a happy tact and ingenuity to tell us what definite things to say and do when the [student] is before us. That ingenuity in meeting and pursuing the [student], that tact for the concrete situation, though they are the alpha and omega of the teacher's art, are things to which psychology cannot help us in the least.
>
> (William James, 1899/2006, p. 8)

William James' words from his well-known *Talks to Teachers* speak across many years to bolster our understanding of the interrelationship between the art and science of teaching. Since his time, a complex field of research and theory about teaching and learning has emerged that reaches beyond psychology to include other perspectives. And often experts in these fields claim that effective teaching is possible only through explicit knowledge based on practical know-how and scientific theory, which Bereiter (2014) called principled practical knowledge. To be sure, James (1899/2006) saw value in these sciences as guidelines, to be used at equal value with ingenuity and tact:

> teaching is an art; and sciences never generate arts directly out of themselves. An intermediary inventive mind must make the application by using its originality. . . . The most such sciences can do is to help us to catch ourselves up and check ourselves.
>
> (p. 7)

We contend that when pedagogical recommendations dictate rules and techniques assuming the superiority of their form of knowing, they go too far.

A phenomenological approach helps us as teachers achieve balance in our focus on the utilitarian role of higher education teaching. For we are increasingly called to be more accountable in using researched-based

164   *Contributions to Higher Education Pedagogy*

practices (e.g., learner-centered, active learning, experiential methods) that replace the traditional lecture/test approach to teaching (Fink, 2013). Fink acknowledges that most higher education teachers have a limited understanding of the science of pedagogy. As teachers are encouraged to adopt trendy methods and techniques, they may begin to doubt the value of their intuitive way of teaching. But only by honoring the lifeworld of the classroom can a teacher determine "what to say and do" when with students, they craft teachable moments. And that is exactly where a phenomenological approach has tremendous value—for it informs the art of teaching. It provides a framework through which teachers can reflect on their teaching in relation to students learning and have some guidelines to help determine what is best in the moment. In writing this book, we have drawn lines from philosophy as applied theoretically to education, research, and practice with the goal of becoming aware of the lifeworld of the classroom and how it connects to teaching and learning abstract knowledge in higher education.

We believe the art of teaching is manifest in the all-important, in-the-moment decisions effective teachers make as they sensitively, intuitively, and creatively engage with students around the course content within the lifeworld of the classroom. To be clear, we are not suggesting that intuition replaces critical reasoning. Rather, we believe that teachers and students can reason better when open to curiosity about the world, when open to alternative views, when engaged in exploring their intuitive assumptions. By weaving personal experience with course content, the goal of deep thinking is furthered.

Indeed, we believe the phenomenological approach we developed throughout this text informs the "tact and ingenuity" of the art of teaching. Our case study findings provided a vivid account of the professor's approach in planning, his description of the improvisational jazz style while teaching, and his enactment of his intent. The reciprocal experiences of his students reveal what stood out for them: a freedom to learn, the significance of their experience of other students, and how they transcended the classroom in transformative ways both personal and professional. Further, the experiences of students who felt their teachers messed up provided insight into the meaning of the lifeworld of the classroom. The six course descriptions, direct expressions of first-person experiences, provided insight into other styles of a phenomenological approach in a variety of fields of study. And the connections to existential phenomenology helped us present a cohesive picture of these experiences.

We want to be clear that some or even many teachers in higher education display a phenomenological attitude as part of their art of teaching—at least certain aspects of this attitude. They will read many of our comments and think, "but that is what I do!" And many teachers are on the verge of this approach, lacking only a modest infusion of encouragement and guidelines. But we also agree with Merleau-Ponty (1948/2004) that perception is often "unknown territory" (p. 39) unless one becomes explicitly aware of its significance. And our aim has been to further a more explicit awareness of the primacy of perception in teaching and learning—the influences of embodiment, sociocultural embeddedness, intersubjectivity, and ambiguity—as they relate to perception and intentionality in the lifeworld of the classroom. We believe our phenomenological approach can enrich the phenomenological attitude of any teacher in any field of study teaching any level of students, perhaps especially in higher education.

Our approach is NOT a set of steps, techniques, activities, lecturing styles, or types of assessment. Rather, we seek to make explicit certain implicit aspects of existential phenomenology that, through a phenomenological attitude, can open teachers and students to the lifeworld they share through intersubjectivity, but also experience individually. Together, teacher and students can go to the phenomenological heart of teaching and learning—and the lifeworld of the classroom can come alive.

In this chapter, we first share principles of our phenomenological approach, based on the aspects of existential phenomenology and implications from our research findings that we have discussed throughout the text. Then, we compare and contrast our approach to other higher education approaches for teaching and/or learning that are currently receiving popular attention or are particularly interesting for purposes of comparison—including other phenomenological approaches. We also include several implications for research of teaching and learning that are drawn from our research findings.

Principles of the Phenomenological Heart of Teaching and Learning

We have derived several principles, represented in Table 9.1, from two sources. The first is existential phenomenological ideas that stood out to us, including the phenomenological attitude, the underlying importance of the lifeworld, and the influences on perception and intentionality of sociocultural embeddedness, embodiment, intersubjectivity, and ambiguity (see Chapter 1 and Table 1.2). The second source includes implications from our extensive case study about the first-person experiences of the professor and his students, related research, additional first-person studies of students' experiences of learning, and our personal reflections as we wrote this book. Together, they allowed us to develop a more detailed approach than shared in current literature.

Our principles focus on key aspects of existential phenomenology as they inform the phenomenological heart of teaching and learning. Based on theory and our research findings, the suggestions we include with each principle are open to individual, intuitive, approaches of teachers as they decide what to do and say within the relational context of the classroom.

166 *Contributions to Higher Education Pedagogy*

Table 9.1 Principles at the Phenomenological Heart of Teaching and Learning*

Cultivate a Phenomenological Attitude

1. Increase awareness of your unique, intuitive tact and ingenuity in your teaching. Consider how to honor your *intentionality* and help students understand what *you* are *about* in the lifeworld of the classroom.
2. Realize the *primacy of perception* in the meaning each person finds in the world of course content.
3. Consider how empathy can help you and your students suspend assumptions and broaden perspectives that *sociocultural embeddedness* and *embodiment* would otherwise narrow.

Weave Personal Experience with Course Content

4. *Launch students into the world of course content* by describing your own experiences or those of others (including well-known experts) as they relate to important concepts. When possible, ask students to share their relevant experiences.
5. Help students understand course content at a deeper level by encouraging them to describe personal experiences or examples related to their confusion, misconceptions, or questions —and then elaborate or provide explanations as needed.
6. Consider how to create awareness of assumptions and biases that are often revealed through what stands out in descriptions of experience and then weave this insight with course content.

Adopt an Egalitarian Stance

7. Be open to the *ambiguity* that exists in all course content as well as in communication with others. Consider ways to join with students in making space for alternative views and the mystery of the world in relation to course content beyond *facts*.
8. Become aware of *intersubjectivity*, especially the fellowship created by shared experiences within a class learning community in which student perspectives are as relevant as the teachers.
9. Consider how to provide safety while also challenging students, making space for playfulness, risk-taking, and the rewards of being open to greater freedom.

Be Open to Transcending Course Content

10. *Balance a utilitarian focus* on knowledge, skills, and career goals, with the wonder and mystery of course content in the world. Consider how to make time to explore the *meaning* of abstract knowledge in your and students' lives.
11. Prepare in advance some open, provocative questions that you might weave into the conversation to help students explore meaning at a deeper level beyond the immediate focus.

*See Chapter 1 for explanations of terms.

Our case study professor and six other teachers who shared their phenomenological approaches suggest that these principles can guide teaching of course content, face to face and online, in many fields of study and with students at various levels of preparedness. The case study student participants' experiences suggest their learning was transformative as

Contributions to Higher Education Pedagogy   167

evidenced by their realizations and the ways in which they transcended course content through its integration into their personal and professional lives, often suddenly and with striking clarity: the transformative learning experience. Indeed, we believe the principles included here can help teachers create an environment that enables teachable moments.

These principles reflect the phenomenological attitude described in the literature by various authors about their phenomenological approaches to teaching in higher education courses. It was interesting for us to find only one study (Hultgren, 1987) that focused on using a phenomenological approach in a higher education course that did not have phenomenology as its main subject matter. There is a lack of literature about using a phenomenological approach in a variety of fields of study in higher education. To be sure, many have written about a phenomenological approach in teaching children and youth (e.g., Friesen, Henriksson, & Saevi, 2012; van Manen, 2017). Indeed, Max van Manen (1991, 2014) has shared a vast and valuable body of literature about pedagogical tact focused on how teachers of children and youth can use his approach when considering their teaching, and other works about phenomenological research and reflection. Here we limit our discussion to six articles about approaches reported by higher education teachers when teaching phenomenological methodology—a course similar to that of our case study.

Other Phenomenological Approaches to Teaching

According to Franklin (2013), Hultgren (1995) provided "one of the most comprehensive accounts of instructional planning" from a phenomenological perspective. Within it, Hultgren carefully built on Heideggerian principles of care, dwelling, and becoming to craft a unique seminar in phenomenology for graduate students of education. Her focus, "letting learn," echoes with the kind of freedom described by the participants in our studies that experienced a phenomenological approach. In an earlier article (Hultgren, 1987), she described her approach in a teacher education course, designed with a "phenomenological framework for student teachers." Through it she reveals the openness, vulnerability, and potential for seeing with new eyes that a phenomenological attitude can bring.

We see similarities between her approach and our own, especially in the importance of reflection and how personal experience was woven with the content of the course. However, the primary sharing of personal experiences occurred in Hultgren's course through students' personal, written journaling. In our case study and descriptions provided by other teachers using our approach, personal experience was woven into course content in a manner where all could benefit from others' perceptions and the synergy of learning from other students' experiences and ideas (see Chapters 6 and 8). Hultgren addressed intentionality and perception without mentioning them specifically. Neither did she focus on the power of intersubjectivity

168　*Contributions to Higher Education Pedagogy*

evident in her small cohort's journals. Journaling, as we described it in Chapter 2, is at a particular level of organization as students externalize their inmost thoughts. Along the trajectory that private thoughts take toward intersubjectivity, they undergo successive modifications and their meaning may even change.

Halling, whose phenomenological methods revolve around dialogue (Halling & Leifer, 1991), was more explicit about the ways in which student sharing of experiences can build intersubjectivity. Halling (2012) described his experience in teaching two courses, one an advanced undergraduate and the other a graduate course, both focused on phenomenological research methods. He highlights experience, "not only to what the research students do to get experience, but also to our *collective* [emphasis added] reflection on experience as a source of understanding" (Halling, 2012, p. 1).

Halling (2012) recounted an example of the tendency, even in small groups, for students to want to move quickly into explanations instead of sticking with experience, to jump to theory and avoid exploring experience. As discussed in Chapter 2, we have powerful inborn biases to seek explanations even before all the facts are known. Halling (2012) reported that he uses personal stories to help students get at experience and its power to be both idiosyncratic and universal, an excellent introduction to the tension that accompanies the competing developmental processes of individuation and socialization. Empathy is a key element in Halling's approach along with trust, as he has students discuss personal stories. We see similarities between our approach and Halling's, especially in his engagement of students in sharing personal experiences. Like Hultgren, he displayed a phenomenological attitude similar to our expression of it within our teachers' descriptions (see Chapter 8) and that of our case study professor (see Chapter 3). But like Hultgren, he is not explicit in discussing intentionality or perception and their role in human experience.

Churchill (2012) did explicitly discuss perception as a key element of his phenomenological approach to teaching higher education courses in which the subject matter is phenomenology. His main focus appeared to be on the value of personal experience in opening students to broader perspectives of the world, especially "an empathic presence to the world" (p. 3) as well as on how perception can lead students to new worlds. Like our case study professor, Churchill (2012) strived to embody phenomenological constructs of course content through personal experiences that emphasize the process and help students connect at a deep level. This included for him a focus on an empathic approach to learning from the experiences of others through what he calls "second person perspectivity." Although he uses different language for some phenomenological constructs and describes specific activities that provided first-person experiences for students (trips to the museum or zoo), his phenomenological attitude is also similar to our case study professor's. And his descriptions of student experiences are similarly transformative, if brief. He did not share student experiences in their own words, so we can deduce little about their learning experiences.

Adams and van Manen (2017) described their year-long seminar for teachers on phenomenological methodology. The seminar included numerous philosophical readings, lectures, writing exercises and completion of a publishable research paper by each student. Like our authors (including our case study professor), they reported their focus on helping students develop a phenomenological attitude, one that can't be learned through step-by-step procedures. They concluded that the seminar, for students and teachers, "grants inceptual understandings of the nature of being and becoming human in our increasingly commercial, distracted, and conflicted world" (Adams & van Manen, 2017, p. 781). We find many similarities with our case study even though they engaged students in activities far removed from the classroom, unlike in our case study where the majority of experiential activities were limited to the classroom. (We should note that the case study professor asked students to bring their out-of-class experiences of doing assigned readings into the on-campus seminars by marking the passages to share that "sang" to them personally.)

A major difference was the requirement by Adams and van Manen (2017) of a publishable paper, a demonstration of skills mastery. We agree that phenomenological research can only be learned at a deep level through engaging in the process, and this assignment appeared to provide that opportunity. What we do not know is whether there was a difference in their students' sense of freedom, so powerful for our case study student participants, which they reported as being due in large part to the lack of required activities beyond reading and engaging in dialogue in the weekly seminars.

Selvi (2008) identified similar issues in education to the ones we describe in Chapter 1, particularly that schooling divides abstract knowledge from individual experience. Her focus in phenomenology was on the individual—individual perception, imagining, and creativity. She noted that "phenomenological pedagogy" can help "learning and teaching by emphasizing [teachers' and students'] unique individualities" (p. 42). The possibilities imaginable in explicating this statement are not reached in the article, but she pointed to the potential for self-actualization. Although this author alluded to intersubjectivity briefly, our approach is much more focused on the lifeworld in which teachers and students find themselves.

Selvi (2008) presented four studies in which "phenomenological pedagogy" was researched in both elementary and higher education settings. No specifications for inclusion criteria are given, and *how* the participating teachers qualified their teaching as phenomenological was unclear, save for an example from Moustakas (1994). Her conclusions included a list of specific techniques that are often discussed in other phenomenological

170 *Contributions to Higher Education Pedagogy*

approaches when teaching the methodology of phenomenological research. Items such as "writing about one's experience" and "preparing a research proposal" are representative of the list. Such activities, in our view, are never *essentially* phenomenological, particularly if they are included in a course in which the utilitarian attitude dominates the importance of the lifeworld of the classroom.

Barritt, Beekman, Bleeker, and Mulderij (1984) shared the ways in which they taught writing and analyzing phenomenological descriptions in a seminar on phenomenological research. To do so, they presented a series of descriptions and explicated how the process of analysis should proceed in a group setting. They explored the ways in which descriptions of "being afraid in the dark" can be analyzed to illuminate the meaning of the phenomenon. They included ideas for the implementation of their findings. In concert with our approach, they presented a teaching method that focuses on the *doing* of phenomenology as an essential complement to the *reading* of phenomenological philosophy. Their course, however, appeared to focus mostly on phenomenology as a research method, while our case study course was focused more on understanding phenomenology as a way of being-in-the-world.

Our case study research findings support the reports by other authors discussed above while also providing in-depth empirical data. Our study of the case study professor's planning (see Chapter 3) revealed his phenomenological attitude, even to his frequent proclamation, "But I'm a phenomenologist!" Further, his description of what to say and do while with students provided clear evidence of his phenomenological approach in teaching, as did the transcribed episodes of classroom conversations (see Chapter 4). He shared the same ontological orientation as described by the teachers in the articles discussed above.

These six reports are congruent with our findings that teachers displaying a phenomenological attitude can design courses with unique activities, a degree of dialogue vs. lecture, and readings that result in similar experiences of deeper and broader understanding of the lifeworld. What they did not include was formalized research of the transformative learning of their students; they included only anecdotal information. And, unlike our intent in this book, these authors did not discuss the use of a phenomenological approach in teaching content other than how to conduct phenomenological research, with the exception of Hultgren (1987). Finally, none of these authors, aside from Hultgren (1995), described how they planned their teaching.

Clearly, more research is needed on the use of a phenomenological approach when teaching courses with content focused on subject matter in a variety of fields of study in higher education. Our six course descriptions included in Chapter 8 provide a beginning, and yet are first-person accounts without rigorous interpretation by researchers. And with the exception of Smith (2016), like the authors reviewed above, the course descriptions include only anecdotal information about students' experiences. We need to know much more about the reciprocal relation between teacher and student experiences in such courses.

But how should we consider phenomenological approaches to teaching and learning in relation to other pedagogical methods recommended in the popular literature for higher education teachers? We consider this next.

Relating a Phenomenological Approach With Higher Education Pedagogy

Readers may have noticed that we avoided using the term *pedagogy* in discussing our phenomenological approach throughout this text. As stated above, we believe our approach can enrich pedagogy, not replace it. For we focus on the intuitive and spontaneous lifeworlds of the teacher and student together, of being-in-the-world of the given teachable moment that leads to transformative learning—where the sensitive, mindful, human art of teaching occurs. It is a microcosm of what to do and say—or encourage students to engage in—within the fluid context of classroom learning and the activities that take place during class sessions. Our approach is focused on various aspects of the phenomenological heart of teaching and learning. In contrast, pedagogical approaches focus on methods or practices that can further learning outcomes in a given course or field of study. Most evidence-based practices are derived from learning theories.

For a comprehensive overview of "intended learning outcomes, ways of learning (origins and theory), and common methods" (p. 38), we refer the reader to Davis and Arend's (2013) *Facilitating Seven Ways of Learning*. These authors organize the majority of learning theories discussed in pedagogical literature in a useful manner and call them *ways of learning*: behavioral learning, cognitive learning, learning through inquiry, learning with mental models, learning through groups and teams, learning through virtual realities, and experiential learning.

One pedagogical approach David and Arend omit is that of social constructivism (Driscoll, 2005). Ideas related to the social construction of knowledge focus on the benefits and needs of learning and development that rely on interactions with others, especially Vygotsky's (1980) sociohistorical theory in which he describes the need for more knowledgeable others to help individuals learn and ultimately develop cognitive processes. Social constructivism may be seen by some as an appropriate umbrella for a phenomenological approach, but we believe phenomenology *enriches* social constructivist methods. For example, if a teacher provides opportunity for collaborative learning, a phenomenological approach can help students become more aware of perceptual influences on their understanding of course content and related personal experiences. And that leads to an approach to education most closely aligned with a phenomenological approach in its goals for learning and attention to the lifeworld of the classroom.

172　*Contributions to Higher Education Pedagogy*

We focus here on four types of higher education pedagogy that encompass many of the recommendations for higher education teaching and learning: acquisition of knowledge through cognitive learning, experiential learning, especially that informed by neuroscience research, learner-centered approaches, and contemplative education. With each of these approaches to pedagogy, we discuss the relation of our phenomenological approach and findings from our research.

Acquisition of Knowledge Through Cognitive Learning

This field of study has received a great amount of attention in the literature due to increasing demands on higher education to produce well qualified workers for today's world (Fink, 2013), as well as its carefully researched methods (Ambrose, Bridges, DiPietro, Lovett, & Norman, 2010). We will describe these practices based on the Ambrose et al. (2010) text *How Learning Works: 7 Researched-based Principles for Smart Teaching*, because these authors carefully link a comprehensive discussion of pedagogical practices to research in cognitive learning. We include this area of pedagogical literature particularly because of its explicit emphasis on the utilitarian goal of student mastery of knowledge and skills related to course content.

These authors provide a clear overview of theoretical literature and research from the field of cognitive learning regarding the following: how students use and organize prior and new knowledge, what factors motivate students to learn, how students develop mastery, what kinds of practice and feedback enhance learning, why student development and course climate matter for student learning, and how students become self-directed learners. It is interesting to compare and contrast their perspective with a phenomenological point of view. We provide two examples.

In a chapter focused on their principle, "Students' current level of development interacts with the social, emotional, and intellectual climate of the course to impact learning" (Ambrose et al., 2010, p. 6), they describe a situation in which students became upset with each other as they discussed issues around illegal immigration. The authors use this situation to focus on how young college students are "still developing the full range of social and emotional skills" (p. 156). They conclude, "these emotions can overwhelm students' intellect if they have not yet learned to channel them productively" (p. 157). From our perspective, the importance they place on student emotional development is almost exclusively focused on "shaping the classroom climate in developmentally appropriate ways" (p. 157) to improve learning performance. A teacher using a phenomenologically oriented approach would instead facilitate students' understanding of the lifeworld within the given context—helping students to develop awareness of ways they can contribute to a positive and yet challenging classroom climate.

The outcomes-focused approach of Ambrose et al. (2010), in our view, encourages teachers to move students too quickly past alternative perspectives and "get down to business." As our research indicates, a teacher with a phenomenological attitude can better know what to say and do to foster a climate of freedom to learn from and with others, even in such challenging moments.

Ambrose et al. (2010) suggest various strategies to facilitate transfer. For example, their strategies include "Give students opportunities to apply skills or knowledge" (p. 117) and "specify skills or knowledge and ask students to identify contexts in which they apply" (p. 119). These strategies could include a phenomenological approach if a teacher guided students to connect experience to knowledge and skills. But with a utilitarian focus, it is more likely the strategies they recommend will become assignments in which the awe and wonder of the phenomenological attitude is ignored.

In Chapter 7 we discuss the case study students' experiences in which they integrated course content in their personal and professional lives *without any attempt to use* Ambrose et al. *strategies* by their professor. Instead, there were many experiences shared in class that were examples of how some course concept related to students' professional fields of study or personal life. The "strategies" emerged from the descriptions.

Some additional strategies they recommend (Ambrose et al., 2010, pp. 180–186) resemble a phenomenological approach. Two suggestions speak to ambiguity: "make uncertainty safe" (p. 180) and "resist a single right answer" (p. 181). They also focus on sociocultural embeddedness with strategies such as "examine your assumptions about students" (p. 181) and "do not ask students to speak for an entire (ethnic) group" (p. 182). Intersubjectivity is alluded to through strategies such as "address tensions early" (p. 185) and "facilitate active listening" (p. 186). But we find the *utilitarian* focus may overwhelm the lifeworld of the classroom, deflating the phenomenological attitude of teachers and students. Based on our research, it appears that an intent to use a phenomenological approach can lead to mastery of course content (based on students' reports of transformative learning) without the need for cognitive learning strategies-at least for our student participants.

While some cognitive learning experts emphasize the role of experience in learning, a specific pedagogy of experiential learning, grounded in neuroscience and brain research, exists in the literature. We discuss these practices next.

Experiential Learning and Neuroscience Research

While Davis and Arend (2013) caution against "the tendency to overreach the evidence with elaborate theories and unwarranted conclusions" (p. 257), they derived a number of principles from neuroscience research we believe warrant discussion. These principles are similar to those discussed by other

174　*Contributions to Higher Education Pedagogy*

authors, including Taylor and Marienau (2016). We summarize those we find most applicable to our phenomenological approach. According to Davis and Arend (2013), neuroscience research can be cautiously applied in pedagogy based on the following: learning grows out of experience; is active, multisensory, iterative, spontaneous, and simultaneous; involves making meaning of information; is holistic, and continuous. In contrast, learning is not isolated from experience; is not passive; is not limited to only one sense; is not linear, sequential, the accumulation of information, fragmented, or conclusive (see pp. 256–259). We see support for phenomenological views concerning the lifeworld of the classroom, connection to the world through experience of it, and its potential openness to ambiguity and spontaneous/simultaneous meaning-making that is holistic and continuous.

Interestingly, Davis and Arend (2013) do not directly discuss methods for teaching that incorporate these principles in the day to day life of the classroom. Instead, they focus on a broader set of methods for experiential learning and emphasize "self-discovery and personal growth from real-world experience" that includes reflection, particularly on experiences through "internships, service learning, and study abroad" (p. 243). While we see ways these experiences can be facilitated through a phenomenological approach, we remain focused on the lifeworld of the classroom whether face to face or online.

Taylor and Marienau (2016), however, devote an entire book to methods they connect to implications from brain research for teaching adults. They discuss the brain's internal process of "categorizing and associating new experiences with previous experiences, which is the key to our ability to eventually make conscious meaning" (p. 215). This process allows humans to "revisit and reconsider [experiences], thus gaining the benefit of hindsight when engaging in further learning" (p. 215). Like David and Arend (2013), they focus on self-reflection. Though they discuss provision of teacher feedback, they do not discuss how reflection on experiences can take place during conversations in the classroom, something our approach highlights. For example, our case study research findings could be used to show how the teacher can follow the flow of conversation, weaving experience with course content, while maintaining control that leads to exploration of some important question related to abstract knowledge. With the addition of a phenomenological approach, the methods Taylor and Marienau (2016) recommend might create a powerful synergy in the lifeworld of the classroom.

Learner-Centered Approaches

Approaches that emphasize the need for a more learner-centered focus do not fit neatly into any one theory of learning or body of research (Weimer, 2013). Some are based on cognitive learning practices discussed

Contributions to Higher Education Pedagogy   175

above, and include authors writing about learner-centered approaches, such as Doyle (2011), whose techniques differ from Weimer's. All such approaches draw to some extent on a list of principles of learner-centered teaching developed by a task force of the American Psychological Association (2015). They derived these principles from a huge body of literature related to effective teaching at various levels of learning. Although focused primarily on K-12 education, a number of writers in higher education have incorporated these principles into their approaches. For the purpose of this chapter, we will focus on one of the more comprehensive approaches for higher education, *Learner-Centered Teaching: Five Key Changes to Practice* (Weimer, 2013). A companion guide was written by Blumberg (2017) to assist teachers in personalizing the approach. The practices include (1) function of content as a means of understanding certain aspects of a broader field within the world, (2) role of the instructor to further opportunities for students to actively engage in all aspects of learning, (3) student responsibility for their own learning, including selection of tasks they find helpful, (4) purposes and processes of assessment that go beyond grading and include student peer and self-assessment, and (5) balance of power between teacher and students concerning all aspects of the course.

From a phenomenological perspective, we find these practices can honor the lifeworld of the classroom but that a phenomenological approach can provide guidelines and awareness that further enrich teaching and learning. For example, the case study professor integrated the students' sense of self with the content, literally launching students into the world of the content in all its ambiguity. It would be possible, however, for teachers without this understanding to fall back into presenting some kind of explicit overarching focus that would reduce ambiguity and freedom of thought about it. At the same time, Weimer (2013) and Blumberg's (2017) focus on balance of power shares, potentially, the egalitarian stance that we espouse. However, a phenomenological approach goes further in its assumption that in everyone's experience there is something that can help them grab onto abstract concepts, thus emphasizing the need to follow as well as lead students into exploring personal experience in relation to course content. The case study professor's improvisational jazz style clearly illustrates this egalitarian stance. In addition, our student participants had a powerful sense of their responsibility as shared in their feeling of "freedom to learn." They also felt a responsibility to other students as discussed in Chapter 6, again taking the learner-centered approach farther. Finally, the majority of teachers who use our approach believe in the purpose of authentic assessment, particularly self-assessment. To be sure, the case study professor did not directly assess students or engage them explicitly in self-assessment, yet his students reported transformative learning. Perhaps this indicates a need to reflect deeply on the purposes of assessment in learning and use them with caution and awareness. And it leads us to explore the overlap of our phenomenological approach with contemplative education.

Contemplative Education

Our phenomenological approach is, perhaps, most compatible with the field of contemplative education. Owen-Smith (2018), in a comprehensive overview of the field, states, "Contemplative educators . . . focus on practices of mind and emotion that draw upon the human capacity to know, specifically through stillness, awareness, attention, mindfulness, and reflection" (p. 1). Our phenomenological approach is seldom one of stillness—of prayer, meditation, and silence—but it is mindful all the same as can be seen in our illustrative episodes of classroom conversation. And, our findings suggest similar goals of contemplative education that Owen-Smith (2018) delineates, to "prioritize the transformation of habits of the mind, deepening of attention and insight, understanding of self as influenced by both interiority and exteriority, and commitment to and reflection on the experiential" (pp. 1–2). She shared a categorical list of contemplative practices developed by The Center for Contemplative Mind in Society: "activist (volunteering, bearing witness), creative (journaling, contemplative arts), generative (meditation, visualization), movement (dance, qigong, yoga), relational (dialogue, deep listening, storytelling), ritual or cyclical (retreats, ceremonies), and stillness (quieting the mind, silence)" (Owen-Smith, 2018, p. 25). We contend our phenomenological approach could help teachers better engage students in many of these practices.

Reflection, a practice given some attention in almost every form of pedagogy we reviewed, can become a less meaningful *task* for students when teachers do not understand how to help students develop skills in reflection and engage in it in highly meaningful ways (Owen-Smith, 2018). Contemplative education literature better explains how to help students gain the skills they need. But it can also be seen as it comes to life in research such as ours, through analysis of classroom conversations in which the professor led and followed students into describing personal experience as they reflected on its relationship to their own embodied and embedded knowing. In several of our course descriptions, teachers included reflection as a key practice. Although students engaged in reflection outside of class, our teachers describe how they engaged students through written responses to help them go deeper. According to our research on students' experiences, we infer that those who needed this support were then able to integrate this level of reflection into their personal and professional lives.

Another contemplative practice, listening, is implicit in our phenomenological approach and illustrated through the case study professor's improvisational jazz style of teaching as he listened and, in turn, facilitated students deep listening. Owns-Smith (2018) discusses deep listening as opposed to passive listening, and Berila (2016) emphasizes the need for embodied listening (and reflection), paying attention to the body's sensations and the knowledge available through embodiment. Our authors find the term *listening to be influenced* helpful in overcoming hidden assumptions and biases that can keep one from deep listening.

Our existential phenomenological framework provides a different body of thought related to many of the goals of contemplative education. We find both helpful in honoring the lifeworld of the classroom. Our approach, however, illuminates specifically ways to include the art of teaching in such practices—to know what to do and say in the teachable moment.

Before we conclude this text, we share implications we derived from our case study and related research in higher education. These implications pertain to the field of existential phenomenology but also to the field of teaching and learning in general.

Implications for Higher Education Research

In an effort to honor the ambiguity in our work, we open to exploration of six assumptions related to our findings presented here and their implications for further research. Then, we offer more general implications related to the pedagogy of teaching and learning.

First, **if teaching and learning is a mutual process**, then more research is needed to explore their interrelationships. We hold the belief that all learning encompasses teaching (and all teaching encompasses learning)—even self-learning. In our case study we gathered and analyzed data of the professor and his students' experiences. These results furthered much deeper insight than would be available if we only focused on the teacher or the students. But most educational research is piecemeal, focused on one or more teachers or one or more groups of students. Seldom do researchers study a teacher and his/her students together, especially as their shared lived experiences evolved over an extended period of time.

Second, **if teaching is both an art and a science**, then educational research needs to explore deeply how these aspects of teaching are integrated. The phenomenological approach we developed based on our research, and its relation to existential phenomenology, suggests we are focused more on the intuitive, flexible art of teaching—how to position oneself as a teacher with a phenomenological attitude that honors the lifeworld of each individual student and the class as a whole. We believe that all effective teaching and learning relies on creativity, including intuition and flexibility as well as procedures with demonstrated efficacy. But most educational research addresses the science, related to given theories or research interests, and ignores the art.

Third, **if high quality learning involves *realizing* that goes beyond *knowing* course content**, then we need to explore more fully how this level of

178 *Contributions to Higher Education Pedagogy*

learning develops within students. In our case study, we found that our phenomenological approach led to transformative learning, as our case study student participants transcended the course content in clear and profound ways. They spoke of changing their underlying assumptions and ability to use the abstract knowledge of course content in a creative and flexible manner. The field of transformative learning continues to enlighten our understanding, but the majority of research on pedagogical practices focuses on learning outcomes restricted to mastery of course content.

Fourth, **if one's perceptions affect their understanding of abstract knowledge,** then decisions about higher education pedagogy must foster an awareness of how teachers and learners connect personal experience with course content. We believe that first-person descriptions of the lived experience of teachers and learners enabled us to make better decisions about our phenomenological approach. In this way, the underlying, intuitive beliefs that could have overridden reasoned motives became apparent. For example, while gathering data during our extensive case study, we observed that students consistently shared more after-class written reflections about other students than about the charismatic professor who led the seminar. We enjoyed the unexpected realization that our worldview of teaching and learning did not adequately accommodate the student experience of other students (Sohn, 2016). This led to a new research project to investigate this phenomenon (see Chapter 6). Thus, we reached a broader and clearer understanding of the meaning of the teaching and learning experience occurring in our case study.

Fifth, **if learning outcomes can occur without specified measures,** then it is important to consider multiple ways to study them. In our case study, the professor intentionally refrained from giving students written assignments and used no form of assessment of learning outcomes. And yet, transformational learning was dominant in the first-person experiences reported by our student participants. Students taught by another of our authors indicated similar levels of transformative learning, in a course in which they also were not graded. However, the course differed from the case study in that she *offered* but did not require assignments and provided feedback, but only requested self-assessment of personally set goals by students. These examples suggest the need for further research about freedom in learning. Although there is growing respect for the value of first-person research, there is also value in more clearly defined measures of learning outcomes.

Sixth, **if a phenomenological approach can inform but not dictate the individual style of the teacher,** then we need to better determine its essential qualities. Based on our research of the case study professor, we clearly delineated the qualities of his improvisational jazz style. Further, the descriptions provided by six other higher education teachers indicated a similar phenomenological attitude but with differing styles, from teaching metaphorically depicted as a balancing act, interpretative dance, abstract art, math missionary, cyberspace salon, and getting comfortable in the discomfort. Further research is needed to illuminate other styles and their divergent and convergent elements.

Aside from these six assumptions and their implications for research, we also found several implications for pedagogical practice. A phenomenological approach can be integrated with many pedagogical methods, for it addresses a different need. It is focused on the lifeworld of individuals, teacher and students, in higher education settings—something most practices, except for contemplative education, tend to ignore. As such, it may help alleviate the confusion many higher education teachers feel when pressed to adopt practices that tend to ignore their ongoing art of teaching. Finally, it may help students more easily adapt to new approaches to learning in higher education that honor their lifeworlds and yet reveal a need for deep reflection and how to go about it.

In Conclusion

> If no work is ever absolutely completed and done with, still each creation changes, alters, enlightens, deepens, confirms, exalts, re-creates or creates in advance all the others . . . [Creations] have almost all their life before them.
>
> (Merleau-Ponty, 1964, p. 190)

The years our research team has spent on this project have provided each of us with deep insight, but we do not feel "it is absolutely completed." We remain open to the ambiguity we find in the exploration of the lifeworld of the classroom and the phenomenological heart of teaching and learning. We are in awe of the experience of teaching and of learning. We acknowledge that most authorities in higher education pedagogy do not recognize the need for, or perhaps have no understanding of, the phenomenological attitude. For it is a need long ignored by mainstream views of pedagogy. Owen-Smith (2018) discusses the "legacy of loss" (p. 2) in modern education when this kind of learning experience is ignored. She speaks of the resistance felt by those in her field of contemplative education and also, as she writes, by those involved with the Scholarship of Teaching and Learning (SoTL). And we believe all of us focused on existential phenomenology share this view:

> We are no longer given time and space for imagination, curiosity, and creativity and for the unfolding of what we have always had. The stillness and quiet necessary for thought development and deep intellectual inquiry become nonproductive, a wasting of time, and a squandering of resources. . . . we lose our ability to attend mindfully and to reflect. . . .
>
> (Owen-Smith, 2018, p. 2)

180   *Contributions to Higher Education Pedagogy*

Our students join us in the awe and wonder of making time for contemplation, for describing personal experience in relation to abstract knowledge, for exploring the influences of our sociocultural embeddedness, embodiment, intersubjectivity, and ambiguity on our perceptions and intentionality.

We also take a historical view, in line with Sherman (2014) as he wrote in his text *Refocusing the Self in Higher Education: A Phenomenological Perspective*:

> As we move into the second decade of the twenty-first century, when higher education is under attack from many directions, we need to consider whether the philosophies which have served the academy so far (viz., rationalism, neo-humanism, idealism, pragmatism) are still adequate. We need to consider also whether these philosophies hold the potential to truly unify higher education and render students' experiences meaningful and purposeful. . . . The philosophical developments of phenomenology and post-structuralism which occurred subsequent to these traditionally drawn-upon philosophical schools, do more accurately mirror and account for the conditions of our time.
>
> (p. 70)

We need to heed the call of others who question the push from society to turn higher education towards goals specifically focused on preparation for the workforce—instead of the liberal education of students. In the foreword to Palmer and Zajonc's (2010) *The Heart of Higher Education: A Call to Renewal*, Nepo wrote:

> What you have before you is a thoughtful and grounded invitation to live into the heart of higher education and to deepen our understanding and practice of transformative learning. The magnitude of the issues confronting the world requires whole people with whole minds and hearts to lead us into tomorrow. And that, in turn, requires us to renew the human purpose and meaning at the heart of higher education.
>
> (p. ix)

We invite you the reader to join us in a creation of the phenomenological heart of teaching and learning in higher education.

References

Adams, C., & van Manen, M. A. (2017). Teaching phenomenological research and writing. *Qualitative Health Research*, *27*(6), 780–791.

Adams, H. (2014). Expression. In R. Diprose & J. Reynolds (Eds.), *Merleau-Ponty: Key concepts* (pp. 152–162). New York, NY: Routledge.

Adolphs, R. (2009). The social brain: Neural basis of social knowledge. *Annual Review of Psychology*, *60*, 693–716. doi:10.1146/annurev.psych.60.110707.163514

Allan, E. J., & Madden, M. (2006). Chilly classrooms for female undergraduate students: A question of method? *Journal of Higher Education*, *77*(4), 684–711. doi:10.1353/jhe.2006.0028

Allis, C. D., & Jenuwein, T. (2016). The molecular hallmarks of epigenetic control. *Nature Reviews Genetics*, *17*, 487–500.

Ambrose, S. A., Bridges, M. W., DiPietro, M., Lovett, M. C., & Norman, M. K. (2010). *How learning works: 7 research-based principles for smart teaching*. San Francisco, CA: Jossey-Bass.

American Psychological Association, Coalition for Psychology in Schools and Education. (2015). *Top 20 principles from psychology for preK-12 teaching and learning*. Retrieved from http://www.apa.org/ed/schools/cpse/top-twenty-principles.pdf

Attenborough, F., & Stokoe, E. (2012). Student life; student identity; student experience: Ethnomethodological methods for pedagogical matters. *Psychology Learning and Teaching*, *11*(1), 6–21.

Bach, D. R., & Dolan, R. J. (2012). Knowing how much you don't know: A neural organization of uncertainty estimates (review). *Nature Reviews Neuroscience*, *13*(8), 572–586.

Bakewell, S. (2016). *At the existentialist café: Freedom, being, and apricot cocktails*. New York, NY: Other Press.

Barcio, P. (2016). *How Arshile Gorky discovered abstraction*. Retrieved from www.ideelart.com/magazine/arshile-gorky

Barritt, L., Beekman, T., Bleeker, H., & Mulderij, K. (1984). Analyzing phenomenological descriptions. *Phenomenology and Pedagogy*, *2*(1), 1–17.

Benn, R. (2000). *Exploring widening participation in higher education: Targeting, retention and "really useful knowledge"*. Paper presented at the Seminar presentation, University of South Queensland, Australia.

182 References

Bereiter, C. (2014). Principled practical knowledge: Not a bridge but a ladder. *The Journal of Learning Sciences, 23,* 4–17. doi 10.1080/10508406.2013.812533

Berger, P. L., & Luckmann, T. (1967). *The social construction of reality.* New York, NY: Anchor Books.

Berila, B. (2016). *Integrating mindfulness into anti-oppression pedagogy.* New York, NY: Routledge.

Bickerstaff, S., Barragan, M., & Rucks-Ahidiana, Z. (2012). "I came in unsure of everything": Community college students shifts in confidence. *Community College Research Center, 29*(3), 1–25. Retrieved from http://ccrc.tc.columbia.edu/publications/shifts-in-confidence.html

Biederman, I., & Vessel, E. (2006). Perceptual pleasure and the brain. *American Scientist, 94,* 249–255.

Biggs, J., & Tang, C. (2011). *Teaching for quality learning at university.* Berkshire, England: McGraw-Hill Education.

Blumberg, P. (2017). *Developing learning-centered teaching: A practical guide for faculty.* San Francisco, CA: Jossey-Bass.

Booker, K. C. (2007). Perceptions of classroom belongingness among African American college students. *College Student Journal, 41*(1), 178–186.

Boostrom, R. (1998). "Safe spaces": Reflections on an educational metaphor. *Journal of Curriculum Studies, 30*(4), 397–408. doi:10.1080/002202798183549

Boring, E. (1964). Cognitive dissonance: Its use in science. *Science, 145,* 680–685. doi:10.1126/science.145.3633.680

Brookhart, S. M., Guskey, T. R., Bowers, A. J., McMillan, J. H., Smith, J. K., Smith, L. F., . . . Welsh, M. E. (2016). A century of grading research: Meaning and value in the most common educational measure. *Review of Educational Research, 86*(4), 803–848. doi:10.3102/0034654316672069

Brooks, J. (2015). Learning from the "lifeworld". *The Psychologist, 28*(8), 642–646.

Brown, W. S. (2017). Knowing ourselves as embodied, embedded, and relationally extended. *Zygon, 52*(3), 865–879.

Burghardt, G. M. (1997). Amending Tinbergen: A fifth aim for ethology. In R. W. Mitchell, N. S. Thompson, & H. L. Miles (Eds.), *Anthropomorphism, anecdotes, and animals* (pp. 254–276). Albany, NY: State University of New York Press.

Buzsáki, G., & Llinás, R. (2017). Space and time in the brain. *Science, 358*(6362), 482–485. doi:10.1126/science.aan8869

Cangemi, J. P. (2001). The real purpose of higher education: Developing self-actualizing personalities. *Education, 105*(2), 151–154.

Carel, H., & Meacham, D. (Eds.). (2013). *Phenomenology and naturalism: Examining the relationship between human experience and nature.* Cambridge, England: Cambridge University Press.

Chalmers, D. (1995). Facing up to the problem of consciousness. *Journal of Consciousness Studies, 2*(3), 200–219.

Churchill, S. D. (2006). Phenomenological analysis: Impression formation during a clinical assessment interview. In C. T. Fischer (Ed.), *Qualitative research methods for psychologists* (pp. 79–110). Burlington, MA: Academic Press.

Churchill, S. D. (2012). Teaching phenomenology by way of "second-person perspectivity" (From my thirty years at the University of Dallas). *Indo-Pacific*

Journal of Phenomenology, *12*(Supplement 3), 1–14. doi:10.2989/ipjp. 2012.12.3.6.1114

Churchland, P. (2002). Outer space and inner space: The new epistemology. *Proceedings and Addresses: The American Philosophical Association*, *76*, 25–48. doi:10.2307/3218627

Cobb, P. (2001). Situated cognition. In N. J. Smelser & P. B. Bates (Eds.), *International encyclopedia of the social & behavioral sciences* (pp. 14126–14129). New York, NY: Pergamon.

Coleridge, S. T. (1817). *Biographia Literaria* (Chapter XIV). Retrieved from www.english.upenn.edu/~mgamer/Etexts/biographia.html

Crowther, P. (1982). Merleau-Ponty: Perception into art. *The British Journal of Aesthetics*, *22*(2), 138–149. doi.org/10.1093/bjaesthetics/22.2.138

Cuseo, J. (2007). Defining student sucess: The critical first step in promoting it. *eSource for College Transitions*, *4*, 2–3. Retrieved from http://sc.edu/fye/esource/archives.php

Davis, J. R., & Arend, B. D. (2013). *Facilitating seven ways of learning*. Sterling, VA: Stylus.

Davis, M., Dias-Bowie, Y., Greenberg, K. H., Klukken, G., Pollio, H. R., Thomas, S. P., & Thompson, C. L. (2004). "A fly in the buttermilk": Descriptions of university life by successful black undergraduate students at a predominately white southeastern university. *Journal of Higher Education*, *75*(4), 420–445. doi:10.1353/jhe.2004.0018

Devlin, M. (2013). Bridging socio-cultural incongruity: Conceptualising the success of students from low socio-economic status backgrounds in Australian higher education. *Studies in Higher Education*, *38*(6), 939–949. doi:10.1080/0 3075079.2011.613991

Dewey, J. (1935). The teacher and his world. *The Social Frontier*, *1*(4), 7.

Dillard, S. (2015, December 26). *Why is improvisation important with jazz music?* Retrieved from www.quora.com/Why-is-improvisation-important-with-jazz-music

Dirkx, J. M. (1998). Transformative learning theory in the practice of adult education: An overview. *PAACE Journal of Lifelong Learning*, *7*, 1–14.

Donnison, S., & Penn-Edwards, S. (2012). Focusing on first year assessment: Surface or deep approaches to learning? *International Journal of the First Year in Higher Education*, *3*(2), 9–20. doi:10.5204/intjfyhe.v3i2.127

Dorn, C. (2017). *For the common good: A new history of higher education in America*. Ithaca, NY: Cornell University Press.

Doyle, T. (2011). *Learner-centered teaching: Putting the research on learning into practice Sterling*, VA: Stylus.

Driscoll, M. P. (2005). *Psychology of learning for instruction* (3rd ed.). New York, NY: Pearson.

Eagleman, D. M. (2011). *What scientific concept would improve everybody's cognitive toolkit?* Retrieved from www.edge.org/response-detail/11498

Ellis, K. (2004). The impact of perceived teacher confirmation on receiver apprehension, motivation, and learning. *Communication Education*, *53*(1), 1–20. doi:10.1080/0363452032000135742

Engstrom, C., & Tinto, V. (2008). Access without support is not opportunity. *Change*, *40*(1), 46–50.

184 References

Festinger, L. (1957). *A theory of cognitive dissonance.* Stanford, CA: Stanford University Press.

Feuerstein, R. (1985). *Instrumental enrichment: An intervention program for cognitive modifiability.* Glenview, IL: Scott Foresman.

Fink, L. D. (2003). *Creating significant learning experiences.* San Francisco, CA: Jossey-Bass.

Fink, L. D. (2013). Forward. In J. R. Davis & B. D. Arend (Eds.), *Facilitating seven ways of learning* (pp. ix–xiii). Sterling, VA: Stylus.

Finlay, L. (2008). A dance between the reduction and reflexivity: Explicating the "phenomenological psychological attidude". *Journal of Phenomenological Psychology, 39,* 1–32.

Finlay, L. (2011). *Phenomenology for therapists: Researching the lived world.* West Sussex, England: John Wiley & Sons.

Finlay, L. (2012). Debating phenomenological methods. In N. Friesen, C. Henriksson, & T. Saevi (Eds.), *Hermeneutic phenomenology in education* (pp. 17–37). Rotterdam, The Netherlands: Sense Publishers.

Floyd, K. S., Harrington, S. J., & Santiago, J. (2009). The effect of engagement on perceived course value on deep and surface learning strategies. *Informing Science: The International Journal of an Emerging Transdiscipline, 12,* 181–190.

Franklin, K. A. (2013). *Conversations with a phenomenologist: A phenomenologically oriented case study of instructional planning* (Doctoral dissertation). Retrieved from https://trace.tennessee.edu/utk_graddiss/1721

Franklin, K. A., Dellard, T., Murphy, B., Plaas, K., Skutnik, A., Sohn, B., . . . Thomas, S. (2014). A transformational twist on learner-centered teaching: Experience and existential phenomenology. In *Proceedings of the 6th annual conference on higher education pedagogy* (pp. 343–344). Blacksburg, VA: Conference on Higher Education Pedagogy-VA Tech University.

Friesen, N., Henriksson, C., & Saevi, T. (Eds.). (2012). *Hermeneutic phenomenology in education.* Rotterdam, The Netherlands: Sense Publishers.

Fritschner, L. M. (2000). Inside the undergraduate college classroom: Faculty and students differ on the meaning of student participation. *Journal of Higher Education, 71*(3), 342–362.

Gadamer, H. G. (2013). *Truth and method.* (J. Weinsheimer & D. Marshall, Trans.). New York, NY: Bloomsbury Academic. (Original work published 1960).

Galanes, G. J., & Carmack, H. J. (2013). "He's really setting an example": Student contributions to the learning environment. *Communication Studies, 64*(1), 49–65. doi.org/10.1080/10510974.2012.731464

Garrison, J. (2010). *Dewey and Eros: Wisdom and desire in the art of teaching.* Charlotte, NC: Information Age Publishing.

Goddard, R. (2003). Relational networks, social trust, and norms: A social capital perspective on student's chances of academic success. *Educational Evaluation and Policy Analysis, 25*(1), 59–74.

Goldin, G. A. (2002). Affect, meta-affect, and mathematical belief structures. In G. C. Leder, E. Pehkonen, & G. Torner (Eds.), *Beliefs: A hidden variable in mathematics education?* (pp. 59–72). Dordrecht, The Netherlands: Kluwer Academic Publishers.

Greenberg, K. H. (2014). Cognitive enrichment advantage. In L. Green (Ed.), *Schools as thinking communities* (pp. 91–110). Pretoria, South Africa: Van Schaik Publishers.

References 185

Greenberg, N. B. (1978). Ethological considerations in the experimental study of lizard behavior. In N. Greenberg & P. D. MacLean (Eds.), *Behavior and neurology of lizards* (pp. 204–224). Rockville, MD: NIMH.

Greenberg, N. B. (1986). Science and technology as human endeavors. *Liberal Education, 72*(1), 35–41.

Greenberg, N. B. (1994). Ethologically informed design in reptile research. In C. Warwick, F. L. Frye, & J. B. Murphy (Eds.), *Health and welfare of captive reptiles* (pp. 239–262). London, England: Chapman & Hall.

Greenberg, N. B. (2016). *Art and Organism: Needs for self-actualization.* Retrieved from http://neilgreenberg.com/ao-needs-self-actualization/

Greenberg, N. B. (2018a). *DEEP ethology.* Retrieved from http://neilgreenberg.com/deep-ethology/

Greenberg, N. B. (2018b). *Unity in diversity.* Retrieved from http://neilgreenberg.com/ao-unity-in-diversity

Greenberg, N. B., Carr, J. A., & Summers, C. H. (2002). Cause and consequences of stress. *Integrative & Comparative Biology, 42*, 508–516.

Greenberg, N. B., Deshpande, D., Greenberg, K. H., Franklin, K., Murphy, B., Plaas, K., . . . Thomas, S. (2015). Patterns in transformative pedagogy: Ethological perspective. In *Proceedings of the 8th annual conference on higher education pedagogy* (pp. 67–68). Blacksburg, VA: Conference on Higher Education Pedagogy-VA Tech University.

Greenberg, N. B., Greenberg, K. H., Murphy, B., Plaas, K., Sohn, B. K., & Thomas, S. P. (2016). The natural history of the teachable moment: Exploring practices that enhance profound learning experiences. In *Proceedings of the 8th annual conference on higher education pedagogy* (pp. 13–14). Blacksburg, VA: Conference on Higher Education Pedagogy-VA Tech University.

Greenberg, N. B., Greenberg, K. H., Patterson, R., & Pollio, H. (2015). The natural history of the teachable moment: Exploring practices that enhance profound learning experiences. In *Proceedings of the 7th annual conference on higher education pedagogy* (pp. 98–99). Blacksburg, VA: Conference on Higher Education Pedagogy-VA Tech University.

Greene, M. (1973). *Teacher as stranger: Educational philosophy for the modern age.* Belmont, CA: Wodsworth Publishing.

Greene, M. (1988). *The dialectic of freedom.* New York, NY: Teachers College Press.

Greeno, J. G. (1998). The situativity of knowing, learning, and research. *American Psychologist, 53*, 5–26. doi.org/10.1037/0003-066X.53.1.5

Haidt, J. (2001). The emotional dog and its rational tail: A social intuitionist approach to moral judgment. *Psychological Review, 108*(4), 814–834.

Haidt, J. (2012). *The righteous mind: Why good people are divided by politics and religion.* New York, NY: Vintage.

Halic, O., Greenberg, K. H., & Paulus, T. (2009). Language and academic identity: A study of the experiences of non-native English-speaking international students. *International Education, 38*(2), 74–94.

Hall, R. M., & Sandler, B. R. (1982). *The classroom climate: A chilly one for women? Project on the status and education of women.* Washington, DC: Association of American Colleges. Retrieved from http://eric.ed.gov/?id=ED215628

Halling, S. (2012). Teaching phenomenology through highlighting experience. *Indo-Pacific Journal of Phenomenology, 12*, 1–6.

References

Halling, S., & Leifer, M. (1991). The theory and practice of dialogical research. *Journal of Phenomenological Psychology, 22*(1), 1–15.

Hass, L. (2008). *Merleau-Ponty's philosophy*. Bloomington, IN: Indiana University Press.

Hava-Robbins, N. (2002). *Interpretative dance*. Retrieved from www.snowcrest.net/turningpoint/interpdance.html

Hawkins, D. (1974). *The informed vision: Essays on learning and human nature.* New York, NY: Agathon.

Heart. (2018). *In Merriam-Webster dictionary online*. Retrieved from www.merriam-webster.com/dictionary/heart

Henrich, J. (2017). High fidelity. *Science, 356*(6340), 810.

Henriksson, C. (2012). Hermeneutic phenomenology and pedagogical practice. In N. Friesen, C. Henriksson, & T. Saevi (Eds.), *Hermeneutic phenomenology in education: Method and practice* (pp. 119–137). Rotterdam, The Netherlands: Sense Publishers.

Hinde, R. A. (1973). *Constraints on learning: Limitations and predispositions.* New York, NY: Academic Press.

Holley, L. C., & Steiner, S. (2005). Safe space: Student perspectives on classroom environment. *Journal of Social Work Education, 41*(1), 49–64.

Horton, M., & Freire, P. (1990). *We make the road by walking*. Philadelphia, PA: Temple University Press.

Hultgren, F. H. (1987). The student teacher as person: Reflections on pedagogy and being. *Phenomenology + Pedagogy, 5*(1), 35–50.

Hultgren, F. H. (1995). The phenomenology of "doing" phenomenology: The experience of teaching and learning together. *Human Studies, 18*, 371–388.

Humphreys, P. (2018). *Out of nowhere*. Retrieved from https://aeon.co/essays/atomism-is-basic-emergence-explains-complexity-in-the-universe?utm_source=Aeon+Newsletter&utm

Husserl, E. (1970). *Crisis of European sciences and transcendental phenomenology*. Evanston, IL: Northwestern University Press.

Hut, P. (2001, February). *The role of Husserl's epoché for science: A view from a physicist*. Paper presented at the meeting of the Husserl Circle, Bloomington, IN. Retrieved from http://archive.is/oxDc

Ihde, D. (1986). *Experimental phenomenology: An introduction*. Albany, NY: State University of New York Press.

James, A., & Brookfield, S. D. (2014). *Engaging imagination: Helping students become creative and reflective thinkers*. San Francisco, CA: Jossey-Bass.

James, W. (1911). *Some problems of philosophy*. London, England: Longmans.

James, W. (2006). *Talks to teachers on psychology and to students on some of life's ideas*. Elibron Classics. Boston, MA: Adamant Media Corporation. (Original work published 1899).

Johansson, C., & Felten, P. (2014). *Transforming students: Fulfilling the promise of higher education*. Boston, MA: Johns Hopkins University Press.

Johnson, D. W., & Johnson, R. T. (n.d.). *An overview of cooperative learning.* Retrieved from www.co-operation.org/what-is-cooperative-learning/

Johnson, D. W., Johnson, R. T., & Smith, K. A. (1998). *Active learning: Cooperation in the college classroom*. Edina, MN: Interaction Book Company.

Johnson, M. (2007). *The meaning of the body*. Chicago, IL: University of Chicago Press.

References   187

Kahneman, D. (2011). *Thinking fast and thinking slow*. New York, NY: Farrar, Straus and Giroux.

Kamakawiwo'ole, I. (2010, April 12). *Official somewhere over the rainbow* [Video file]. Retrieved from www.youtube.com/watch?v=V1bFr2SWP1I

Karp, D. A., & Yoels, W. C. (1976). The college classroom: Some observations on the meanings of student participation. *Sociology and Social Research*, 60(4), 421–439.

Karp, M. (2016). A holistic conception of nonacademic support: How four mechanisms combine to encourage positive student outcomes in the community college. *New Directions for Community Colleges*, 2016(175), 33–44. doi:10.1002/cc.20210

Karp, M., & Hughes, K. (2008). Information networks and integration: Institutional influences on experiences and persistence of beginning students. *New Directions for Community Colleges*, 2008(144), 73–82. doi:10.1002/cc.347

Kasl, E., & Yorks, L. (2016). Do I really know you? Do you really know me? Empathy amid diversity in differing learning contexts. *Adult Education Quarterly*, 66(1), 3–20.

King, A. (1993). From sage on the stage to guide on the side. *College Teaching*, 41(1), 30–35.

Kneller, G. F. (1958). *Existentialism and education*. New York, NY: Philosophical Library.

Lakoff, G., & Johnson, M. (1980). *Metaphors we live by*. Chicago, IL: University of Chicago Press.

Laland, K. N. (2017). *Darwin's unfinished symphony: How culture made the human mind*. Princeton, NJ: Princeton University Press.

Langan, D., Sheese, R., & Davidson, D. (2009). Constructive teaching and learning: Collaboration in a sociology classroom. In J. Mezirow, E. W. Taylor, & Associates (Eds.), *Transformative learning in practice: Insights from community, workplace, and higher education* (pp. 46–56). San Francisco, CA: Jossey-Bass.

Lathey, J. (2014, October 6). Teaching math to people who think they hate it. *The Atlantic*. Retrieved from www.theatlantic.com/education/archive/2014/10/teaching-math-to-people-who-think-they-hate-it/381125/

Laureys, S., & Tononi, G. (Eds.). (2008). *The neurology of consciousness: Cognitive neuroscience and neuropathology*. New York, NY: Elsevier.

Lawrence, J. (2002). *The "deficit discourse" shift: University teachers and their role in helping first year students persevere and succeed in the new university culture*. Paper presented at the meeting of the Pacific Rim First Year Higher Education, Christchurch, New Zealand.

Lawrence, J. (2005). *Addressing diversity in higher education: Two models for facilitating student engagement and mastery*. Paper presented at the meeting of HERDSA, Sydney, Australia.

Lebab (1890). In Strong, J. (Ed.) *Strong's exhaustive concordance of the Bible*. Nashville, TN: Abingdon Press.

Levin, K. (2016). Aesthetic movements of embodied minds: Between Merleau-Ponty and Deleuze. *Continental Philosophy Review*, 49(2), 181–202.

Levins, R., & Lewontin, R. C. (1985). *The dialectical biologist*. Cambridge, MA: Harvard University Press.

Macann, C. (1993). *Four phenomenological philosophers: Husserl, Heidegger, Sartre, and Merleau-Ponty*. London, England: Routledge.

188 References

Macdonald, H. M. (2013). Inviting discomfort: Foregrounding emotional labour in teaching anthropology in post-apartheid South Africa. *Teaching in Higher Education, 18*(6), 670–682. doi.org/10.1080/13562517.2013.795938

Mackh, B. (2018). *Higher education by design: Best practices for curricular planning and instruction.* New York, NY: Routledge.

Marconi, D. (2012). Quine and Wittgenstein on the science/philosophy divide. *Humana Mente Journal of Philosophical Studies, 21,* 173–189.

Maslow, A. H. (1943). A theory of human motivation. *Psychological Review, 50*(4), 370–396. doi:10.1037/h0054346

Mayo, C. (2010). Relationships are difficult. In G. S. Goodman (Ed.), *Educational psychology reader: The art and science of how people learn* (pp. 426–437). New York, NY: Peter Lang.

McEwen, B. S., & Sapolsky, R. M. (1995). Stress and cognitive function. *Current Opinion in Neurobiology, 5*(2), 205–216. doi.org/10.1016/0959-4388(95)80028-X

McKay, J., & Devlin, M. (2014). "Uni has a different language . . . to the real world": Demystifying academic culture and discourse for students from low socioeconomic backgrounds. *Higher Education Research & Development, 33*(5), 949–961. doi:10.1080/07294360.2014.890570

Mentkowski, M., & Associates. (2000). *Learning that lasts: Integrating learning, development, and performance in college and beyond.* San Francisco, CA: Jossey-Bass.

Merleau-Ponty, M. (1962). *Phenomenology of perception.* (C. Smith, Trans.). London, England: Routledge. (Original work published 1945).

Merleau-Ponty, M. (1964). The primacy of perception and its philosophical consequences. (J. M. Edie, Trans.). In J. M. Edie (Ed.), *The primacy of perception and other essays on phenomenological psychology, the philosophy of art, history, and politics* (pp. 12–42). Evanston, IL: Northwestern University Press.

Merleau-Ponty, M. (1965). *The structure of behavior.* (A. L. Fisher, Trans.). London, England: Methuen. (Original work published 1942).

Merleau-Ponty, M. (1968). *The visible and the invisible: Followed by working notes* (C. Lefort, Ed., A. Lingis, Trans.). Evanston, IL: Northwestern University Press.

Merleau-Ponty, M. (2004). *The world of perception.* (O. Davis, Trans.). New York, NY: Routledge. (Original work published 1948).

Merleau-Ponty, M. (2007). *The Merleau-Ponty reader.* Evanston, IL: Northwestern University Press. (Original work published 1958).

Merleau-Ponty, M. (2012). *Phenomenology of perception.* (D. A. Landes, Trans.). New York, NY: Taylor & Francis. (Original work published 1945).

Milton, O., Pollio, H. R., & Eison, J. A. (1986). *Making sense of college grades.* San Francisco, CA: Jossey-Bass.

Moran, D. (2000). *Introduction to phenomenology.* New York, NY: Routledge.

Moret, L. (2018, June). *"Get comfortable in the discomfort": Dialogue with novice graduate student researchers.* International Human Science Research Conference, Wofford College, Spartanburg, SC.

Morris, V. C. (1990). *Existentialism in education: What it means.* Prospect Heights, IL: Waveland Press. (Original work published 1966).

Moustakas, C. (1994). *Phenomenological research methods.* London: Sage.

Muller, J. T. (2015). *Intergroup dialogue in multicultural psychology education: Group climate development and outcomes* (Unpublished doctoral dissertation). University of Tennessee, Knoxville, TN.

Muller, J. Z. (2018). *The tyranny of metrics*. Princeton, NJ: Princeton University Press.

Nagel, T. (1974). What is it like to be a bat? *The Philosophical Review, 83*(4), 435–450. doi:10.2307/2183914

NASA. (2018). *Astrobiology at NASA*. Retrieved from https://astrobiology.nasa.gov/research/astrobiology-at-nasa/

Natanson, M. (1973). Phenomenology and the social sciences. In M. Natanson (Ed.), *Phenomenology and the social sciences* (pp. 3–44). Evanston, IL: Northwestern University Press.

Neem, J. N. (2013). Experience matters: Why competency based education will not replace seat time. *Liberal Education, 99*(4). Retrieved from www.aacu.org/publications-research/periodicals/experience-matters-why-competency-based-education-will-not-replace

Nepo, M. (2010). In P. J. Parker & A. Zajonc, *The heart of higher education: A call for renewal.* (pp. v–xii). San Francisco, CA: Jossey-Bass.

Noddings, N. (1992). *The challenge to care in schools: An alternative approach to education*. New York, NY: Teachers College Press.

O'Gara, L., Karp, M., & Hughes, K. (2009). Student success courses in the community college: An exploratory study of student perspectives. *Community College Review, 36*(3), 195–218.

Owen-Smith, P. (2018). *The contemplative mind in the scholarship of teaching and learning*. Bloomington, IN: Indiana University Press.

Palmer, P. J. (2003). Teaching with heart and soul: Reflections on spirituality in teacher education. *Journal of Teacher Education, 54*(5), 376–385.

Palmer, P. J. (2007). *The courage to teach: Exploring the inner landscape of a teacher's life*. San Francisco, CA: Jossey-Bass.

Parsons, A. (2016). *Lifeworld (Lebenswelt; Umwelt)*. Retrieved from http://compendium.kosawese.net/term/lifeworld-lebenswelt-umwelt/

Paulus, T. M., Bichelmeyer, B., Malopinsky, L., Perreia, M., & Rastogi, P. (2005). Power distance and group dynamics of an international project team: A case study. *Teaching in Higher Education, 10*(1), 43–55.

Petitot, J., Varela, F. J., Pachoud, B., & Roy, J. M. (Eds.). (1999). *Naturalizing phenomenology*. Stanford, CA: Stanford University Press.

Piaget, J. (2003). *The psychology of intelligence*. (M. Piercy & D. E. Berlyne, Trans.). New York, NY: Routledge. (Original work published 1947).

Plato. (n.d.). *Phaedrus*. (B. Jowett, Trans.). Retrieved from http://classics.mit.edu/Plato/phaedrus.html

Pollio, H. R., & Beck, H. P. (2000). When the tail wags the dog: Perceptions of learning and grade orientation in, and by, contemporary college students and faculty. *The Journal of Higher Education, 71*(1), 84–102. doi.org/10.2307/2649283

Pollio, H. R., Graves, R., & Arfken, M. (2006). Qualitative research methods. In F. Leong & J. Austin (Eds.), *The psychology research handbook: A guide for graduate students and research assistants* (pp. 254–275). Thousand Oaks, CA: Sage Publications.

Pollio, H. R., Henley, T. B., & Thompson, C. J. (1997). *The phenomenology of everyday life*. Cambridge, England: Cambridge University Press.

References

Race, P. (2010). *Making learning happen: A guide for post-compulsory education.* London, England: Sage Publications.

Rader, S., & Summerville, T. (n.d.). *Creating dialogue in the classroom.* Retrieved from www.unbc.ca/sites/default/files/assets/centre_for_teaching_and_learning/tips/creating_dialogue.pdf

Robinson, O. (2012). A war of words. *The Psychologist, 25*(2), 164–166.

Robinson, S., & Robinson, M. M. (2013). Exploring Gadamer's *Truth and method: Elements of a theory of hermeneutic experience* [Review of Chapter 4 of *Truth and Method*, by H. G. Gadamer (2nd ed.)]. Retrieved from https://transitionconsciousness.wordpress.com/2013/03/27/exploring-gadamers-truth-and-method-elements-of-a-theory-of-hermeneutic-experience

Rogers, C. (1969). *Freedom to learn: A view of what education might become.* Columbus, OH: Merrill.

Rousmaniere, K. (2000). From memory to curriculum. *Teaching Education, 11*(1), 1–12.

Saldaña, J. (2016). *The coding manual for qualitative researchers.* San Francisco, CA: Sage Publications.

Sartre, J. P. (1956). *Being and nothingness.* (H. E. Barnes, Trans.). New York, NY: Routledge. (Original work published 1943).

Schacter, D. L., & Addis, D. R. (2007). The cognitive neuroscience of constructive memory: Remembering the past and imagining the future. *Philosophical Transactions of the Royal Society B: Biological Sciences, 362*(1481), 773–786.

Searle, J. R. (1999). *Mind, language and society.* London, England: Weidenfield & Nicolson. Retrieved from http://human-brain.org/searle.html

Selvi, K. (2008). Phenomenological approach in education. In A. Tymieniecka (Ed.), *Education in human creative existential planning* (pp. 39–51). Dordrecht, The Netherlands: Springer.

Sherman, G. (2014). *Refocusing the self in higher education: A phenomenological perspective.* New York, NY: Routledge.

Shettlesworth, S. J. (1998). *Cognition, evolution, and behavior.* New York, NY: Oxford University Press.

Sidelinger, R. J., & Booth-Butterfield, M. (2010). Co-constructing student involvement: An examination of teacher confirmation and student-to-student connectedness in the college classroom. *Communication Education, 59*(2), 165–184. doi.org/10.1080/03634520903390867

Silverstein, A. (1988). An Aristotelian resolution of the idiographic versus nomothetic tension. *American Psychologist, 43*(6), 425–430.

Smith, J. T. (2016). *Stories of success: A phenomenological study of positive transformative learning experiences of low-socioeconomic status community college mathematics students* (Doctoral dissertation). Retrieved from http://trace.tennessee.edu/utk_graddiss/4168

Smith, J. T. (2018, February 22). People watching. *The New York Review.* Retrieved from www.nybooks.com/articles/2018/02/22/helen-levitt-people-watching/

Sohn, B. K. (2016). *The student experience of other students* (Doctoral dissertation). Retrieved from http://trace.tennessee.edu/utk_graddiss/3748

Sohn, B. K. (2017). *Coming to appreciate diversity: Ontological change through student-student relationships.* Manuscript submitted for publication.

Sohn, B. K., Plaas, K., Franklin, K., Dellard, T., Murphy, B., Greenberg, K. H., . . . Thomas, S. P. (2016). Freedom to connect: Insight into the existential dimension of transformative learning in a graduate seminar. *Journal of Transformative Education, 14*(3). doi:10.1177/1541344616631425

Sohn, B. K., Thomas, S. P., Greenberg, K. H., & Pollio, H. R. (2017). Hearing the voices of students and teachers: A phenomenological approach to educational research. *Qualitative Research in Education, 6*(2), 121–148. doi:10.17583/qre.2017.2374

Sokolowski, R. (2000). *Introduction to phenomenology*. Cambridge, England: Cambridge University Press.

Spinney, L. (2014, January 15). Talent for prejudice: Why humans dehumanize others. *New Scientist*. Retrieved from www.newscientist.com/article/mg22129520-800-talent-for-prejudice-why-humans-dehumanise-others/

Stein, B. E., Stanford, T. R., & Rowland, B. A. (2014). Development of multisensory integration from the perspective of the individual neuron. *Nature Reviews Neuroscience, 15*(8), 520–535.

Sternberg, R. (1997). Concept of intelligence and its role in lifelong learning and success. *American Psychologist, 52*(10), 1030–1037. doi:10.1037/0003-066X.52.10.1030

Stolz, S. A. (2015). Embodied learning. *Educational Philosophy and Theory, 47*(5), 474–487. doi.org/10.1080/00131857.2013.879694

Switzer, R. (2001). Together in the flesh: Ethics and attunement in Hume and Merleau-Ponty. In D. H. Davis (Ed.), *Merleau-Ponty's later works and their practical implications* (pp. 253–290). Amherst, NY: Humanity Books.

Taylor, E. W. (2009). Fostering transformative learning. In J. Mezirow, E. W. Taylor, & Associates (Eds.), *Transformative learning in practice: Insights from community, workplace, and higher education* (pp. 3–17). San Francisco, CA: Jossey-Bass.

Taylor, E. W., Cranton, P., & Associates (Eds.). (2012). *The handbook of transformative learning: Theory, research, and practice*. San Francisco, CA: Jossey-Bass.

Taylor, K., & Marienau, C. (2016). *Facilitating learning with the adult brain in mind: A conceptual and practical guide*. San Francisco, CA: Jossey-Bass.

Tennenhouse, E. (2017). It's a no-brainer. *New Scientist, 235*(3134), 5–57.

Thomas, S. P. (2005). Through the lens of Merleau-Ponty: Advancing the phenomenological approach to nursing research. *Nursing Philosophy, 6*(1), 63–76.

Thomas, S. P. (2010). Merleau-Ponty and James Agee: Guides to the novice phenomenologist. In L. Embree, M. Barber, & T. J. Nenon (Eds.), *Phenomenology 2010: Selected essays from North America, Part 2: Phenomenology Beyond Philosophy* (Vol. 5, pp. 281–308). Bucharest, Romania: Zeta Books.

Thomas, S. P., & Davis, M. (2000). *Enhancing success of Black nursing students: Project success*. Paper presented at the meeting of the American Academy of Nursing, San Diego, CA.

Thomas, S. P., & Pollio, H. R. (2002). *Listening to patients: A phenomenological approach to nursing research and practice*. New York, NY: Springer.

Thomas, S. P., Thompson, C., Pollio, H. R., Greenberg, K. H., Conwill, W., Sall, A., . . . Dias-Bowie, Y. (2007). Experiences of struggling African American students at a predominantly white university. *Research in the Schools, 14*(2), 1–17.

References

Thompson, C. J., Locander, W. B., & Pollio, H. R. (1989). Putting consumer experience back into consumer research. *Journal of Consumer Research*, 16(2), 133–146.

Thoreau, H. D. (1962). *The journal of Henry D. Thoreau* (Vol. 2). New York, NY: Dover. (Original work published 1855).

Tinbergen, N. (1963). On aims and methods of ethology. *Zeitschrift für Tierpsychologie*, 20, 410–433.

Tuan, Y. (1977). *Space and place: The perspective of experience*. Minneapolis, MN: University of Minnesota Press.

van de Goor, J., Sools, A. M., Westerhof, G. J., & Bohlmeijer, E. T. (2017). Wonderful life: Exploring wonder in meaningful moments. *Journal of Humanistic Psychology*, 1–21. Retrieved from http://journals.sagepub.com/doi/pdf/10.1177/0022167817696837

van Manen, M. (1991). *The tact of teaching*. Albany, NY: State University of New York Press.

van Manen, M. (2014). *Phenomenology of practice: Meaning-giving methods in phenomenological research and writing*. Walnut Creek, CA: Left Coast Press.

van Manen, M. (2017). *Pedagogical tact: Knowing what to do when you don't know what to do*. New York, NY: Routledge.

Varela, F. J., Thompson, E., & Rosch, E. (2016). *The embodied mind*. Cambridge, MA: MIT Press. (Original work published 1991).

von Uexküll, J. (1982). The theory of meaning. *Semiotica*, 42(1), 25–82.

Vygotsky, L. S. (1980). *Mind in society: Development of higher psychological processes*. M. Cole, V. John-Steiner, S. Scribner, & E. Souberman (Eds.). Cambridge, MA: Harvard University Press. Watt, W. W. (1957). *An American rhetoric*. New York, NY: Rinehart.

Weimer, M. (2013). *Learner-centered teaching: Five key changes to practice*. (2nd ed.). San Francisco, CA: Jossey-Bass.

Wiggins, G. P., & McTighe, J. (2005). *Understanding by design* (2nd ed.). Alexandria, VA: Association for Supervision and Curriculum Development.

Willis, P. (2012). An existential approach to transformative learning. In E. W. Taylor, P. Cranton, & Associates (Eds.), *The handbook of transformative learning: Theory, research, and practice* (pp. 212–227). San Francisco, CA: Jossey-Bass.

Wilson, R. A., & Foglia, L. (2017). Embodied cognition. In E. N. Zalta (Ed.), *The Stanford encyclopedia of philosophy*. Retrieved from https://plato.stanford.edu/archives/spr2017/entries/embodied-cognition

Xin. (2018). *In Han Trainer Dictionary.com*. Retrieved from https://dictionary.hantrainerpro.com/chinese-english/translation-xin_heart.htm

Yoshimi, J. (2011). Phenomenology and connectionism. *Frontiers in Psychology*, 2(288). https://doi.org/10.3389/fpsyg.2011.00288

Zahavi, D. (2003). Intentionality and phenomenality: A phenomenological take on the hard problem. *Canadian Journal of Philosophy*, 29(Supplement 1), 63–92.

Zuniga, X., Nagda, B., & Cytron-Walker, A. (2007). Intergroup dialogue in higher education: Meaningful learning about social justice. *ASHE Higher Education Report*, 32(4), 1–128.

Index

Page numbers in italics indicate figures; page numbers in bold indicate tables.

abstract art, teaching as 153–154
accommodation 28, 103
active learning 101; *see also* free to learn
adaptations: change 39; contribution to fitness 33; evolution 45; traits 40, 45, 48
aesthetic: appreciation for 129, 130–131; dimensions 39; experience 130–131
African American students: experience of 141, 142–144, 148, 160; invisibility/supervisibility theme 142
ambiguity 12; case study 19–20; cognitive learning 173; phenomenological concept **11**, 45, 171, 173; teaching and learning 165, **166**; different from other courses; free and open
American Psychological Association 175
Arendt, Hannah 105
Aristotle 44
art: appreciation for 130–131; of teaching 164–165, 177
Art and Organism (A&O) 153
asking/ask back 76, 91, 150
assessment 13, 27; cheat-proof systems 51; classroom 125–126; grading and 62, 105; measurable outcomes 125; self-, 151, 175, 178; student performance 154; types of 165
assumptions 12, 14–16, 78, 161; about students 173; biases and 106, **166**, 177; course content 149, 177–179; intuitive 65, 164;

operating about cognition 30; questioning 19, 92, 130; research context 158–159; *see also* bias(es)
assuring: as a descriptor of the professor's classroom facilitation *energized* theme 80; professor and student descriptors **82**, **83**, **85–88**
authenticity 35; authentic relationships 140, 145–146; free to be authentic 103; of group 104, 122; relationships 138–139
authority 30, 91, 97
autonomous small groups 150
autonomous student development 52

balancing act, teaching as 154–155
being-in-the-world 7, 10, 14, 34, 128, 171; human being-in-the-world 10, 24, 34
bias(es) 16, 30, 33, 106, 129, 144, 157; assumptions and 106, **166**, 177; confirmation 93; congenital and acquired 37, 39; implicit 15, 33, 45; unconscious 15; *see also* assumptions
biological needs 32, 40–41, 43, 44, 47
biology of art and aesthetic experience 153
black students experience 142–144
bodily attunement 16
bracketing 7, 39, 112, 159; *see also* epoché
bridling beliefs 159

Cartesian dualism 30, 33
case study 4–9; ambiguity 19–20; classroom context 67–69;

194 Index

comparing findings to extant literature 61–63; course and its professor 6–7; data analysis 7–9; data collection 7, **8**; embodiment 16–18; goals of 5; intentionality 20–22; intersubjectivity 18–19; intertwined influences of perception 12–14; phenomenological attitude 11–12; research findings 69–78; research questions 7, **8**; sociocultural embeddedness 14–16

categorization: comparison or 117; limits of experience 103–104

Center for Contemplative Mind in Society, The 176

certitude 103

challenges: art and poetry 131; attitudes 127; beliefs 114, 127; in learning 19, 43, 110, 150; values 127

Chalmers, David 37

changes in being personal and professional 24, 127–128, 173

check-ins 150, 151, 154, 161

classroom: atmosphere 74, 101; climate 24, 38, 110, 111, 119–120, 172–173; episode of teacher and student dialogue with humor 74–75; classroom participation 157–159; safety: student interactions 110–111

co-creation of knowledge 64

cognition 10, 22; complex protean concept 47; consciousness and 31, 35–37, 49; effect of stress on 47; embodied 30, 34–35, 38; perception and 38

cognitive dissonance 47, 102

cognitive learning knowledge acquisition 172–173

Cohen, Leonard 66

collaborative 23; balance with ambiguity, safety and comfort 95, 104–106; implications of, and connected 104–106; learning 27, 96, 111, 120, 171; theme 99–100, **102**

comfortable in discomfort, teaching as getting 157–159

common existential project 24, 99, 124

common good 126

compartmentalization 129, 137, 155

compensation for change 45

competition 53, 95; antithesis of community 123; extra-group 121; freedom from **102**; kinds of 105; lack of 99; sources of 105

comprehensive 4, 23, 54, 66, 167, 171

condescension 142

conflict 18, 25, 73, 123–124

connected 15, 23, 66; collaborative and 95; *see also* collaborative

connectedness: biological organization 39; of knowledge 153

connoisseurship 4, 25–26, 71, 162

consciousness 9, 18, 30, 39, 47–48, 74, 106; cognition and 35–37; hard problem of 37; unity of 120

consolidation of responsibility 110

constraints 53, 103, 108; on behavior 42, 48–49; freedom from 96, **102**; sense of 46

contemplative education 172, 176–177, 179

cooperative and collaborative learning students 109–111

Cornell University 156

corporatization 126

Courage to Teach, The (Palmer) 92

course content: openness **166**; personal experience and **166**; realizing 128, 177–178

creativity **11**, 32, 122, 131; growth dimension 43; memory and 36; teacher 63; teaching and learning 177, 179

critical moments 155

critical reasoning 164

cultural incongruity 145

cyberspace salon, teaching as 152–153

DEEP: acronym 34; ethology 40–41, 41; deployment of DEEP thinking 29; development 42–43; ecology 43–45; evolution 45–46; physiology 46–47

deep learning 64

delve deeply into concepts 96, 98

de Mille, Agnes 149

Descartes, René 73, 100, 121

describing: as descriptor of the professor's classroom facilitation *free-flowing journey* theme **80**; professor and student descriptors **82**, **83**, **85**–**87**

descriptive 4

development, DEEP ethology 42–43
dialectic/dialectical 33, 73, 81
dialogue: energized theme 73–75; energizing with humor 74–75; free-flowing journey 71–73; professor as traffic controller of 77–78, 80; verbal interaction 68–69
different from other courses: implications of 101–103; theme 95–96, **102**
dispensing facts 61, 77
disrupting, as descriptor of the professor's classroom facilitation *energized* theme 80, 81, 85–88, 98, 103
disruptions **102**, 103, 155
diversity 117, 119; coming to appreciate 116–119; seeing and appreciating 122–124; seeing variations 117–118
dramatizing 74, as descriptor of the professor's classroom facilitation *energized* theme 80, 81; professor and student descriptor **82, 83,** 85–88, 90

ecology 22, 34, 40; DEEP ethology 43–45
ecphory/ecphoric 28, 38
egalitarian stance 10, 18, 21, 77; adopting an **166**; awareness of intersubjectivity **166**; fellow travelers in life's journey 18, 77, 91; improvisational jazz style illustrating 71, 175; learners among learners 76; open to ambiguity **166**; professor displaying 73, 76, 77
elaborate/elaborated/elaborating 35; as descriptor of the professor's classroom facilitation *free-flowing* journey theme 80, 81; professor and student descriptors **82–84**, 85–89, **166**, 173
Eliot, T.S. 59
embeddedness 38, 66, 72; academic 107; social 131; sociocultural **10,** 12, 14–16, 90, 101, **102**, 106, 121, 122, 149, 159–160, 165, **166**, 173, 180
embodied cognition 34, 38; theory of 35
embodied mind 30

embodiment 12, 34–35; case study 16–18; cognitive learning 172; collaborative and connected **102**; concept of 157; phenomenological concept **10**; safe and comfortable **102**; student research participants 161; teaching and learning 165, **166**
emergent/emergence 31, 36–37
empathic space 121
empathic understanding 108
empathy 24, 39, **166**; building 133; intersubjectivity and 18; sense of 12, 129, 133; trust and 168
empirical 4
enemy, identification of common 121
energized: professor 84, 90; as theme of the professor's classroom facilitation 69, *70* 73–75, 79, **80**
energizing 37, 39; acting vocative questions 76; connections 28; dialogue with humor 74–75; motivational systems 47
engagement: active 101; emotional 115, 121, 149; intellectual 55; students 7, 17, 34, 36, 114–115, 117, 121, 145, 168
entertaining 74–75; as a descriptor of the professor's classroom facilitation *energized* theme 80, 81; professor and student descriptors **83, 88**
epigenetics 42
epiphany 28, 34, 103
epoché 5, 39; *see also* bracketing
error detection 46, 47
ethogram 32
ethology 27; integrative biology of 49; *see also* DEEP ethology
everyday life 1, 31, 90, 156; ambiguity of 19, 104, 130; greater awareness of 129–130
evidence-based practices 5, 171
evolution 22, 33, 41; DEEP ethology 45–46
existentialism 9, 29–30; existence of 30
Existentialism and Education (Kneller) 126
Existentialism in Education: What It Means (Morris) 128
Existential Phenomenological Psychology (seminar) 6

196 Index

existential phenomenology 5, 29–30, 179; approach 2; course and professor 6–7; embodied cognition 34; field of 8–9, 177; framework 92; integrative biology and 31–41; intimate nature of questions of 98; learning 104, 149, 179; perspective on 9–22; phenomenological attitude 11–12; philosophy 49; understanding of 159–160, 162, 164

experiences: life-changing 24, 128–129; professor and students 1–2; transformative learning 48–49; *see also* first-person experience; personal experiences; student experiences

experiential learning, neuroscience research and 173–174

explorations of self 105, 114, 120, 154, 161

facilitate: active listening 173, 176; classroom 79, **80**; dialogue 68, 91, 147–148, 156; learning 34, 48, 64, 92, 95, 108–109; lifeworld of classroom 78; teaching as 50, 65

Facilitating Seven Ways of Learning (Davis and Arend) 171

feedback 62–63, 110, 151, 154, 172, 174, 178

figural themes: instructional planning 54, 55–60; *see also* instructional planning

first-person experience: class session 55–56; listening to patients 133; students 40, 66, 91, 160, 164; teaching and learning 3–4, 9, 11, 165, 168, 170, 178

first-person perception 100

first-person perspective 2, 20, 98, 103, 107; African American students 142; LSES student 145

Fly in the Buttermilk metaphor 142

following: as a descriptor of the professor's classroom facilitation *traffic control* theme **80**; professor and student descriptors **82**, **83**, **85**, **86**, 87

Franklin, Karen 54

free and open: implications of 103–104; theme 96–97, **102**

freedom, share contributed by 106

Freedom to Learn (Rogers) 108

free-flowing journey: controlling 77; as theme of the professor's classroom facilitation 69, *70, 71–73,* 75, 78, 79, **80**, **82**, 84

free to learn 23, 96–100, 150, 175; collaborative and connected theme 99–100; different from other courses 95–96; implications of different 101–103; implications of free and open 103–104; implications of relevant and applicable 106–107; implications of safe and comfortable, collaborative and connected 104–106; phenomenological approach 101–107; relevant and applicable theme 100; safe and comfortable theme 97–99; themes 95–101; themes and concepts of phenomenology **102**

Freire, Paulo 153

genetics 42

genuineness 98

gestalt: experience 69, 91, 95, 101; holistic 92; perception 82; student experience of other students (SEOS) 119; teaching/learning 64

Gestalt psychology 21

go somewhere to answer a BIG question: as ground/context of the professor's classroom facilitation *70, 70–71*

go with the flow 91

grades 45, 62, 95, 99, **102**, 105, 111, 143, 152

grading 51–53, 62–63, 93, 98, 105, 175

Graham, Martha 149

ground 7; figure 21, 82

guide from the side 151, 153

habit 43

hard problem 37

Heart of Higher Education, The (Nepo) 180

heart of teaching and learning 2, 3, 11, 25, 51, 92, 141, 149, 159, 162; intentionality 20–21; principles of 165–171, **166**

Heidegger principles 167

helmsman 64

hermeneutic: circle 7, 33, 42; phenomenological approach 5

higher education, 21st century workforce 126

higher education pedagogy: acquisition of knowledge through cognitive learning 172–173; contemplative education 176–177; experiential learning and neuroscience research 173–174; implications for research 177–179; learner-centered approaches 174–176; phenomenological approach 171–177; *see also* pedagogy

hive mentality 121

holism 33

homeostasis 40, 46

How Learning Works (Ambrose) 172

human development, individuation and socialization 44

humor 97, 100; class discussion 123; classroom discussion 17–18; intersubjectivity and 119–120; professor using 74–75, 81, 84, 119–120, 121, 160; self-deprecating 53, 156; teacher and student energizing dialogue with 74–75

Husserl, Edmund 20, 31, 40, 100, 118

imaginative variation 118

implicit bias 33

improvisational jazz: illusion as illusion 82–84; my time vs. external time 85–89; process codes relation to themes 79–81; process coding of classroom conversation 81, 89–90; professor's teaching style 78–90, 91; teaching as 23, 65–66

individuation 44–45, 48, 168

inner landscape 141

institutional role of student 23, 95

instructional planning 63–64; all the stuff 59; blow them away 57–58; characteristics of well-designed experiences 52; comparing findings to extant literature 61–63; contextual factors in 53; figural themes of 54, 55–60; first-person experience 55–56; going with the flow 59–60; good question 58–59; narrowing focus to 51–52; personal factors in 53–54; planning with possibilities 56–57; post-class reflection by Dr. Pollio 60–61; practices of master teacher 54–61; teaching preparation 50–51; *see also* master teacher

instructor, label 3

integration: idea of 128; of information 37; inner and outer influences 42; internal and external 48–49; learner's experience 127; of learning 127; personal and professional lives 167; social 144

integrative biology 49; existential phenomenology and 31–41; teaching and learning 22

intentionality 11, 12, 93; case study 20–22; perception and 101, 165, 167–168, 180; phenomenological attitude **166**; phenomenological concept **10**; subjective states of 66; of teacher and students 90, 160

interceptors 34

interconnectedness of all things 129, 136–139; academic disciplines 136–137; authentic relationships for connecting 138–139; breaking down silos 137–138; concept of 136

intergroup dialogue (IGD) 147, 148

international students: experiences of 146–148, 159, 160, 161; intergroup dialogue (IGD) 147, 148

interpretative dance, teaching as 66, 149–152

interrelationships 163, 177

intersubjectivity 12; case study 18–19; cognitive learning 172; collaborative and connected **102**, 104; creating positive 119–124; hive mentality 121; phenomenological concept **10**; play and intimacy 120–121; safe and comfortable **102**, 104; teaching and learning 165, **166**

intimacy 98, 114–115; play and 120–121

intra-teach sessions 52

intuition 2, 15, 17, 22; biological needs 40; intuitive beliefs 30, 178; replacing critical reasoning 164; teaching and learning 25, 34, 177

invisibility/supervisibility theme, black student experience 142–143

inviting students, professor **82–83**, 84, 87–88, 90

James, William 36, 46, 56, 115, 163

Johnson, Mark 39

joining: as a descriptor of the professor's classroom facilitation *traffic control* theme 80; professor and student descriptors **82, 83, 85,**

198   *Index*

87, 150; professors and students 65; students as learners 19, 68

journaling 63, 167–168, 176

judgment 38, 145; assumptions and 93; freedom from **102**, 104; lack of 98, 109; nonjudgmental 110, 120

Kant, Immanuel 100

knowledge: acquisition through cognitive learning 172–173; multiple ways of knowing 135–136; perception and understanding abstract 178; transmission of 59, 63

labels, teacher *v* instructor 3

language, interpersonal communications 44–45

launched into the world, students 14, **122**, **166**

leading: as a descriptor of the professor's *traffic control* theme 80; professor and student descriptors **82–84**, **86–89**

learning: appreciation for aesthetic 130–131; experiential, and neuroscience research 173–174; greater awareness of everyday life 130; interconnectedness of all things 136–139; learner-centered approaches 174–176; learning that lasts 127; life-changing experience of 128–139; a new way of seeing 129–132; openness 132–136; outcomes 178; outcomes from phenomenological approach 125–127; profound people 126; realizing course content 128; research-based principles 25, 163–167, **166**; teachable moment 29; transformative 27–29; understanding of sociocultural context 131–132; *see also* free to learn

learning by doing 63

learning community 44, 144, 146–147, 149–150, 160, **166**

learning environment *see* messed-up learning environment

lebah (heart) 25

Lebenswelt 1, 31

legacy of loss 179

lethargy of custom 43

levels of organization 37–40; communication within and between 39

l'existemce précède l'essence, motto 39

lifeworld 17; art of teaching 162, 164; of the classroom 1–4, 12, 14; compared to *umvelt* 31; concept of 90–91; of course content 1; dimension of ecology 44–45; diversity and 122; energizing the 73–75; experiences of 155, 159–160, flow of journey 71–73; healthy relationships in 146; higher education 25, 171–175, 177, 179; idea of 31; ideal place of 71; incorporating, 31; of individuals 179; intersubjectivity 18–19, 92, 172; in-the-moment aspects of 70; meaning and importance of 11; mess-ups and 162; organization of 38–40; perception of students and teachers 21, 65–66, 90–91, 149, 165, 169; phenomenological concept 10; questions within questions 69, 70, 75–76

listening: better 132–136; contemplative practice 176–177; facilitating active 173; listen to be influenced 12, 65, 91, 150, 177

lived experiences: African American students 142; ambiguity 19; embodiment 10, 17–18; human-being-in-the-world 10; intentionality 21; intersubjectivity 90; lifeworld 31, 90; physical and psychological aspects of 70–71; professor and students 4–5, 177–178; space and place in 14

looking, how we are 10, 20

low socioeconomic status (LSES) students experiences 144–146, 148, 159, 160, 161

Mackh, Bruce 50

Maslow, Abraham 40

mastered competencies 125

master teacher: designation 54; ground of phenomenological attitude 55; instructional planning practices of 54–61; themes of instructional planning 55–60

math-hater 156

math missionary, teaching as 156–157

meaning 39, 49; ambiguity 19; anticipation of 33; course content 102, 104, 106, **166**; free to learn 95; instructing 3; intersubjectivity

18; learning 27–28; lifeworld 11, 21, 164; marginalization 8; perception and 84, 92, 160, **166**; shared understanding 44; space and place 14; teachable moment 29; of time 65, 66

measurable outcomes 125

Merleau-Ponty, Maurice 2, 6, 9–21, 25, 27, 30–34, 36, 48, 55–57, 65–66, 71, 76, 90–91, 94, 97, 100–102, 106, 109, 118, 120, 126, 130–131, 136, 138, 152–153, 157, 164, 179

messed-up learning environment: African American student experiences 142–144; experiences of low socioeconomic status (LSES) students 144–146; international student experiences 146–148; teacher attitude 145

messing about 24–25, 141; phenomenological approach to teaching 149–159; teaching and learning 162; teaching as abstract art 153–154; teaching as a cyberspace salon 152–153; teaching as balancing act 154–155; teaching as getting comfortable in discomfort 157–159; teaching as interpretative dance 66, 149–152; teaching as math missionary 156–157

metaphor for teaching, helmsman 64

mind-maps 153–154, 161

mini-lectures 7, 56, 60, 68, 77, 89

mismatch 46–47

motivation 18, 21, 40, 46–47, 50, 107, 131, 144, 155

mystery **11**, 19–20, 155, 161, **166**

naturalizing phenomenology 30–31

needs, biological 32, 40–41, 43, 44,47

network of relations 11, 20

neuroscience research 172; experiential learning and 173–174

online courses 24–25, 51, 150, 160, 166, 174; asynchronous 152–153; discussion prompt 156–157; synchronous 149–152

opening: classroom dialogue 71, 79; concept 157; as a descriptor of the professor's *traffic control* theme 79, **80**, 81; professor and student

descriptors **82**, **85**, 123; students to world perspectives 168

openness 132–136; better listening 132–133; greater appreciation of differing perspectives 134–135; to others 132; to critical reflexivity 132; transcending course content **166**; valuing multiple ways of knowing 135–136

optimality 39, 43

Palmer, Parker 50, 92, 123, 141

Parsons, Alan 31

pedagogy: evidence-based 5, 171; phenomenological 169; science-based practices 163–164, 177; term 171; *see also* higher education pedagogy

perception: cognition and 36–37; descriptive philosophy of 36; instructional planning 57; intertwined influences of 12–14; phenomenological concept **10**; primacy of 66, 90, 160, 165, **166**

perpetual beginner, role of 130

personal 4

personal experiences 3, 7, 128; class episode of teacher and student 74–75; classroom 49; course content **10**, 22, 89–90, 92–93; free-flowing journey theme **80**, 91, 149, 164, **166**, 174; sharing 68, 74, 77, 79, 80, 150; weaving 80, 81, **82–84**, 84, **85–89**; *see also* experiences

phenomenological approach 4; free to learn 23; messing about with, to teaching 149–159; students' needs and teachers' adaptation 24–25; teaching as abstract art 153–154; teaching as a cyberspace salon 152–153; teaching as a math missionary 156–157; teaching as balancing act 154–155; teaching as getting comfortable in discomfort 157–159; teaching as interpretative dance 66, 149–152

phenomenological attitude 4, 29, 65; cultivating **166**; openness 132–136; professor displaying 65–66, 90; qualities of 129; teaching 156–157; wonder and openness 172–173

phenomenological heart of teaching and learning 3, 162; designing

200   *Index*

courses embracing 141; higher education 21; insight about 159; messing about with 149; principles of 165–167, **166**
phenomenological interviewing 107
phenomenological philosophy 55, 64, 91, 170
phenomenological research 3–4; features of 5; methodology of University of Tennessee 4–5
phenomenology 9; biological needs 40–41; cognition and consciousness 35–37; embodiment 34–35; existential 29–30; exploring existential 159–160; focus on individual 169; interpretation within ethology and 33; levels of organization 37–40; naturalizing 30–31; science and 27; teaching approach **10–11**; teaching and learning 126–127, 155
Phenomenology of Perception, The (Merleau-Ponty) 30–31, 100
physiology 22, 34, 41, 46; DEEP ethology 46–47
Piaget, Jean 110, 123
place 71; meaning of 14; psychological structure 70
Plato 110, 123
playful/playfulness/playful manner 7, 75, 79, 81; energized *70*, **80**; possibilities 56–57; sitting around the fire with others 120–121
pleiotropic 38
Pollio, Howard R. xi–xiii, xv–xvi, 14, 19, 54, 60–61, 112
polygenic 38
positionality 7, 134, 158
post-class reflections 150, 154
preparation for teaching 22–23; contextual factors in instructional planning 53; focus on instructional planning 51–52; personal factors in instructional planning 53–54
pressure to perform, lack of 98
presuppositions 122, 158
principled practical knowledge 163
prizing acceptance and trust 108
process coding/code: analysis of 23; classroom conversation 81, **82–84**, 84, 89–90; relation to themes 79–81; transcript from graduate seminar dialogue **82–84**, **85–89**

Process-Oriented Guided Inquiry, peer learning 111
professor, label 3
professor's perspective: energized *70*, 73–75, 80; free-flowing journey 71–73, 80; illusion in illusion 81, **82–84**; launching students into world 69–78; my time vs. external time **85–89**; process coding of classroom conversation 81–82, 89–90; questions within questions *70*, 75–76, 80; themes 69, **80**; to go somewhere to answer a BIG question *70*, 70–71; traffic control *70*, 77–78, 80
profound people 126
proprioceptors 34

qualitative research 29, 105, 139, 152; course 157–159; methodology 135, 153
quantitative analysis 135, 136
questions: choice as a descriptor of the professor's *questions within questions* classroom facilitation theme 80, 81; as a descriptor of the professor's *questions within questions* classroom facilitation theme 80, 81, **82–83**, 84, **85–89**, 89; good 58–59; open-ended 5, 75–76, 107, 159; professor and student descriptors **82**, 84, **85**, **88**; provocative **166**; questioning 19, 77, 130; research, and data collection 7, 8; rhetorical 76; vocative 76
questions within questions: as theme of the professor's classroom facilitation 69, *70*, 75, 76

Race, Phil 51
realizing 127; course content 127, 128; realization 14, 28, 92, 161, 167, 178; shift from knowing to 28
realness 108
reasoned motives 178
reasoning 34, 126, 164
reductionism 33
reductive physicalist 32
reflection, contemplative practice 176
reflexivity 129–130, 132, 159
Refocusing the Self in Higher Education (Sherman) 180
relational stance 12, 16, 99

Index 201

relationships 15; authentic 138–139, 140, 145–146; figure-ground 21; intentionality 20–22; interdependent 127; LSES students 144–146; personal 127, 132; professional 127, 132; student-student 18, 160; teacher striving for, with students 160
relevant and applicable: implications of 106–107; personally and professionally relevant 23, 95, 101; relevance and applicability 100, 107; theme 100, **102**
research: learning principles 7, 165–167, **166**, 172; qualitative 157–159; quantitative 105, 135, 136
revelations 57, 155
Rogers, Carl 108

safe and comfortable: implications of 104–106; theme 97–99, **102**
safe classrooms 43, 104, 110, 155
sage on the stage 50, 53, 61, 64, 153
Sartre, Jean-Paul 30, 100
Scholarship of Teaching and Learning (SoTL) 179
science 32; phenomenology and 27; of teaching 2, 163, 177
second person perspectivity 168
selection pressure 45
self-actualization 12, 40, 49, 140, 169
self-actualizing personalities 140
self-assessment 151, 175, 178; *see also* assessment
self-reflection, professor's practice of 62–63
sensory world 31, 38
September 11, 2001 terrorist attacks, perception 98–99
shared worlds, understanding of 39–40
situated cognition 35, 38
situation: dramatizing a 81; embarrassment in social 104; experience in **89**; individual 106; learning and grading 62; meaningful connections in 58–59; opportunity in 72, 77; share contributed by the 106; student awareness of 16, 20, 26
social brain 44
social constructivism/constructivist 69, 171
socialization 44–45, 48, 168

sociocultural context, better understanding of 131–132
sociocultural embeddedness 12; case study 14–16; cognitive learning 173; phenomenological concept **10**; relevant and applicable **102**; student in case study 106; teaching and 160; teaching and learning 165, **166**
sociohistorical theory 171
Socrates 29
solidarity 75, 111–112
space 32; meaning of 14; psychological structure 70; time and 41, 116, 179
statistics course 156–157
stories *see* personal experiences
Strand Mark 122
stress 46–47
Strogatz, Stephen 156
student experiences 24, 95; of learning 102; African American students 142–144; better listening 132–133; classroom safety 110–111; first generation community college 24, 141, 144, 159, 161; freedom 96; ground of 95; group work 52, 56, 105, 109–111, 124; interaction in higher education 109–111; interconnectedness of all things 136–139; international students 146–148; low socioeconomic status (LSES) students 144–146; messed-up learning environment 141–148; multiple ways of knowing 135–136; new way of seeing 129–132; non-native English speaking 160; openness 132–136; personal transformation 140; struggling students 143, 152; valuing multiple ways of knowing 135–136; *see also* free to learn; messed-up learning environment
student experiences of other students (SEOS) 99, 109; all together in this space 112, *112*, 113; changes in being 118–119; coming to appreciate diversity *112*, 113, 116–119; completely caught up *112*, 113, 115–116; creating positive intersubjectivity 119–124; diversity 117; genuine investment *112*, 113, 114–115; methodology and results 112–119; play and intimacy 120–121; power of

202 *Index*

connection 111–112; seeing and appreciating diversity 122–124; seeing variations 117–118; student interaction 109–111; thematic structure of *112*
student needs, phenomenological approach 24–25
student reports, transcending the classroom 24
supervenient 36, 38

Talks to Teachers (James) 163
teachable moments 22, 27, 29, 37, 43–46, 48, 48–49, 155, 160, 164, 167, 171, 177
teacher(s): adaptations 24–25; caring 58–59, 61, 68, 99, 155, 157, 167; label 3; uncaring 143–144
teaching and learning: phenomenological research 3–4, 165–167; principles at phenomenological heart of **166**
teaching as: abstract art 153–154, balancing act 154–155; cyberspace salon 152–153; getting comfortable in the discomfort 157–159; improvisational jazz 65–93; interpretative dance 149–152; math missionary 156–157
teaching practices and approaches: active learning 101, 164; cognitive learning 171, 172–173; contemplative education 176–177; experiential learning 173–174; learner-centered approaches 174–176; outcomes-based 171, 173, 178; phenomenological approaches to 167–171; phenomenological concepts **10–11**; preparation for 22–23; sense of embodiment 161; traditional lecture/test 161, 164; *see also* preparation for teaching
teaching styles: as abstract art 153–154; art of 164–165; as balancing act 154–155; as cyberspace salon 152–153; improvisational jazz as 23, 65–66, 78–90, 91; interpretative dance as 66, 149–152; math missionary as 66, 156–157; phenomenological approach and 178–179
team-building activities 122
themes *see* instructional planning

therapeutic/therapy 98–99, 107, 130, 133
time, class episode exploring meaning of 66
Tinbergen, Nico 41
traffic control: theme of the professor's classroom facilitation 69, *70,* 77–78, **80**
transcendental idealist 32
transcendental phenomenology 30
transcending the classroom 24, 128
Transdisciplinary Phenomenology Research Group (TPRG) 6, 7, 8, 69, 78, 141
transfer of learning 28
transformational learning: experience 145–146, 149, 167, 170, 171, 175, 178; learning 27–29, 48–49, 127; realizing course content 127, 128; students' transformations 128, 140, 158
true truth 32
trust 108
trusting the process 72, 77
twenty-first (21st) century workforce 126

umwelt 31
unassigned assignments 151
unconscious/implicit bias 15, 33, 45
unhelpful help 143
unification 36
unity in diversity 41
University of Tennessee, Knoxville (UTK) 4, 5
unorthodox 96, 98
utilitarian approach 149; balance 141, 154–155, 163, **166**; higher education 163, 172–173
utilitarian attitude **11**, 13, 76, 91, 170
utilitarian focus 3, **166**, 173

van Manen, Max 167
von Uexküll, Jacob 31

walking in another's shoes 39–40
weaving: descriptor of classroom facilitation 79, **80**, 81; as a descriptor of the professor's classroom facilitation *free-flowing journey* theme **80**, 81, **82–84**, 85–89, 91, 149, 164, 174; personal

experience with course content **166**; professor and student descriptors **82**

Weimer, Maryellen 50

wonder 22; attitude 65; attitude of 121, 172–173; awe and 55, 173, 180; everyday life 130; mystery and **166**; openness 11–12, 19, 130, 173; sense of 11, 12, 55, 129

worldview 10, 42, 45, 80, 81, 102, 107, 121, 178; *see also* sociocultural embeddedness

xin (heart and mind) 25